Migration at Work

Migration at Work

Aspirations, Imaginaries and Structures of Mobility

Edited by
Fiona-Katharina Seiger
Christiane Timmerman
Noel B. Salazar
Johan Wets

LEUVEN UNIVERSITY PRESS

The publication of this work was supported by the Research Foundation-Flanders (FWO) Project G.0759.14N, the Erasmus Open Access Fund and the KU Leuven Fund for Fair Open Access.

Published in 2020 by Leuven University Press/Presses Universitaires de Louvain/Universitaire Pers Leuven. Minderbroedersstraat 4, B-3000 Leuven (Belgium).

ISBN 978 94 6270 240 0 (Paperback)
ISBN 978 94 6166 344 3 (ePDF)
ISBN 978 94 6166 345 0 (ePUB)
https://doi.org/10.11116/9789461663443
D/2020/1869/41
NUR: 756

Layout: Coco Bookmedia
Cover design: Johan Van Looveren

In Memoriam Christiane Timmerman

This book is dedicated to the late Professor Christiane Timmerman, who passed away on 10 February 2019. She was one of the promotors of the project behind this book and one of the book's editors.

Christiane Timmerman (born in 1959) was a Belgian psychologist, anthropologist and migration expert. She was a member of the Faculty of Social Sciences of the University of Antwerp where she lectured in migration and integration. Since 2006 Christiane had been the director of CeMIS, the Centre for Migration and Intercultural Studies, an interdisciplinary research centre of the University of Antwerp.

Christiane studied at the University of Leuven (KU Leuven) where she obtained Master's degrees in Psychology (Clinical Psychology and Experimental Social Psychology) in 1983 and in Social and Cultural Anthropology in 1987. Later she embarked on a PhD in Social and Cultural Anthropology, which she completed in 1996.

She had gained professional experience with civil society organisations working with migrants before starting her academic career. Her research trajectory took her to the University of Leuven and then to the University of Antwerp. There, she took over the directorship of UCSIA, the University Centre Saint Ignatius Antwerp in 2004 (until 2011), before co-founding CeMIS.

Under her leadership, CeMIS became an internationally recognised leader of and partner in various large-scale international research projects. CeMIS also joined the IMISCOE network, the largest European network for migration, integration and social cohesion. Christiane put migration and integration research in Flanders and in Belgium firmly on the map.

Table of contents

Acknowledgments

The editors would like to thank The Research Foundation – Flanders (FWO) for funding the "Migration at Work" workshop during which many of the papers included in this volume were presented. Moreover, the editors would like to thank the FWO, the Erasmus University Open Publication Fund, and the KU Leuven Fund for Fair Open Access Publishing for making open access publishing possible for this volume.

Introduction

Fiona-Katharina Seiger, Noel B. Salazar and Johan Wets

International migration is in the news almost daily and has risen up the political agenda of national governments and supranational organisations. Migration affects sending as well as receiving countries and is an inherent part of current processes of globalisation and internationalisation. In recent decades, international migrations have been characterised by profound changes. Global migration resulted in the transformation of societies and cultural diversity within specific countries. If the number of migrants in a country is high, this group automatically becomes relevant for multiple societal actors. People in the industrialised world struggle with questions of integration, political incorporation, undocumented immigration, and who could/should be allowed in and who should be refused. Countries in the "Global South" see needed trained professionals leave for opportunities envisaged as elsewhere in the world.

Migration research is gaining interest. But there is no encompassing coherent theory about international migration, only a series of partial ideas and models that have been separately developed, often divided by different disciplinary viewpoints, borders and goals (De Haas, 2010). All this is logical because the diverse approaches to migration were developed to study specific phenomena, without consideration for universal applicability. Research questions did not fit within any discipline's traditional boundaries and no single discipline had an overall stake in the results of the study. Research on human migration within social sciences is thus multidisciplinary. Different disciplines put forward different theoretical explanations, using different levels of analysis, different approaches, stressing different research questions, and this results in a large variety of viewpoints and positions. Massey et al. (1993, p. 432) state that "a full understanding of contemporary migratory processes will not be achieved by relying on the tools of one discipline alone, or by focusing on a single level of analysis". To this end, a multidisciplinary and multilevel approach must be used, presenting theories from sociology, political science, economics, psychology, anthropology, social geography, development studies and environmental studies and deriving its findings from micro-, meso- and macro-level contexts. Researchers also struggle with methods as they attempt to fit the "unwieldy questions of immigration into patterned disciplinary methodological techniques" (DeSipio et al., 2007). International migration includes processes as diverse as colonising movements, refugee migration, migration of ethnic and/or religious minorities, employment-related migration involving people with various levels of education and training, student mobility, family migration and intra-European mobility. The focus of this volume is on one of the many processes: labour-related migration.

Research by social scientists into international migration and the mobility of people has constantly been growing: more people are involved, more research projects are conducted, and more articles and books are published. Yet, apart from "still lack[ing] a body of cumulative knowledge to explain why some people become mobile, while most do not, and what this means for the societies where migrants come from, pass through and settle in (not forgetting that most societies are all of these to some extent)" (Castles, 2010), we do not even have a common definition of a migrant. The International Organization for Migration (IOM) defines a migrant as "any person who is moving or has moved across an international border or within a State away from his/her habitual place of residence". The International Labour Organization (ILO) defines migrant workers – the main actors in labour migration – as "[…] all international migrants who are currently employed or unemployed and seeking employment in their present country of residence" (ILO, 2015). The United Nations Department of Economic and Social Affairs's definition of who is an international migrant is quite broad: "any person who changes his or her country of usual residence" (UN DESA, 1998).

These rather broad definitions immediately highlight that human movement is at the core of what is commonly known as migration. The kind of geographical mobility that migrants become associated with is usually limited in terms of time, but it shapes their lives significantly (Hage, 2005). Indeed, the migrant is a "figure least defined by its being and place and more by its becoming and displacement; by its movement" (Nail, 2015, p. 3). However, while centring the definition of a "migrant" on movement through social and geographical space we should not forget that numerous forms of mobility entail such movements, and that the multitude of terms used to describe these mobilities reveals the differing social values associated with the former and those who engage in them (Salazar, 2018; Sandoz, 2019). For instance, relatively recent debates about whether refugees should be considered migrants reflect implicit and explicit normative stances on who is "deserving" of international protection and who is not.[1] Other discussions have similarly upheld normative stances on who merits hospitality and who does not by erecting a dichotomy between voluntary and involuntary migration (Bivand Erdal & Oeppen, 2018; Carling, 2017, p. 3). In this volume we opt for an inclusive definition of the "migrant", focused on the act of leaving one's habitual place of residence, rather than on the motives and drivers for that move. The latter are discussed in terms of imaginaries and aspirations that shape migratory trajectories, together with the regimes of mobility that enable, disable and structure mobilities involved in labour-related migration projects. With geographical mobility at its core (Salazar & Jayaram, 2016), migration is entangled with other forms of mobility too, including labour flexibility, seasonal and temporary mobility for work, regular cross-border commuting, (im)mobility within countries tied to residence requirements, as well as processes of up- and downward socio-economic mobility entrenched in geographical movement.

Labour-related mobilities exist in many shades and colours. Just as the temporal patterns of work have been diversifying, so too have its spatial patterns. Karl Marx (1906) as early as in the nineteenth century described how human mobility contributes to a reserve labour army, which facilitates the low wages necessary for the growth of capitalist industry. Labour-related mobilities are thus by no means new (Prothero & Chapman, 1985). However, because of processes of globalisation, increased levels of education, the proliferation of global media, improved transport systems and the internationalisation of business and labour markets, the nature and purpose of such mobilities are becoming increasingly complex.

Labour mobility is positively valued by respected international organisations such as the OECD (Dayton-Johnson et al., 2007) and the UNDP (UNDP, 2009). As with mobility in general, work-related mobility is intimately intertwined with the promise of economic and symbolic mobility. This is based on the assumption that a position elsewhere is "a source of exceptional learning [...] that allows individuals to enhance their employability over time" (Williams, 2009, p. 23). As a result, "mobility itself becomes a valued measure of individual achievement; people point out the obstacles they had to overcome to make each successive move" (Ossman, 2004, p. 117). One can see labour mobility as a response to a neoliberal requirement for employment flexibility, which is believed to be a prerequisite for "success" (Sennett, 1998).

Nicholas De Genova points out how "free" and mobile labour, produced by the evolution of capitalism, is "a distinctly circumscribed" form of freedom (De Genova & Peutz, 2010, p. 56)—the "freedom" to move about and sell one's labour is produced by the lack of freedom to withhold one's labour. Mobility is, then, a contradictory form of freedom, produced by the needs and effects of global capital, yet resistant to total control by capital or the state. Labour mobilities, marked by the imposition of restrictive regulation, are entirely consistent with neoliberal labour regimes and their need for flexible, docile and expendable labour. The intersection of mediating influences such as the changing social divisions of labour, regulation and institutions, and issues of social identities, social recognition and discrimination determines whether transnational mobility leads to labour market entrapment or potential stepping-stones for individuals.

While labour mobility involves migration, the willingness to migrate in search of employment is insufficient to compel anyone to move. Other processes related to the existence (or lack) of opportunities in both sending and receiving countries and regions, the imaginaries one has of life as a migrant, and the many different rules and regulations that hinder, facilitate or even stimulate (cross-border) movement are all of great importance in the decision-making process of migrants and those who aspire to become such. Clearly, the dynamics of labour mobility are not solely dependent on workers' readiness to migrate. They are also heavily influenced by the opportunities perceived and the imaginaries held by both employers and regulating authorities in relation to migrant labour. Imaginaries, understood as socially shared and transmitted representational assemblages that interact with people's personal imaginings and are used as meaning-making and world-shaping devices (Salazar, 2018, p. 162), indeed play a central role in how potential destinations are pictured as greener pastures or in the romanticising of the homeland (Glick Schiller & Salazar, 2013, p. 194). At the same time, the predominance of a "migration culture" does not necessarily spawn greater readiness to seek employment overseas (Timmerman et al., 2014). It is thus of great importance to approach migration and labour mobility from a more encompassing and wider perspective.

This volume comprises chapters based on research conducted in different geographical contexts, including the European Union, Turkey and South Africa, and tackling the experiences and aspirations of migrants from various parts of the globe. In doing so, the authors weave their analyses from two distinct yet intertwined vantage points: the role of structures and regimes of mobility on the one hand, and aspirations as well as migrant imaginaries on the other. As the different chapters show, these intertwine to make and shape movements in space. These two conceptual vantage points allow the exploration of how cross-border mobilities that are usually experienced as personal, bottom-up desires are strongly shaped by top-down (infra-)structures. More importantly though, while the studies featured in this volume build around these seemingly dichotomous analytical entry points, the authors disrupt this dichotomy by pointing to the malleability and fragility of mobility regimes in the face of emancipatory and agentic action (see chapters by de Sousa Ribeiro, Lulle, Ncube& Mkwananzi, Wajsberg), while showing how the aspirations of migrants and their imaginaries are circumscribed by and feed back into how labour mobility is structured (see chapters by Di Martino et al., Dimitriadis, Moderbacher and Ayaydin). We opted for a division of the volume into two separate but related sections to reflect the privileging of either one of these vantage points in the analyses featured in the different chapters.

The first part of this book focuses more on the structures and "regimes of mobility" that underpin how people embark on their migration trajectories and offers insights into how the former enable and delineate forms of cross-border and internal mobility. In this context, "regime" refers to "the role both of individual states and of changing international regulatory and surveillance administrations that affect individual mobility" (Glick Schiller & Salazar, 2013, p. 189). The contributions in this section notably deal with issues of deskilling, brain waste, the proliferation of precarious employment, as well as the role of gender in structuring mobility, at the intersection of regimes of mobility and flexibility.

Lulle (Chapter 1) argues that labour migration theories ought to be read critically through the lens of care. She discusses how the need and desire among Latvian labour migrants to provide co-present care, meaning by being physically present, affect their decisions about the location and length of their stays abroad. The need to travel home regularly patterns their mobility, rendering migration often temporary, seasonal or requiring a supportive network of co-workers and employers to allow for longer absences from work. Advancing that migration is not solely an economic endeavour but also a care-giving project, Lulle critically evaluates migrants' ability to make use of their rights as workers when the regimes that enable their mobility also restrict it; despite entitlements to holiday and compassionate leave, her data show that migrant workers frequently feel that if they were to claim these rights they would quickly be replaced by someone else.

The enabling and disabling qualities of regimes of mobility are also discussed by de Sousa Ribeiro (Chapter 2). Here, such regimes include regulations pertaining to the recognition of skills that are directly linked to social mobility. Situating her discussion in Portugal, where she looks at the experiences of healthcare workers from Eastern Europe who arrived in the 1990s, she explores the interrelations between regulation regimes (e.g. admission policies, academic institutions' procedures, professional bodies' rules) and emancipation structures (e.g. regularisation programmes, subsidised re-accreditation programmes, fast-track diploma recognition) to discuss how initiatives at various levels have contributed to institutional change.

Structuring mobilities, whether spatial or socio-economic, are influenced not only by regimes but also by social factors that work in everyday interactions and influence ideas of what is desirable, appropriate or possible (e.g. gender). Following the capabilities approach (Sen, 2001; Nussbaum, 2011) and looking at the influence of migration as a gendered endeavour, Ncube and Mkwananzi (Chapter 3) discuss how migration has allowed female sub-Saharan economic migrants in South Africa to be agentic and interrupt ascribed traditional gendered roles and stereotypes.

The tension between structure and agency is also explored by Wajsberg (Chapter 4). She analyses narratives of (im)mobility as experienced by West African migrants during their migration trajectories within Europe. Wajsberg disentangles the various navigational tactics her interlocutors have engaged in to achieve both spatial and socio-economic mobility despite their immobilisation by restrictive national and supranational migration policies within the European Union. These include individuals side-stepping some of the residence requirements that tie them to a particular place, to organising and participating in grassroots movements challenging the rules and regulations that immobilise them.

The authors featured in this first part of the book notably draw our attention to the tensions between migrants' aspirations vested in their migratory endeavours and the structures and regimes that circumscribe their mobilities. Agency and emancipation feature in all four chapters, as the authors explore how immobilising structures are negotiated and challenged by their respondents, potentially contributing to change (see de Sousa Ribeiro, this volume). These efforts are part and parcel of ongoing migratory projects that did not end with border-crossing; the projects continue in the form of struggles to find access to the labour market and to benefit from it so as not to reproduce the sort of stasis many wanted to get away from by leaving their places of origin.

Bottom-up initiatives, such as interest groups and movements formed through social media (see de Sousa Ribeiro; Wajsberg, this volume), play an important role in dealing with the circumstances of labour migration, as do offline social ties (see Lulle, this volume). Migrant networks are an important resource to negotiate or (attempt to) disrupt mobility regimes and surmount immobilisation. As de Sousa Ribeiro and Lulle have shown, these networks not only help to deal with what immediately concerns people's ability to be spatially mobile (i.e. material and legislative circumstances) but, beyond that, with the rules and regulations that relate to work, such as the transferability and accreditation of skills, as well as workers' rights. In recognition of the interrelationship of spatial and socio-economic mobility, which is not exclusive but definitely central to migration for work, we may think of structures and regimes of mobility as including not only migration policies and the policing of borders and border-crossings on the ground, but also the rules and regulations surrounding flexible work and the acceptance and recognition of academic and professional credentials and experience.

The second part of the book focuses on the imaginaries driving desires and decisions to migrate. Imaginaries of "other" places are at the root of many travels, including labour migration (Salazar, 2011, p. 575). People seldom travel to *terrae incognitae* these days, but instead journey to places they already "know" through the imaginaries that circulate about them (Salazar, 2013). These intuitions and rumours of "the other side" (Glick Schiller & Salazar, 2013, p. 195) can include general expectations of achieving "better lives" through employment opportunities leading to social and economic mobility, but may also include images that deter individuals from embarking on such journeys (Timmerman et al., 2014). Migratory mobilities are as much about these underlying imaginaries as they are about actual physical movements. In other words, "movement is not just the experience of shifting from place to place, it is also linked to our ability to imagine an alternative" (Papastergiadis, 2000, p. 11). Aspirations come close to a concept of imaginaries as historically laden, socially shared and transmitted.

Imaginaries, in turn, play an important role in the formation of aspiration, influencing why people aspire to move and where they aspire to move to.

Aspirations to migrate are often developed with reference to common narratives surrounding labour mobility to improve one's life, or stories told by migrant kin, or through imageries purported by media. Employers and authorities also act based on their own imaginaries of what migrants may bring to the job: for instance, migrants from certain (ethnic, religious, regional, etc.) backgrounds are expected to be hard working, whereas others are perceived as fortune-seekers. The contributions in this section thus explore how expectations of greater opportunities and better employment conditions set people in motion, how imaginaries of places and people persist over time despite changing migratory patterns and motives, and how expectations of a better life may also be disappointed as migrants find themselves immobilised by regimes of (im)mobility.

Di Martino et al. (Chapter 5) examine how highly educated migrant women negotiate their careers considering structural constraints. Focusing on coping strategies of European and Latin American women in the Basque Country, the authors analyse their respondents' experiences through the lens of migratory careers; they show how opportunities and challenges are made sense of and dealt with as their private and professional trajectories abroad unfold. In the process, aspirations initially lodged in the migratory project evolve to achieve job matching and work-life balance.

Moderbacher (Chapter 7), too, points to the important nexus between imaginaries vested in mobility and structural realities gradually disrupting the former at various instances. She illustrates how certain migrants are systemically immobilised through governmentally prescribed training programmes that keep participants busy but fail to convey skills that are applicable in the labour market. The case studies presented by Di Martino et al. and Moderbacher show that labour market integration and the structural opportunities or constraints mediating that process are central to social mobility and to the fulfilment of aspirations to improve one's life that frequently drive cross-border migration in the first place.

Such aspirations and underlying imaginaries of more desirable locations for work propel onward migration, as Dimitriadis (Chapter 6) shows in his study of Albanian migrant construction workers in Italy and Greece. Similarly, negative perceptions – such as fears of racism or of having to settle for less favourable lifestyles – can work as deterrents. Migrant imaginaries, Dimitriadis concludes, can thus explain decisions regarding mobility on top of economic explanations, notably so in cases where staying put seems counter-intuitive if looked at solely in terms of income differentials and job availability.

Migrant imaginaries, this time projected upon migrant workers by prospective employers, fuel and structure the care labour industry in Turkey (Ayaydin, Chapter 8). Filipino nannies occupy a privileged niche in the racialised hierarchy of foreign child-carers in Turkey. Placement agencies market Filipino women's English-language proficiency, their modernity and their supposed cultural predisposition to providing good child care, thereby branding Filipina nannies as the "Mercedes" among nannies and turning them into repositories for upper-middle-class desires of class actualisation. This has by consequence driven the demand for female workers from the Philippines in that sector.

In sum, the chapters in this volume illustrate how mobility is co-produced by migrants' imaginaries, their subsequent aspirations to move, as well as by regimes of mobility that are similarly underpinned by images of desirable and undesirable migrants. As a process, mobility not merely encompasses migrations from A to B, but keeps developing along migratory routes involving moments of limited mobility and stuckedness. Imaginaries are rectified in the process of migration and new possibilities arise through the accumulation of knowledge, contacts and social networks, making it conceivable to move on to further destinations. Placing an emphasis on migrants' experiences, this book investigates the meaning of mobility to those on the move while keeping in mind that mobility and immobility remain embedded in unequal relationships of political, social, cultural and economic power that unfold differently in various local contexts.

Contemporary labour migration research often revolves around one aspect of migratory processes, such as a specific group of migrants, the core motivations to migrate, expectations involved in the process of migration, or issues surrounding the integration of migrants in receiving societies. This volume aims – in an attempt to contribute to a broader understanding of the phenomenon as described earlier – to lay out a more encompassing perspective to labour migration by bringing together discussions of the phenomenon emanating from different disciplines and focusing on international labour mobility, that having been generally ignored in migration studies (King & Skeldon, 2010). Based on an array of case-studies examining migratory movements in various contexts, this volume aims to draw cross-contextual parallels by addressing the questions of the role played by opportunities in mobilising people, how structures enable, sustain and change different forms of mobility, and how imaginaries fuel labour migration and vice versa. In doing so, this volume also aims to tackle the interrelationships between imaginaries driving migration and shaping "regimes of mobility", as well as how the former play out in different contexts, shaping internal and cross-border migration.

Note

1 For more information on these debates see the project entitled "the meaning of migrants": https://meaningofmigrants.org/, accessed 25.03.2020.

References

Bivand Erdal, M., & C. Oeppen. (2018). "Forced to leave? The discursive and analytical significance of describing migration as forced and voluntary". *Journal of Ethnic and Migration Studies*, 44:6, pp. 981–998. DOI: 10.1080/1369183X.2017.1384149.

Carling, J. (2017). "Refugee Advocacy and the Meaning of 'Migrants'". PRIO Policy Brief (02/2017).

Castles, S. (2010). "Understanding Global Migration: A Social Transformation Perspective". *Journal of Ethnic and Migration Studies*, 36:10, pp. 1565–1586.

Dayton-Johnson, J., L.T. Katseli, G. Maniatis, R. Münz & D. Papademetriou. (2007). *Gaining from Migration: Towards a New Mobility System*. Paris: OECD Development Centre.

De Genova, N., & N.M. Peutz (eds.). (2010). *The Deportation Regime: Sovereignty, Space, and the Freedom of Movement*. Durham, NC: Duke University Press.

De Haas, H. (2010). "The internal dynamics of migration processes: A theoretical inquiry". *Journal of Ethnic and Migration Studies*, 36: 10, pp. 1587–1617.

DeSipio L., M. Garcia y Griego & S. Kossoudji (eds.). *Researching Migration: Stories from the Field*. New York: Social Science Research Council. www.ssrc.org/publications/view/42451838-264A-DE11-AFAC-001CC477EC70/.

Glick Schiller, N., & N.B. Salazar. (2013). "Regimes of Mobility Across the Globe". *Journal of Ethnic and Migration Studies*, 39:2, pp. 183–200.

Hage, G. (2005). "A not so multi-sited ethnography of a not so imagined community". *Anthropological Theory*, 5:4, pp. 463–475.

ILO. (2015). *ILO Global estimates of migrant workers and migrant domestic workers: results and methodology*. Geneva: International Labour Office.

King, R., & R. Skeldon. (2010). "Mind the gap! Integrating approaches to internal and international migration". *Journal of Ethnic and Migration Studies*, 36:10, pp. 1619–1646.

Marx, K. (1906). *Capital: A Critique of Political Economy* (E. Untermann, Trans.). Chicago, IL: C.H. Kerr & Co.

Massey, D. S., J. Arango, G. Hugo, A. Kouaouci, A. Pellegrino & J. E. Taylor. (1993). "Theories of International Migration: A Review and Appraisal". *Population and Development Review* 19:3, September, pp. 431–466.

Nail, T. (2015). *The Figure of the Migrant*. Stanford, CA: Stanford University Press.

Nussbaum, M. (2011). *Creating Capabilities: The Human Development Approach*. Cambridge, MA: Harvard University Press.

Ossman, S. (2004). "Studies in Serial Migration". *International Migration*, 42:4, pp. 111–121.

Papastergiadis, N. (2000). *The Turbulence of Migration: Globalization, Deterritorialization, and Hybridity*. Cambridge: Polity Press.

Prothero, R. M., & M. Chapman (eds.). (1985). *Circulation in Third World Countries*. London: Routledge.

Salazar, N. B. (2011). "The Power of Imagination in Transnational Mobilities". *Identities*, 18:6, pp. 576–598.

Salazar, N. B. (2013). "Imagining Mobility at the 'End of the World'". *History and Anthropology*, 24:2, pp. 233–252.

Salazar, N. B. (2018). "Theorizing Mobility through Concepts and Figures". *Tempo Social*, 30:2, pp. 153–168.

Salazar, N. B., & K. Jayaram (eds.). (2016). *Keywords of mobility: Critical engagements*. Oxford: Berghahn.

Sandoz, L. (2019). *Mobilities of the Highly Skilled towards Switzerland. The Role of Intermediaries in Defining "Wanted Immigrants"* (Springer IMISCOE Series). Town: Springer Open.

Sen, A. (2001). *Development as freedom*. Oxford and New York: Oxford University Press.

Sennett, R. (1998). *The Corrosion of Character: The Personal Consequences of Work in the New Capitalism*. New York: Norton.

Timmerman, C., K. Hemmerechts & H. M. De Clerck. (2014). "The Relevance of a 'Culture of Migration' in Understanding Migration Aspirations in Contemporary Turkey". *Turkish Studies*, 15:3, pp. 496–518.

UN DESA. (1998). "Recommendations on Statistics of International Migration: Revision 1". Statistical Papers, series M no. 58, Rev 1.

Williams, A. M. (2009). "Employability and international migration: Theoretical perspectives". In S. McKay (ed.). *Refugees, Recent Migrants and Employment: Challenging Barriers and Exploring Pathways* (pp. 23–34). New York: Routledge.

Part I:
Projects, structures and regimes of labour mobility

Temporary Labour Migrants from Latvia Negotiate Return Trips for Care: Distributing Resources Across Borders

Aija Lulle

Introduction

In this chapter I unpack how existing structures in 'regimes of mobility' for work fail to consider migrants as caring agents. The gap between literatures of temporary migration and care both is obvious and begs to be bridged. The free movement the EU has experienced for exponentially more than a decade, though, has mainly created flexibility for employers. However, migrants do carve out time and space, and forge relationships to fulfill, at least partially, their crucial needs to care for family members and other relevant people in their lives. I discuss pathways of relationships between temporary migration and care. I explore how interrelationships between Latvian migrants, their employers and their family members are shaped by "regimes of mobility" across borders as well as other (infra)structural constraints. Hence, this chapter centres on the notion of "regimes of mobility" (Salazar & Glick Schiller, 2014), which I explore both as a form of limitation and opportunity in temporary labour migration. I define "regime" as structural sets of rules and regulations at transnational, national and local levels and also as informal regulations and interpersonal contracts between people. Supranational laws envisage free movement of labour in the case of the European Union. Therefore, labour migration in such legal setting primarily involves employers and employees, while in family relations such rules play out not just as money-earning projects. I argue that caring across borders is a part of the temporary labour migration project, e.g. to earn money in order to provide a better life for family members. Accordingly, labour mobility may conflict with care needs and expectations of time devoted to work and to family members abroad.

I draw on fieldwork conducted in two sites covered in my research. The first site is Guernsey – a British Crown dependency which subscribes to the EU principles of the free movement of labour but does not give full social rights to temporary migrant workers. The second is Finland, a full member of the EU. While it was not possible to claim child benefits in Guernsey (the island is not part of the EU), temporary labour migrants in Finland, according to the EU regime, usually did claim child benefits for their children who remained in Latvia.

In migrants' views, temporary migration for work purposes is crucially linked to and motivated by care responsibilities. Although classic migration literature on target earners and theories on household economies emphasise the economic side of migration motivations, from the migrants' perspective motivation to engage in temporary work is crucially linked to care arrangements. Temporality and timing are relevant: migrants may need to travel back home for "hands-on" care and to be together with their family members. But care can take many forms and involve spatial and temporal arrangements. The care provided can be direct, in immediate need and out of compassion, or it can be indirect, such as emotional support provided from a distance and through gifting (Bonizzoni & Boccagni, 2013; Hochschild, 2000). Care can also be expressed in the form of the sending home of money (Lulle, 2014). Moreover, care can express itself in more socially oriented collective investment back "home". It is important to note that the participants in my research (located on the island of Guernsey and in Finland) did not invest in community infrastructures.

In this complex care provision system, my research participants were mostly concerned about their ability to visit their relatives whenever necessary. To return home for care purposes migrants negotiate these trips with (1) employers, (2) co-workers and (3) family members, with varying degrees of success. To illustrate these three modes of negotiation I draw on my long-term research among Latvian labour migrants in the UK and Nordic countries. Migrants' ability to negotiate such trips varies considerably and changes over time. I pay special attention to how migrant workers achieve travel rhythms and conditions which satisfy their needs, and why and in what situations they are denied holidays for care purposes in another country. I conclude with suggestions for future research avenues on how existing prominent labour migration theories ought to be critically read and updated through the lens of care relations, time and material resources distribution across borders from migrants' point of view.

Rereading temporary mobility regimes through classic theories

Arguably the largest and longest-lived theoretical model on migration theory is the so-called push-pull model (Lee, 1966). This model presumes economic reasons to be the primary drivers of migration: people move when there are economic push factors and go to places where they can earn more. Hence, the model somewhat implies a "calculative migrant". A migrant assesses "costs and benefits" before moving or before returning "home" (Bogue, 1977; Sjaastad, 1962). A similar model uses the notion of an "intervening opportunity" (Stouffer, 1960) when people move to places where there are the specific opportunities they seek, such as housing or work. These models must be critiqued for a number of reasons. Firstly, they are a-temporal, as they presume that people make calculated decisions about where to move based on negative and positive factors found in particular places, but fail to account for how long people remain in those places when the factors that initially attracted them cease to exist. Secondly, migrants are seen as "target earners" (Piore, 1979), who ideally earn a set amount of money they wish to have, and return "home" when that target is reached. Thirdly, the above classic theories overlook immediate and extended family relations that span borders. Most importantly, care is missing in these models.

The migration theory has recognised these shortcomings in the so-called new economics of labour migration. This model presumes that migration stems from decisions made within the family or household to maximise income (Taylor, 1999). Furthermore, more theoretical attention has been paid to the gradual opening of international labour markets as a consequence of neoliberal globalisation with its flexible economic relationships and subsequent impact on increased temporal forms of international migration (Castles, 2006; Iglicka, 2001; Venturini, 2008). Economic connectivity is clearly the main emphasis in efforts to define circular migration (Newland et al., 2008; Triandafyllidou, 2013), while other non-economic factors such as education, meeting family members' needs and so forth are also recognised. The migration and development perspective even characterises circular migration as a triple-win solution: for sending and receiving countries, and also for migrants and their families (EC, 2005a; EC, 2005b; IOM, 2005; Ruhs, 2006; United Nations, 2006; World Bank, 2006). Again, care as both an individual need and a project of a household is rather absent from these ideas.

I argue that such flexible, temporal relationships give preference to fast recruitment and lay-offs, and provide quick solutions in cases of fluctuating labour demand and supply. In other words, theoretical interpretations of migration need to be linked to other forms of mobilitiy: transport, tourism, social mobilities between employment sectors but, importantly, to underlying necessity and willingness to care for significant others across borders. Skeldon (2012) particularly emphasises *free* movement: people move back and forth between two or more countries and are free to return to their home countries *at any time*. He notes that flexibility and circularity are the main characteristics of these movements, where people engage in "regular and repetitive outward movements between an origin and a destination or destinations; and that the circular migrant is free to return at any time" (Skeldon, 2012, p. 47). The interlinkages between those who left and those who stayed put again remained overlooked. However, this has been further recognised in a break-through approach to migration networks (Boyd, 1989; Fawcett, 1989). This approach emphasises interdependence and reciprocity, and some strands of this approach do incorporate families across borders and important realities of migrant worlds. However, "flexible" types of migration such as short-term and seasonal migration necessitate thinking more widely about this phenomenon in relation to care needs in distant places.

Mobility regimes and care

The "mobility turn" urging researchers to see mobilities and migration as an integral part of social life (Sheller & Urry, 2006) is the most recent and most promising paradigm through which to understand the links between temporary labour migration, care and the negotiation of travel back and forth among various actors. People move back and forth, and for some this mobility has become a major resource in the twenty-first century (Cresswell, 2010, p. 22). The term "space of possibility" was coined by Morokvasic (2004), who famously stated that the newly opened borders to the European Union and their novel and relatively stable legal status as EU citizens offered a space of possibility for Eastern Europeans. These "new" EU citizens became free to leave, free to return and free to use the European space through transnational mobility in order to help them to adjust to changes in post-socialist countries. Engbersen and Snel (2013) have even called such mobility "liquid". Families and workers travel, and engage in transnational parenting (Bonizzoni & Boccagni, 2013). Hence, we need to include the concept of transnational families in understanding temporary migration motivations and arrangements. Some forms of care (e.g. money) can circulate, while others (direct care) cannot (Baldassar & Merla, 2014). Migrants are manoeuvring various option of transnational parenting, especially that of mothers, navigating through gender norms and expectations (Parrenas, 2005). Migrants also care for their ageing parents (Baldassar, Baldock & Wildin, 2007).

Migrant workers develop new modes of temporalities, especially in the demanding domestic care sector, where women care for children or the elderly in an immigration country but need to go back to their own families both to recuperate from demanding paid care work and to engage in their unpaid family care work. Marchetti (2013) has described, for example, how Eastern European care providers have developed job sharing among themselves, replacing each other regularly. However, these relatively regular travels home for care needs in different job sectors remain underexplored. Even less researched are questions around how negotiations regarding such travels fail or succeed between a migrant worker and an employer.

Theoretically, the gap between care literature and temporary labour migration is obvious: the former focuses on sets of family norms and arrangements, while the latter primarily discusses economic rules and regulations. I argue for the need to bridge this gap and aim to do so through the notion of "regimes of mobility". Empirically, the conflict lies in family ideals of care and employers' ideals of profit. Families hope that temporary work abroad will bring in more money at the expense of the absence of one (or all) care provider(s). Employers hope that they will maximise their profit from employing migrant workers intensively for a short time. Complex everyday care needs shatter these "ideal" constructions. Migrants need to travel back home for short periods too, but these travel needs for care are usually not taken into account by their employers. The question is, how do migrants negotiate their care needs within these constrains and what opportunities are provided by intra-European regimes of mobility?

Methodology

The case studies presented here derive from my long-term engagement in fieldwork with Latvian migrants travelling between the UK and Latvia (2010–2014) and between Finland and Latvia (2016–2018). The first study was my doctoral project, while the second case study was conducted as part of the project entitled "Inequalities among Transnational Families in Nordic-Baltic Space", funded by the Academy of Finland, whose Principal Investigator was Prof. Laura Assmuth of the University of Eastern Finland. The former resulted in a large qualitative database of 96 interviews with migrants, plus18 interviews with experts and employers, while the latter comprises 20 interviews which were long-term ethnographic engagements with migrants across three generations as well as with non-migrants who were significant in the migrant participants' lives. Castles (2012, pp. 8, 23) underlines that each qualitative migration research initiative should develop concepts and use methods which allow the understanding of, first, how individuals are linked to social structures in changing historical contexts and, second, what the "prevailing character types" or dominating ideas are in each society. Besides, research should build on new knowledge rather than on existing knowledge. This long ethnographic engagement across three different spatial contexts allowed me to discern how some dominant types of travel for care occur.

The following empirical sections explore to what extent power inequalities between employers and employees can be considered part of regimes whereby intra-European mobility for work has created opportunities for (temporary) labour migrants but has also exposed them to vulnerabilities tied to an "endless" supply of migrant labour to replace them. Moreover, a lack of familiarity with local labour laws and thin social networks often render temporary migrants unable to claim protection and their rights. Most importantly, temporary migration status has created uncertain situations where social rights are reduced even within the EU (Lafleur & Mescoli, 2018). The cases outlined below are illustrative of the care arrangements of many of the temporary migrants involved in my research.

Negotiating cross-border mobility and child care

I interviewed Sanita several times in the UK. She was in her forties when she worked on the island of Guernsey in 2010–2014. Sanita was a high-school graduate, holding several professional diplomas, but had for a long time been the stay-at-home mother of her twins. After she had divorced and her ex-husband refused to provide maintenance for their children, Sanita started studying in Latvia to gain confidence and restructure her life. At the same time, she worked in a local municipality to earn a daily income. Prior to finding a job on Guernsey, she had worked on a Greek island as part of her internship training in tourism and hospitality studies in 2004, while her mother looked after the twins who were early teenagers at the time. In 2005 she moved to London and worked as the domestic carer of a child for a year. She described London as a good choice: there were relatively cheap flight connections every day. From the very beginning she negotiated with her employer – a young mother – that she would travel back to Latvia at least twice a month to look after her own children. But after a year in London she moved to Germany and to Sweden for shorter periods owing to personal relationships she had made. When she worked in Sweden, her partner proposed that she should bring her children along and settle there, but it was clear after just a few months that the relationship would not work out. Upon returning to Latvia in 2007, she considered a vacancy in a regional municipality and was shortlisted for interview, but finally decided not to take the job because travelling back and forth between her proposed workplace and her home locally would involve expenditures of time and money which she considered too high. There was no chance of negotiating shorter work hours or teleworking locally. "I would not see my children anyway, so I did not even go to the second interview", she justified her decision. Sanita again went abroad, this time to Ireland. Her earnings in Ireland and good air transport connections in 2007 allowed her to visit her home in Latvia every month, enabling her to complete her final year at college in Latvia. Her children were also growing up and becoming increasingly independent. Her mother lived near the children and visited them often. After the economic crisis in Ireland in 2008, Sanita returned to Latvia, and soon afterwards embarked on the trip to Guernsey again to search for employment. Her children were finishing high school and planning for higher education, so pressures to provide monetary support for their plans were even greater. Travelling to and from Guernsey, however, was not easy: Sanita had to use a connecting flight via London and travelling door to door could take all day. Sanita was working in a hotel at the time, with a regular total of four weeks' holiday a year. Besides, since the main aim was to provide care in the form of money in light of her physical absence, for several years she travelled back home only once a year, while her children came to visit her also once a year.

Hospitality, agriculture, packaging goods and cleaning services were among the most popular employment sectors for Latvian migrants throughout the 2000s and the early 2010s. But unlike hospitality, the other mentioned sectors were organised according to short-term contracts in Guernsey: a migrant could work for up to nine months on the island but had to leave for at least three months thereafter. Moreover, while these are usually entry-level jobs for migrants, I emphasise that research participants were consciously *temporary* –

they did not want to stay abroad permanently and thus did not invest so much in their career prospects. Their family members did not usually relocate with them, which would have been a typical pathway out of temporary into more permanent migration and care arrangements.

I found that many women working in these sectors preferred such regulations precisely because they matched their need to return home to provide care in person. Working abroad was negotiated with family members. Ideally, those who were working on shorter contracts of up to nine months could spend at least three months a year at home, which is considerably longer than the typical four weeks a year in most permanent jobs. For instance, Skaidrīte, a woman in her thirties, periodically worked in a seed packaging company on Guernsey and did not work when she was back in Latvia. "I live at home with the children, take them to school, and then back home. The money that I earned is distributed during those months [while back home]". Another woman, Zelma, in her early forties, broke her six-month contact after her daughters called and cried about how much they were missing their mother. She was "free to return" at any time (cf. Skeldon, 2012) but at the expense of the loss of a contract and income. Zelma usually worked for six to nine months on Guernsey and lived on savings while back in Latvia. This time, instead of the envisaged six months of income from abroad, she lived on her small savings in Latvia and provided "hands on" care and presence to her daughters.

Cases like these, where migrant employers rely on labour contracts or residence requirements operating within loosely defined informal arrangements (as in the case of child care and free days allocated for a carer) and where care is distributed among other family members when the earner is away can enrich our understanding of what drives and structures migration beyond the classic models of the new economics of labour migration (cf. Stark & Bloom, 1985) and "target earners" (Piore, 1979). Moreover, targets themselves may need to be re-theorised: care is crucial and often a primary target of such economics. This care target is clearly influenced by geographical distance, ease of transport, and the opportunities granted by particular regimes of mobility. Also, care targets are shaped significantly by employer-migrant employee relations. Finally, the nature of work is important, as I demonstrated in the case of Sanita: in some sectors more holidays can be negotiated, while in others (also in case of Zelma, who was packaging seeds during a season of high demand, longer absences for care abroad are not negotiable.

Emergency travel home

On a European scale, the free movement of people allows for relatively easy border-crossing; good transport connections and relatively cheap airline tickets enable travel which was not possible several decades ago. However, attention to constraints allows us to appreciate that migrants are not free-floating agents who can return home whenever they wish without serious consequences such as losing their jobs. Quite the opposite: return visits are severely constrained by available financial resources and by the obligations an individual has as a worker. Distance matters too. This can best be seen in cases when a person needs to visit family for urgent reasons. Let us consider Maija's experience. In her twenties, she arrived on Guernsey where she started working in restaurants. However, Maija had not yet worked long enough to qualify for annual leave when a death occurred in the family:

> My dearest grandmother died in August [...] I was searching for tickets to go to Latvia but could not go. I wanted a week off, but the boss said: "Do you think that you can do whatever you want just because you are a Latvian?" [...] But it really hurt me that I was not able to attend the funeral. [...] I went later in autumn; I had a week off. I did not tell anybody that I was coming. I arrived with presents; I saw my dad crying for the first time in my life. Mom even did not talk to me, she turned her back and started crying. And then they told me that the other grandmother was in hospital. I went to the graveyard, but mainly spent time at the hospital visiting my grandmother and met friends just for a few hours [...] went out on Friday night, met friends again on Saturday and had a flight to Stansted on Sunday, waiting very long there for the next day's flight at 6 am. On Tuesday my mother called and said that grandmother died on Monday. [...] It is very hard not to be able to go to the funeral and say the last goodbye.

There can be other urgent needs that require a return to Latvia, and so the conditions under which a migrant worker is allowed to be absent from work must be negotiated with an employer. Although the interviews reveal a generally high degree of understanding from and an individualised attitude of employers towards the need of migrant workers to go back home, flexibility is not limitless, not least due to the easy availability of replacements as other migrant workers are constantly searching for jobs. Urgent home visits can cause conflicts with employers, and in some urgent cases a migrant worker may have to resign from work, such as in Ginta's case. Ginta, a woman in her late twenties, worked in a shop. She had pre-planned annual leave but received a wedding invitation and wanted to combine her visit home with a health check she thought would be more specific than one she could receive on Guernsey. Going just for a weekend for the wedding was too expensive for Ginta but negotiations with her employer over changing her annual leave dates failed:

> The boss said there is no person who can replace me, which was just pretence. Anybody from our company could replace me, but she simply did not want to show me a human attitude and let me go for just two weeks. So, I resigned.

Ilmars' need to return home temporarily to provide care in person was also dismissed. In his fifties, he worked in the transport sector and had to resign to go to Latvia just for a few days, but was invited to apply for the same job again once he got back. Although he had qualified for several days' annual leave due to his employment history of almost four months, his employer did not want to grant him a holiday. The supply of temporary migrants is relatively high owing to intra-European labour mobility regimes, so employers see migrants like Ilmars as replaceable workers. Following Marxist critique, Miles (1986) notes that migrants are seen as a "reserve army" and are hence exploited.

Ilmars resigned and upon his return searched for another job, as his employer's lack of flexibility had left him resentful. These situations reveal that a migrant worker can end up in precarious employment situations, where visits home can endanger his/her ability to continue working abroad. Employers may benefit greatly from the flexible recruitment of migrants: they are easy to hire in busy times and easy to fire during economic downturns. But care – reproductive work – does not follow the same logic as the one flexible mobility regimes are catering to. Again, this reality is due to the framing of labour migrants as purely "labour", where their care obligations across borders are seen as incompatible with their status as labour migrants. Spatial capitalist relations can assume that workers will be more productive when they are away from reproductive duties. Therefore, distances are constitutive to regimes of labour mobility. Regimes of transnational mobility clearly play a role here: migrants need more time to travel and reach home compared to locals, but giving more "out of work" time to migrants is not in employers' interests. Hence, I argue that means of transport and distances should also be included in an analysis of regimes of mobility.

Some trips home are also inevitably related to emergency, illness and death, as in one case already discussed above. If employed in a small-scale business where employers develop almost familial relationships with their employees, my findings showed that the latter had more bargaining power as they could leverage on their good relations. For instance, when Alma's mother died in 2011, her boss immediately bought expensive tickets on her behalf, and Alma embarked on her "holiday" at home.

My sole thought from the time I woke up, while I worked, and when I went to bed was of my mother [...] I trembled every time the phone beeped (conversation with Alma, in her sixties, Guernsey, March 2012).

I did not come across the notion of compassionate leave before speaking to my participants who were employed mainly in service and physically intensive work in the UK. Su, labour migration theories do need a nuanced reworking in terms of labour sectors and class sensitivities in cases of care needs.

Frequent travel home

The third case I would like to introduce is the experience of Armands, 27, who worked in construction in Finland. He entered the path of migration as soon as he turned 18. Armands' mobility narrative is entwined with the search for a better life of which care is an irreducible part (Kilkey, Plomien & Perrons, 2014). He had worked in several EU countries. During one of his trips home to Latvia, he met a young woman whom he started dating and with whom he maintained a long-distance relationship while based in the UK, the Netherlands and in Denmark, where he was intermittently working on short-term contracts. While they were expecting a baby, Armands found employment in Finland because he needed to earn money to renovate the apartment the couple had inherited from relatives. The contracts were longer and new construction jobs were constantly available. During the first two years, all of Armands' savings went into new walls, the bathroom and furniture for the flat. During his third year abroad, Armand saved for their wedding. When they got married, the couple were already expecting their second child.

His wife and two small children remain in Latvia. Although she considered relocating the entire family to Finland, she eventually abandoned the idea because of the cold weather conditions. These, according to Armands, made her change her mind and decide that she felt better in their renovated flat back home.

Armands travels every two to three weeks to spend a long weekend of three to four days at home. In order to do so, he needs to work more hours on some days, including at weekends. His bosses are also from a post-Soviet country and almost all the workers are migrant men. Male employers and employees support each other in care and solidarity. Life is more difficult for his wife with two children as she is de facto a single mother when Armands is working abroad:

> She constantly tells me: "Come home, money is not so important, we will manage somehow". But how? I have been home, and I know that I still need some years abroad to save up more money. Especially now with two kids, expenses are high.

In order to save up, he lives in a shared house in Finland with five other men, two of whom are his relatives. The negotiation of care duties and travel are two-fold, according to Armands. Firstly, bosses acknowledge that men with families need to travel home and allow working hours to be flexible. Secondly, those who are young and strong help those who are older and physically weaker but do not travel back home often. For instance, at the time of the interview (2018) Armands was helping a man in his early sixties who still needed to work a couple more years before reaching pensionable age. Since the older man had recently suffered a stroke and had back problems, the younger man thus took over physically demanding jobs, while the older man covered Armands' shifts when he was away.

Conclusion

In this chapter I have applied the conceptual lens of "regimes of mobility" (Salazar & Glick Schiller, 2014) to account for motivations other than economic when migrants engage in temporary migration. Temporary migrants continuously negotiate their need to travel to give care. Also, needs to provide care change over time. During some years care is provided to grandparents, during others it is provided to children, parents, or a relative who has fallen ill. These negotiations take place in families, with fellow employees and with employers. The travel for short term, hands-on care is the "soft" spot in the current era of the flexibilisation of the migrant labour regime. Granting or not granting permission to take leave mainly remains subject to the moral understanding of an employer, thus also affecting people's mobility. While this is the case for any employee – migrant or not – migrants are still more vulnerable owing to the distance factor. Multiple care duties can be combined with paid work if a family lives nearby, which is not the case with many temporary migrants.

Overcoming the constraints of labour mobility regimes and carving out time to travel home to give care require active agency. However, I argue that no research on labour mobility regimes and care needs spanning borders can ignore mobility-constraining and enabling structures. These are, firstly, global neoliberal structures of flexible employment that do not consider flexibility regarding the need to provide care. State governments and employers benefit from temporary labour migrants' work and usually place constraints on family reunions, but they do not consider migrants as providers of care. Secondly, these are national level structures governing working time and how days off can be accumulated. Thirdly, these are workplace structures with their internal culture of (not) recognising migrant employees' needs to care across borders.

From the migrants' point of view, travelling for care includes calculating costs and benefits (cf. Sjaastad, 1962) but, unlike the original model, includes care costs. Those are the costs of reproductive work they do across borders. In the first case discussed here, travelling back home to care goes hand in hand with children's or parents' life course needs. Migrants use tactics and, if they can, choose to work in places which are well connected to home by way of infrastructure to enable them to travel more frequently. When hands-on care is not the primary concern, but earning money is, the emphasis shifts to higher wages instead of transport connectivity. Hence, as temporary migrant travels for care contain a strong element of "calculatedness", the desire to procure care needs to be seriously incorporated into classic models in migration theory. Migration theory needs not only to incorporate diverse and culturally shaped family structures and strategies of temporary labour migrants (Harbison, 1981; Goldring, 2004; Zontini, 2001) but to do so in line with analyses of cross-border realities where care work spans borders and requires a migrant worker to cross them occasionally. The realities of temporary migration do not support a triple-win scenario (World Bank, 2006) fully as all costs of care and the negotiation of care needs are shouldered by migrants.

In the second case I discussed emergency travel, which can or cannot be granted through the discretion of employers. Migrants are imagined as productive only and granting emergency trips home is a compassionate step rather than a matter of workers' rights. Thirdly, I have discussed how migrants develop a culture of helping those who need support and develop reciprocal support arrangements (Marchetti, 2013, on job sharing among migrant women; Lulle, 2014, on helping those most in need). Such arrangements can be found regardless of gender, with men and women helping one another to fulfil caring requirements. Such tactics could be considered in terms of a moral economy of doing good deeds for each other. Global or national economies as well as individual enterprises benefit from temporary labour migrants in terms of increased capital gain.

Summing up the cases discussed above, I argue that travelling for care is not only a moral economy. It ought to be reconceptualised as a political economy of national and individual rights and the protection of temporary labour migrants across borders. In order for that to happen, structural change in legislation and cultural change in workplace practices is required, rather than just relying on migrants' own compassion and morality of mutual support. For instance, the European Commission (EC, 2005a) does not define circular migration; however, it indirectly notes that circularity comprises regular moving between two or more countries and encourages governments to ensure conditions under which people who move regularly across international borders can keep their jobs. Care in such legislation need to be taken seriously. The social protection (Alpes, 2015; Lafleur & Mescoli, 2018) of temporary migrant workers remains very little understood and advocated for at the levels of legislation and organisational cultural change in enterprises.

Finally, care is not "liquid" mobility, meaning that it is not a highly flexible process in contrast to labour mobilities in the EU regime (see Engbersen & Snel, 2013). The basis of the mobility paradigm about places and people who stay put in order to facilitate mobility for others is a fruitful starting point. But to recognise termporay migrants' rights to give care, not only through economic remittances but through physical mobilities too, is more difficult at the present time and at various scales: global, regional and at the workplace.

References

Alpes, M. J. (2015). "Social protection and migration control: The case of migrant care workers and Parisian welfare hotels". *Transnational Social Review* 5:3, pp. 1–16.

Baldassar, L., & L. Merla. (2014). *Transnational Families, Migration and the Circulation of Care. Understanding Mobility and Absence in Family Life*. London and New York: Routledge.

Baldassar, L., C. Baldock & R. Wildin. (2007). *Families Caring Across Borders: Migration, Aging and Transnational Caregiving*. London: Palgrave MacMillan.

Bogue, D. J. (1977). "A migrant's-eye view of the costs and benefits of migration to the metropolis". In A. A. Brown and E. Neuberger (eds). *Internal Migration: A Comparative Perspective* (pp. 167–182). New York: Academic Press.

Bonizzoni, P., & P. Boccagni. (2013). "Care (and) circulation revisited: A conceptual map of diversity in transnational parenting". In L. Baldassar and L. Merla. *Transnational Families, Migration and the Circulation of Care. Understanding Mobility and Absence in Family Life* (pp. 76–91), New York: Routledge.

Boyd, M. (1989). "Family and personal networks in international migration: recent developments and new agendas". *International Migration Review,* 23:3, pp. 638–670.

Castles, S. (2006). "Guestworkers in Europe: a resurrection?". *International Migration Review,* 40:4, pp. 741–766.

Castles, S. (2012). "Understanding the relationship between methodology and methods". In C. Vagas-Silva (ed.). *Handbook of Research Methods in Migration* (pp. 7–25). Cheltenham: Edward Elgar Publishing.

Cresswell, T. (2006). On the Move: Mobility in the Modern World. London: Routledge.

EC. (2005a). "Migration and Development: Some concrete orientations". European Commission, Communication from Commission (COM) 390.

EC. (2005b). "Policy plan on legal migration". European Commission, Communication from Commission (COM) 669.

Engbersen, G., & E. Snel. (2013). "Liquid migration: dynamic and fluid patterns of post accession migration". In B. Glorius, I. Grabowska-Lusinska and A. Rindoks (eds.). *Mobility in Transition: Migration Patterns after EU Enlargement* (pp. 21–40). Amsterdam: Amsterdam University Press.

Fawcett, J. T. (1989). "Networks, linkages and migration systems". *International Migration Review,* 23:3, pp. 671–680.

Goldring, L. (2004). "Family and collective remittances to Mexico: a multi-dimensional typology". *Development and Change,* 35:4, pp. 799–840.

Harbison, S. F. (1981). "Family structure and family strategy in migration decision making". In G. F. DeJong and R. W. Gardner (eds.). *Migration Decision Making: Multidisciplinary Approaches to Microlevel Studies in Developed and Developing Countries* (pp. 225–251). New York: Pergamon Press.

Hochschild, A. R. (2000). "Global care chains and emotional surplus value". In W. Hutton and A. Giddens (eds.). *Global Capitalism* (pp. 130–46). New York: The New Press.

Iglicka, K. (2001). "Shuttling from the former Soviet Union to Poland: from 'primitive mobility' to migration". *Journal of Ethnic and Migration Studies,* 27:3, pp. 505–518.

IOM. (2005). *World Migration 2005: Costs and Benefits of International Migration*. Geneva: International Organization for Migration.

Kilkey, M., A. Plomien & D. Perrons. (2014). "Migrant men's fathering narratives, practices and projects in national and transnational spaces". *International Migration*, 52, pp. 178–191.

Lafleur, J.-M., & E. Mescoli. (2018). "Creating undocumented EU migrants through welfare: a conceptualization of undeserving and precarious citizenship". *Sociology*, 52:3, pp. 480–496.

Lee, E. S. (1966). "A theory of migration". *Demography*, 3:1, pp. 47–57.

Lulle, A. (2014). "Shifting notions of gendered care and neoliberal motherhood: from lives of Latvian migrant women in Guernsey". *Women's Studies International Forum* 47, pp. 239–249.

Marchetti, S. (2013). "Dreaming circularity? Eastern European women and job sharing in paid home care". *Journal of Immigrant & Refugee Studies* 11:4, pp. 347–363.

Miles, R. (1986). "Labour migration, racism and capital accumulation in western Europe since 1945: an overview". *Capital & Class*, 10:1, pp. 49–86.

Morokvasic, M. (2004). "Settled in mobility: engendering post-wall migration in Europe". *Feminist Review*, 77, pp. 7–25.

Newland, K., D. Agunias & A. Terrazas. (2008). *Learning by doing: Experiences of circular migration*. Washington, DC: Migration Policy Institute.

Parrenas, R. S. (2005). *Children of global migration. Transnational families and gendered woes*. Stanford, CA: Stanford University Press.

Piore, M. J. (1979). *Birds of passage: Migrant labour in industrial societies*. Cambridge: Cambridge University Press.

Ruhs, M. (2006). "The potential of temporary migration programmes in future international migration policy". *International Labour Review*, 145:1–2, pp. 7–36.

Salazar, N. B., & N. G. Schiller (eds.). (2014). *Regimes of Mobility: Imaginaries and Relationalities of Power*. London: Routledge.

Sheller, M., & J. Urry. (2006). "The new mobilities paradigm". *Environment and Planning A*, 38:2, pp. 207–226.

Sjaastad, L.A. (1962). "The costs and returns of human migration". *Journal of Political Economy*, 70:1, pp. 80–93.

Skeldon, R. (2012). "Going round in circles: Circular migration, poverty alleviation and marginality". *International Migration*, 50:3, pp. 43–60.

Stark, O., & D. E. Bloom. (1985). "The new economics of labor migration". *The American Economic Review*, 75:2, pp. 173–178.

Stouffer, S. A. (1960). "Intervening opportunities and competing migrants". *Journal of Regional Science*, 2:1, pp. 1–26.

Taylor, J. E. (1999). "The new economics of labour migration and the role of remittances in the migration process". *International Migration*, 37:1, pp. 63–88.

Triandafyllidou, A. (2013). *Circular migration between Europe and its neighbourhood: Choice or necessity?* Oxford: Oxford University Press.

United Nations. (2006). *International migration and development: Report of the Secretary-General.* New York: United Nations General Assembly.

Venturini, A. (2008). "Circular migration as an employment strategy for Mediterranean countries". CARIM/RSCAS Anlytic and synthetic notes No 39.

World Bank. (2006). *International labor migration: Eastern Europe and the former Soviet Union.* Washington, D.C.: The World Bank, Europe and Central Asia Region.

Zontini, E. (2001). "Family formation in gendered migrations: Moroccan and Filipino women in Bologna". In R. King (ed.). *The Mediterranean Passage: Migration and New Cultural Encounters in Southern Europe* (pp. 231–257). Liverpool: Liverpool University Press.

Regulatory Regimes and (Infra)Structuring Emancipation Dynamics: The Case of Health Workers' Migration

Joana de Sousa Ribeiro

Introduction

Migration and healthcare are socio-political phenomena that are governed by national and supra-national inter-related regulatory frameworks. On the one hand, the politics of admission into a country remain largely a matter of national regulation, despite the international recognition of the right to migrate as a Human Right (Universal Declaration of Human Rights, Article 13). On the other hand, International Health Regulations (IHR) are part of a supranational legal framework (WHO, 2005) that came into force in June 2007. The IHR, with the aim of preventing and responding to the international spread of diseases and other health risks, represent a common national effort to notify an international organisation such as the World Health Organisation (WHO) about specific public-health events, such as emerging infectious diseases.

While regulation tends to be a field of analysis in migration (Geddes & Korneev, 2015) and health studies (Chamberlain, Dent & Saks, 2018), emancipation remains an under-researched area, notably as regards its structural settings.[1] Based on a case study addressing health workers' migration to and from a Southern European country, Portugal, this chapter aims to debate the regulation-emancipation tensions, articulations and transactions through the concept of "(infra-)structuring emancipation", which attempts to consider "emancipation" as a dynamic feedback mechanism in the overall migratory process.

The cross-cutting analysis of these two areas – international migration and international health – is an important challenge for the inter- and intra-play[2] of regulation and emancipation. Indeed, this case study provides us with an opportunity to explore different fields of transnational practices (international recruitment practices, re-accreditation processes of foreign-trained professionals, as well as matters of the portability of qualifications or the sustainability of the health workforce) which helps to comprehend the inter- and intra-relations of regulation and emancipation. Taking into account the interrelatedness of several dimensions of regulation[3] and the emancipatory potentials within each field of transnational practices (such as international recruitment, re-accreditation, portability of qualifications and a sustainable health workforce), this chapter envisages the relevance of a relational approach concerning the regulation-emancipation debate.

This regulation and emancipation division is analysed bearing in mind social transformations occurring in a capitalist society, where the labour market is organised via brokers and intermediaries (through international job fairs or recruitment by private agencies) and is affected by the role of social media networks in international recruitment processes. Additionally, institutional (infra-)structures, such as specific professional inclusion programmes and Offices, specific institutional networks, national legal frameworks, plus global health governance tools, are also taken into account.

I thus propose a re-evaluation of de- and re-regulation of mobility regimes *vis-à-vis* emancipatory mobility structures through the notion of '(infra-)structuring emancipation', which reintroduces the longstanding sociological dilemma of structure *versus* agency and its capacity, or not, of convergence. This includes debating the possibilities of blurring this binary as, for instance, "the cumulative effect of independent decisions may, over time, alter the decision making context" (Massey, 1990, p. 9). When on e is aware of this dynamic, the tensions between regulatory regimes and mobility structures for emancipation become more visible, at least in its (dis)continuities.

Exploring the inter- and intra-relations of regulatory regimes and the "(infra-)structuring emancipation" dynamics related to the international mobility of health workers from and to Portugal, this chapter seeks to answer the following questions: how does the migration of health workers inter-play with regulatory regimes and structures of mobility? At what point are changing social transformations (e.g. the privatisation of intermediaries, the digitalisation of networks and informal recruitment channels) relevant contextual and cumulative causation mechanisms for migration and do they consequently present themselves as specific fields of transnational practices for de(re-)regulation and emancipation? How can this case-study contribute to overcoming the traditional social sciences dilemma regarding structure and agency?

The chapter is divided into four sections. First, it briefly describes the context that frames the research analysis, namely Portugal as a country of immigration and emigration. Second, the paper highlights the general conceptual framework behind the analytical approach. This section, in particular, argues for a new concept: "(infra-)structuring emancipation" dynamics. This is followed by a section where the fields of transnational practices under this notion are described in more detail. The final section summarises and concludes the discussion.

The Inter- and Intra-Play among Regulation and Emancipation

Regulation and emancipation processes are generally understood as diametrically opposed processes in social theory such as the Marxism, Critical Theory, Political Economy, Feminist Studies and Subaltern Studies approaches, to name a few. Considering regulation as the "mechanisms of social control, including unintentional and non-State processes" (Baldwin et al., 1998, p. 4) and emancipation as "freeing those outside established structures of power from the constraints that hold them back from realising their potential" (Fierke, 2010), both concepts are essential for an analysis of cross-border labour mobility and its relation to decent international recruitment practices, effective knowledge transfer and a sustainable health workforce. In the framework of this debate and drawing on either capabilities theory or the agency-structure sociological division, emancipation is usually conceived as the opposite of regulation, reinstating in this way the dichotomous discourse of modernity.

In this regard, the migration literature tends to value a one-sided perspective (structure or agency) over one that effectively incorporates both sides (agency-structure) or, at least, one that illustrates the negotiation process driven by the agency.[4] In this line, the concept of "relational agency" (Burkitt, 2015) presents an alternative approach that underlines the relational view and considers individuals as"'interactants' rather than as singular agents or actors" (Burkitt, 2015, p. 2). In the process, the notion of "structure" is replaced by multiple relational links, "webs of interdependence" (Burkitt, 2015, p. 14) or networks, not confined to a fixed space or time. Apart from this argument, the contribution of Karen Barad

(2007) is also relevant, especially if an explanation of the inter-action and intra-action of constraints and enablers of mobility is envisaged.

To provide an explanation of the inter-action and intra-action of constraints and enablers of mobility, I also draw upon structuration theory (Giddens, 1984) and morphogenesis analysis (Archer, 1982), which redirect the focus towards a methodological and an analytical dualism respectively. The critical realist approach to migration studies (Bakewell, 2010) and the theorisation of agency and structure as phenomena that are interrelated and mutually informing (Sewell, 1992) endorse the possibilities of an integrative response in a specific area of studies such as migration.

Therefore, in order to contribute to a relational approach that considers the inter- and intra-play dynamics of structure and agency and drawing on the concept of "structures of opportunity" (Itzigsohn, 2000), usually referring to political participation resources, I propose the notion of (infra-)structuring emancipation. By that I mean the emergence of (infra-)structures that envisage the turning over of social and institutional constraints to mobility.[5] The emphasis on "(infra-)structuring" in its verb condition translates an open-ended, dynamic and dialogical process of inter- and intra-relations of organised practices and webs of resources, in this case related to the study of international recruitment practices, transnational knowledge transfer and the sustainability of the health workforce.

The flowchart below (Flowchart 1) seeks to translate the inter- and intra-play among regulation and emancipation, having as a mediator "emancipatory infra-structures" dynamics, namely social media networks, job fairs, specific programmes and offices, specific institutional networks, the national legal framework and toolkits. Thus, this proposal represents an interstitial linkage that comprises regulation and emancipation approaches, considering multiple dimensions of regulation (supranational regulation, multilateral regulation, re-regulation, soft regulation, self-regulation, de-regulation), without neglecting the emancipatory dynamics that each field of transnational practices (international recruitment, re-accreditation processes, the portability of qualifications and a sustainable health workforce) contemplates.

Therefore, an attempt to consider regulation and emancipation in its (dis) continuous inter- and intra-play instead of diminishing tensions and articulations is an alternative proposal to explore the channels of cross-transactions among the two (Dépelteau, 2008). The question of such (dis)continuity gains even more relevance in the exploration of the international migration of health workers,

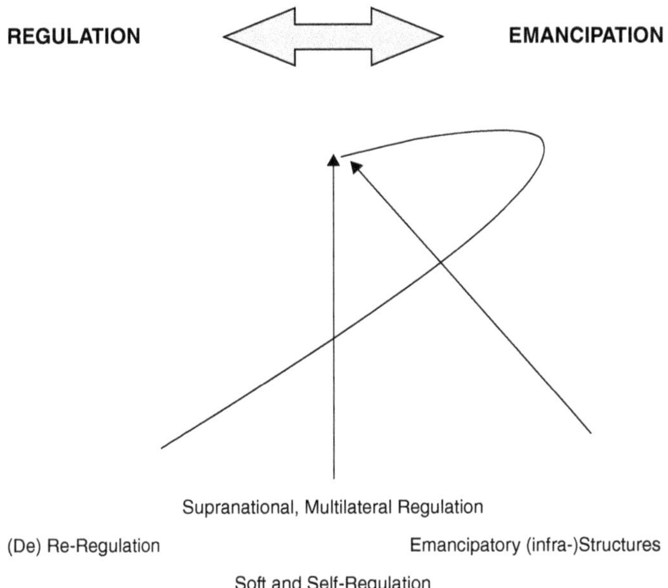

Flowchart 1: Inter- and Intra-Play among Regulation and Emancipation

as the study of migration is too often based on deterministic proposals, such as those concerning "push-and-pull" models.

Indeed, instead of studying labour migration (in this case health workers' migration) as an international labour flow between two places (and the respective pull-push motivations), the approach advocated in this chapter turns to a dialogic dynamics under the labour migration process, which involves several state and non-state agents, with a regulatory and an emancipatory scope. This constellation of interests and strategies is based on an inter-mediation of power relations often neglected in skilled migration research.[6] However, besides that, an (intra-)mediation relationship between regulation and emancipation is also essential to consider. Thus, "(infra-)structuring emancipation" is a way to respond to the challenge of an integrative approach without being exclusively over-determined by a middle range focus.

Setting the Context

This case study[7] is embedded in the analysis of "overstayer"[8] and "overqualified" migrants' experiences, such as those of: a) Eastern European migrants who came to Portugal during the late 1990s on tourist visas and who took jobs below their educational qualification level before their qualifications were recognised and b) overqualified Portuguese emigrants who, in the aftermath of the 2008 economic, social and financial crisis, migrated to escape from reduced career prospects, underemployment and unemployment. In both cases, migration is tied to experiences of overqualification in Portugal where the public welfare and healthcare systems suffered from disinvestment during the austerity period,[9] affecting recruitment and job opportunities. Between the late 1990s and the beginning of the twenty-first century, Portugal, along with other Southern European countries, received a large immigrant population from countries in Eastern Europe with which it had had no prior social, economic, historical or cultural privileged relations (Baganha, Marques & Góis, 2004). As a member of the Schengen agreement, Portugal turned into an attractive country for immigration, especially when the secondary labour markets in Italy and Spain became saturated and these traditional immigration countries implemented control policy measures.[10] Indeed, with an immigrant population rising from approximately 50,000 individuals in 1980 to almost 480,300 in 2018 (SEF, 2019), Portugal began to imagine itself at the centre of an Intra-EU mobility regime (Peixoto, 2009), whose differentiation, stratification and contradictions were pointed out by some authors (Engbersen et al., 2017).

Additionally, the "relatively strong historical propensity for intra-European Union (EU) mobility" (Holland & Paluchowski, 2013, p. 4) from Portugal was evident during the 2008 economic and financial crisis. Indeed, the available data report around 100,000 exits in both 2011 and 2012, a figure that surpasses the international flows during the dictatorship period of the 1960s. During the 2008–2011 period, Portugal was the only Southern European country where the percentage of Portuguese emigrants having less than three years of migration and higher qualifications almost doubled (from 14% to 27%), which reveals a structural change in the profile of the Portuguese emigrant population (Holland & Paluchowski, 2013). Moreover, unemployment increased significantly during the austerity period (from 12.7% in 2011 to 16.2% in 2013), affecting in particular young workers under 25. For instance, during that period an estimated 7,000 to 9,000 nurses were unemployed.

Therefore, the dual migratory profile of Portugal as an immigrant and an emigrant country has become more obvious. As such, this coexistence has been called a "mixed regime" (Peixoto, 2007; 2009). This singularity of the

Portuguese migratory experience also applies to the health sector. On the one hand, the international outflow of doctors and nurses was in part a consequence of the economic and financial crisis. For instance, the data from the Portuguese Nursing Council showed that, in 2010, 179 Portuguese nurses requested a Certificate of Good Standing for working abroad, a required document for working in EU countries which, at least, reveals the intention to migrate, while a year later, precisely at the beginning of the "Troika" period, when Portugal signed two Memoranda of Understanding,[11] that number had risen to 1,775. The following three years (2012–2014) reported more than 2,500 and, in 2017, 1,286. Additionally, data from the Medical Council registered that between 2014 and 2017 nearly 1,219 people left the country. On the other hand, it is important to remark that precisely at that time (in 2017) there were 3,103 foreign health professionals working in Portuguese NHS institutions (2.4% of the total staff), mostly doctors (58.9%) and nurses (17.6%) (ACSS, 2018).

Fields of Transnational Practices in Health Workers' Migration

The case-study under analysis aims to translate the intertwined relationship embedded in the regulation-emancipation tensions. This case of healthcare workers migrating to and from Portugal gives us an opportunity to analyse international recruitment practices, the re-accreditation processes of foreign-trained professionals, the portability of qualifications and the sustainability of the health workforce in line with the de(re-)regulation regimes and the emergent emancipatory (infra-) structures (Table 1). Indeed, and for the purposes of this chapter, these matters are important fields of transnational practice for studying the relationship between regulation and emancipation. Therefore, taking into account examples of supranational regulation, multilateral regulation, "soft regulation", self-regulation, (de)re-regulation processes and emancipation structures (Table 1), the relevance of an inter- (but also intra-) relational approach for the regulation-emancipation debate becomes more obvious.

Having said that, several fields of transnational practices related to the institutional regulation of healthcare migration (international recruitment practices, re-accreditation processes, the portability of qualifications and a sustainable health workforce) are analysed below, in order to show the inter- and intra-play between regulation and emancipation.

Table 1   Fields of Transnational Practices, Regulatory Regimes and Emancipatory (Infra-)Structures

Fields of transnational practices	Regulatory regimes	Emancipatory (infra-)structures
International recruitment	Soft regulation *(WHO Global Code of Practice and the International Recruitment of Health Personnel)* Multilateral regulation *(bilateral agreements)* De-regulation and Re-regulation *(recruitment agencies)*	Social media networks *(Facebook groups)* Jobs Fairs (virtual or not)
Re-accreditation	Self-Regulation *(professional bodies: Ordem dos Médicos and Ordem dos Enfermeiros)*	Specific programmes and offices *(programmes for foreign-trained doctors and nurses; support office for academic and skills recognition)*
Portability of qualifications	Supranational regulation *(Directive 2005/36/EC and the amending Directive 2013/55/EC)* Re-Regulation *(Law Act nº 341/2007)*	Specific institutional networks *(ENIC and NARIC)* National Legal Framework *(Law Act nº 341/2007)*

Fields of transnational practices	Regulatory regimes	Emancipatory (infra-) structures
Sustainable health workforce	Soft Regulation (*Towards a sustainable health workforce in the WHO European Region: framework for action*)	Toolkit (*Toolkit for a Sustainable Health Workforce in the WHO European Region*)

International Recruitment Practices

The recruitment of healthcare professionals in Portugal has gone through a process of increasing privatisation and informality; from bilateral agreements to international recruitment agencies, from talent searching to social media and social networking, the process of international recruitment is becoming an increasingly selective and non-state-driven process. Therefore, a WHO Global Code of Practice on the International Recruitment of Health Personnel was adopted by the sixty-third World Health Assembly on 21 May 2010 and serves as a guide for ethical and decent international recruitment practices. Portugal was one of the signatory countries; by then the state's role in international recruitment was still launched through bilateral agreements.

Indeed, in 2008 the Portuguese Ministry of Health established bilateral agreements with Cuba (44 physicians in 2009; contracts were renewed in 2012, not necessarily with the same group) and Colombia (82 physicians in 2011). Additionally, a formal permit for healthcare professionals from Costa Rica (14 physicians in 2008, nine in 2011) and a cooperation healthcare agreement with Uruguay for three-year periods (15 physicians in 2008) were launched. The medicine regulatory body (Ordem dos Médicos, OM) was sceptical about this solution. As the former president of the OM stated:

> We had colleagues who wanted to be hired under the same conditions and we were not given these same conditions. So, there was a positive discrimination of those colleagues who were proactively imported.

At the same time, specialised job fairs, organised by international companies such as Careers and White and MedPharmJobs, were launched in hotels in Porto, Coimbra and Lisbon and, increasingly, in virtual space to attract Portuguese graduate students and healthcare professionals (mainly doctors and nurses) to work abroad. This corresponds to a process of cross-border recruitment de(re)regulation. Following Mackenzie and Lucio (2005), I prefer the term "re-regulation" precisely because it involves a change of the regulatory functions of actors. For instance, recruitment agencies (some of them based in the Portuguese cities of Porto, Viseu and Lisbon) have assumed the role of gatekeepers as they are responsible for the selection, registration, advising, and initial introduction of recruits to the technical language and caregiving culture of host countries such as the United Kingdom, France, Belgium, the Netherlands and Denmark. These agencies are represented at job fairs and other recruitment events, while also organising promotion events in hotels, hospitals, medical schools and nursing schools. The recruitment agencies interviewed pointed out that their recruitment work was not as welcome in public hospitals and education institutions. Indeed, an employee of one of the recruitment agencies recounted the case of a nursing school professor who was not happy about the launching of an international recruitment drive at the nursing school:

> [...] for him, we were draining people. What he wanted to say is that we were the ones to blame [...] Even when I asked him about the working conditions for nurses in Portugal – the lack of a labour contract, the lump sum contracts, the amount of payment for each hour – he said that the current situation was not so bad.

Thus, an entire international recruitment industry has flourished, involving a range of activities and services, indcluding the recruitment process, language-learning schools, translation, document authentication services and career guidance. This "migration industry" (Castles & Miller, 2003, p. 27) also targets the best qualified segment of the migrant population, the "skilled workers". Locating the concept in the migration systems theory framework, the above authors underlined the importance of a "meso-structure" in understanding the (re)production of the migration process. However, the analysis of "migration intermediaries" within a skilled "migration industry" remains rare (Tissot, 2018).

Moreover, the expansion and use of personal networks through social media open up new ways of understanding the importance and role of weak ties (Granovetter, 1973) in job-seeking. The case of the Portuguese healthcare professionals abroad demonstrates the relevance of Facebook groups (such as *Internato Médico no Estrangeiro, Médicos Portugueses no Estrangeiro, Médicos Portugueses Residentes no Estrangeiro* and *Diáspora dos Enfermeiros*) in the process of seeking information about jobs overseas. The *Diáspora dos Enfermeiros* (Nurse Diaspora) Facebook group is a noteworthy case, because it started as a social media group and later emerged as a collective association (*Saúde além Fronteiras*). This association addresses not only Portuguese nurses abroad but also potential emigrants. Then, the coordinator of *Saúde além Fronteiras*, himself a former emigrant and one of the first Portuguese health-sector migrants in the United Kingdom, began to engage in consultancy and international recruitment. Currently, he is considering returning to nursing practice in Portugal because, "here [in Portugal] the potential talent is wasted ... we don't have the possibility to be recognised as a professional group".

To sum up, it is important to note the relevance of intermediary infrastructures as meso-level practices and resources that enclose new forms of de(re-)regulation regimes and the emergence of "emancipatory (infra-)structures" (social media networks, international job fairs, specific programmes and offices, specific institutional networks, national legal frameworks and toolkits) that could serve not only as facilitators but also as gatekeepers[12] of a selective recruitment process.

Subsidised Programmes for Foreign-Trained Doctors and Nurses
Special reaccreditation programmes were created to address situations of overqualification among foreign-trained professionals working in Portugal in the secondary labour market (Baganha et al., 2004). First, the Project to Support the Professionalisation of Immigrant Doctors (PAPMI, 2002–2005) was piloted and coordinated by civil society organisations. Its main aim was to facilitate the recognition of the qualifications of foreign doctors in order for them to be able to practise in Portugal. The main challenges in the implementation of this project were related to unfamiliarity with the regulatory bodies, employers and academic institutions, not knowing about the occupation-specific language, a lack of recognition of or pertaining to professional experience gained outside Portugal, institutional discrimination against older female applicants, difficulties in adjustment to the Portuguese workplace culture, and not understanding the caregiving culture.

After this initial pilot project there was another project targeting the reaccreditation of foreign-trained doctors (Professional Integration of Immigrant Doctors, PIPMI, 2008–2009), which received sponsorship from the Health Ministry. This project was a collaboration by the Ministry with several organisations that had already been involved in the pilot project, including an established international Catholic organisation, a foundation, medical and nursing schools, medical and nursing professional councils, embassies and consulates, and the Borders and Foreign Bureau (SEF). Nursing, too, received special attention regarding the recognition of qualifications. Indeed, a project aimed at the recognition of nursing qualifications was developed between 2004 and 2007. This project comprised Portuguese language courses and the provision of social services to facilitate family inclusion in Portugese society.

The assessment of diploma equivalence is a long process as it involves the need to gather all the required documents (and their translations), the delivery of the documentation to a medical faculty and nursing school, a waiting period, attendance at Portuguese-language training courses, a training period (four months for nurses, four to six months for physicians), several exams (a language exam as well as theoretical and clinical diagnosis exams), registration with the medical and nursing council, and a professional internship (if a licence is to be issued).

The organised civil society that coordinates and implements the above projects performs important roles during the re-accreditation process, from service provision to bridging and bonding social capital, promoting connections among the applicants for the projects and even mentoring newcomers. The organisations involved in the projects act as certifiers of the whole of the recognition process, which is essential for public recognition of the re-accreditation process as a societal added value.

The above experiences were also incorporated at a governmental level, as the High Commissioner for Migration (ACM) created a Support Office for Academic and Skills Recognition. This Office's purpose is to make available an integrated structure which could respond to the barriers previously identified during the launching of the projects: gathering all the documentation required for the application process in the country of origin (namely the syllabus programme), the translation and authentication of all the documents, and registration with professional associations. As stated by the Office coordinator, the aim of the Office is to:

> Show all the options, to state what is possible, what is not possible; so, when the applicant decides, he could decide in a responsive way [...] because if the goal is to work as a doctor, he or she has to know that there is a regulator body that rules the procedures.

As I have argued elsewhere (Ribeiro, 2018), the implementation of the ACM Office is an example of a bottom-up institutionalisation process of non-state actors' initiatives. This institutional response, in conjunction with the subsidised Programmes for Foreign-Trained Doctors and Nurses, represents a turning point in the process of re-accreditation, which could be considered as a new (infra-) structuring dynamic as regards the recognition of migrants' qualifications, although not extended in all its dimensions, such as the inter-recognition one (Ribeiro, 2019).

Frameworks Supporting the Portability of Qualifications
One of the main pillars of the European Union project is the free movement of European citizens, namely the right of entry to any Member State, whatever one's social condition, regardless of professional status or illness. The regulatory regime of the Professional Qualifications Directives (Directive 2005/36/EC and the amending Directive 2013/55/EC) allows for the automatic recognition of professional qualifications in regulated professions (doctors, dentists, pharmacists, nurses, midwives, veterinary surgeons and architects), thereby facilitating free movement (European Commission, 2011). Overall, the provision of qualifications recognition is thus an opportunity to extend the accessibility of the internal labour market to certain EU-EEA professionals.[13]

While the 2005 Directive simplified the legislative framework adopted since the 1960s, the so-called "modernised Directive" (Directive 2013/55/EC) adjusted it to a digital age, incorporating measures that facilitate the recognition procedures. Indeed, both the use of the Internal Market Information System (IMI) as an effective alert system about professional malpractice and the introduction of a European Professional Card[14] increased the transparency of the recognition process. These initiatives are among the new measures provided for by the 2013 Directive. This amending Directive also addresses the question of linguistic proficiency. Language proficiency tests are envisaged in the case of professions that deal with patient safety. These tests are implemented after the recognition of qualifications but before a professional licence is issued by a regulatory body.

In the Portuguese case, the year 2007 marks an important turn in the process of recognition of educational qualifications issued in countries that are incorporated in the European Network of Information Centres (ENIC),[15] which reigns supreme in the EU-EEA region. That year, a national regulation (Law Act n° 341/2007) was implemented to govern the process of diploma recognition in terms of academic titles. This regulation simplified the recognition of foreign academic degrees by removing lengthy bureaucratic procedures and can thus be considered part of either an emancipatory (infra-)structure or a re-regulatory regime. According to the Portuguese National Academic Recognition Information Centre (NARIC), the above national legal framework gained international recognition as a good practice and could be transferred to other national legal frameworks. In this regard, this specific institutional network and the above national legal framework correspond to a new (infra-)structuring dynamic regarding knowledge transfer.

Sustainable Health Workforce
"Towards a sustainable health workforce in the WHO European Region: a Framework for Action"[16] outlines an international instrument advocating for a sustainable health workforce in the WHO European Region. The above document is aligned with the main guidelines of the *Global Strategy on Human Resources for Health: Workforce 2030* (2016)[17] and the *Working for Health and Growth: Investing in the Health Workforce* (2016),[18] both perceived as a paradigm shift in health workforce policy. Moreover, the need to sustain a transformed and effective health workforce within strengthened health systems is also underlined in the 2030 agenda goals.

In an international context, a sustainable and resilient health workforce[19] is considered one of the main drivers for health system strengthening in the European Region. To obtain such a workforce several challenges need to be addressed: supply and demand imbalances, gender inequality and gender imbalances, achieving an appropriate skill mix, geographical maldistribution, gaps in attaining decent working conditions, and improving recruitment and retention. The internal imbalances within the EU, a social effect of regional socio-economic asymmetries (in favour of Northern and Western Europe), make effective actions across various sectors and institutional actors even more urgent. To understand this question fully it is important to note that in 2010 the WHO adopted the *Global Code of Practice for the International Recruitment of Health Personnel*, which corresponds to a "soft regulation" to prevent international recruitment from countries of the metaphorical Global South, notably those with critical staff shortages. Consequently, Southern and Eastern European countries have been perceived as potential source countries, aggravating the inequalities in the distribution of health workers within the EU.

During the Fourth Global Forum on Human Resources for Health (Dublin, 13–17 November 2017), a *Toolkit for a Sustainable Health Workforce in the WHO*

European Region was developed, revealing the importance of health workforce sustainability in a region such as Europe, where the regional inequalities remain. This toolkit was created in order to support Member States and other stakeholders in the implementation of several strategic objectives (education and performance, planning and investment, capacity-building and analysis and monitoring), as well as collecting policy-evidence resources, such as international and national Human Resources for Health strategic documents (WHO Studies and Recommendations, *European Union Joint Action on Health Workforce Planning and Forecasting* disseminations, data from the European Commission Expert Group on European Health Workforce), analytical, planning and management tools, as well as case studies from within the WHO European Region and other research material. This tool is a valuable resource for Member States, including employers in the public and private sectors, non-governmental organisations, professional associations, educational and training institutions, trade unions and civil society organisations, to assess their health workforce policies within a local context.

This Framework for Action for a WHO region (Europe), where the reliance on foreign-trained health workers in some countries is evident, as it is in Portugal (Wismar et al., 2011), is a "soft regulation" initiative.[20] However, with the creation of the above toolkit (*Toolkit for a Sustainable Health Workforce in the WHO European Region*) a further step was taken towards a common transnational (infra-)structure addressed to the sustainability of the health workforce.

Concluding Remarks

In the case analysed – healthcare migration to and from Portugal – the reported social transformations (the privatisation of intermediaries, digitalisation of social networks and informal recruitment channels) are mainly related to the replacement of state (infra-)structures with non-state ones, driven by the market or organised via civil society networks. This social change poses new challenges regarding the equation of regulation regimes and mobility structures; among them, the emergence of an (infra-)structuring process that inter- (intra-)mediates regulation and emancipation.

Therefore, the given examples (social media networks, job fairs, specific programmes and offices, specific institutional networks, national legal frameworks and a toolkit) provide us with relevant settings for the analysis of the proposed term "(infra-)structuring emancipation", it being a facilitator (but also a gatekeeper) of the structure of mobility. Additionally, the processes of de(re-)regulation that the intermediaries of international recruitment envisage replace state mechanisms in the admission procedures with other channels of transaction of a corporate nature, for instance international recruitment agencies or social media networks.

Thus, as this case study illustrates, emancipatory (infra-)structures and de(re)regulation regimes assume an important role regarding a regulation-emancipation (dis)continuum process. In that, specific social transformations, for instance, growing privatisation, digitalisation of social networks and the increase of informal recruitment channels, should be understood as part of a continued, mutually constitutive, inter- (intra-)relationship of structure and agency.

In line with Salazar and Smart (2011), this chapter intends to go beyond the lack of balance of mobility with freedom, by illustrating new confinements that produce new modes of power relations, for instance among them the emergence of market mechanisms and the processes of de(re-)regulation. Indeed, looking at "emancipatory (infra-)structures" allows us to visualise other actors, processes and outcomes, which render visible the (dis)articulations that undergird the regulation *versus* emancipation binary. The dichotomy logic in mobility studies was problematised by some authors (i.e. Glick Schiller & Salazar, 2013), but the "regulation *versus* emancipation" dimension has not been given much attention.

In times of heightened cross-border mobility (Urry, 2008), the (de)commodification of labour intersects with state and non-state initiatives, and with structures of mobility which also have emancipatory potential. In this way, the term "regimes" in migration studies, drawing on Esping-Andersen's (1990) seminal work, implies a constellation of institutional, social and technological actors and processes that lead not only to varying degrees and forms of regulation but also to emancipation. The concept of "(infra-)structuring emancipation" introduced in this chapter seeks to capture this phenomenon.

To sum up, this chapter has sought to contribute to the structures and regimes of mobility debate, presenting a proposal that envisages inter- and intra-relations between constraining and enabling resources, the "(infra-)structuring emancipation". Like the frameworks of other regimes, such as care regimes (Lutz, 2017; Anderson, 2012), it encompasses the structures and regimes of mobility with a sliding scale of regulation that addresses "emancipatory (infra-)structures". Thereby it looks at a dialogical and open-ended combination of regulation and emancipation that needs further analysis in the future concerning, for example, its extension beyond healthcare contexts.

Notes

1 Among the exceptions please consider the debate initiated by Boaventura de Sousa Santos more than 20 years ago (Santos, 1995) and the international project coordinated by him at the Centre for Social Studies, University of Coimbra, Portugal, from January 1999 to December 2001 and entitled "Reinventing Social Emancipation": https://www.ces.uc.pt/emancipa/en/team/index.html.
2 To best reflect the simultaneity of both processes I employ the expression 'inter- (intra-) play'.
3 Such as supranational regulation, multilateral regulation, 'soft regulation', self-regulation, and de(re-)regulation.
4 Please consider one of the exceptions, namely Mainwaring (2016).
5 In my view, other proposals such as "Migrant Infrastructure" (Xiang and Lindquist, 2014), "Critical Infrastructure" (Korpela, 2016), "Infrastructuring Environments" (Blok, Nakazora & Winthereik, 2016) or "Arrival Infrastructure" (Meeus, Arnaut & van Heur, 2019; Sauders, 2010) do not emphasise enough the emancipatory dynamics (the dialogic potential for enabling transformation). Instead the focus is on the materialities.
6 Among the exceptions are Groutsis, van den Broek & Harvey, 2015; van den Broek, Harvey & Groutsis, 2016 and, more recent, Sandoz, 2019.
7 This chapter is based on longitudinal doctoral research. It is supported by biographical interviews with nurses and doctors who came from non-EU countries (Moldova, Russia and Ukraine), alongside accounts collected from Portuguese working abroad. Additionally, semi-structured interviews with international recruitment agencies and several national and international institutional actors were carried out; and official documents from the last decade concerning immigration, emigration and health policies were analysed. All quotations are selected from the interviews conducted as part of the PhD research.
8 Drawing on Maria Ioannis Baganha's proposal to distinguish five types of "foreign illegal workers" (Baganha et al., 1999), the category of "overstayer" corresponds to the person who comes to Portugal on a short-term visa (usually a tourist visa) and then remains in the country.
9 Indeed, the 2011–2014 period was marked by intense austerity policymaking.
10 In the case of Italy, after the restrictive Bossi Fini law (Law 189/30 July 2002), voted in by the then centre right government in 2002, a so-called "security package" from the Minister of Interior, Roberto Maroni, was introduced (Law 125/24 July 2008 and Law 94/15 July

2009) (Triandafyllidou & Ambrosini, 2011). Regarding Spain, the launching of a control policy was informally achieved after every period of regularisation (1985/1986, 1991, 1996, 2000, 2001 and 2005).

11 One of them with the European Commission and the European Central Bank (the Memorandum of Understanding on Specific Economic Policy Conditionality (MoU)) and the other with the International Monetary Fund (the Memorandum of Economic and Financial Policies (MEFP)).

12 This gatekeeping role occurs due the fact that the emancipation dimension under analysis in this article is sustained on infra-structures configurations and not on superstructures ones, following the Marxist terms. Therefore, it does not analyse the structural transformation of the societal configuration but just the overpassing of social and institutional constraints, a selective process then. In this case, the elected ones are the included on the social and institutional networks or who have a diploma in medicine or nursing areas and are selected for specific recognition programmes.

13 This EU legal framework also applies to third-country nationals who are members of the family of an EU citizen exercising their right to free movement within the European Union; who have the status of long-term residents; or who have refugee status in a Member State. Those conditions are accepted when the qualification is obtained in an EU Member State.

14 The European Professional Card (EPC) is an electronic certificate to be exchanged between competent authorities through the Internal Market Information System (IMI). This professional mobility tool has been available since 18 January 2016 for five professions (general care nurse, physiotherapist, pharmacist, (real) estate [the term 'real estat6e' is an American one. In English it is real property or land. But we do have a profession of 'estate agent', which is why I have put the 'real' in brackets] agent and mountain guide).

15 To implement the Lisbon Recognition Convention (Council of Europe, 1997), the Council of Europe and UNESCO launched the ENIC Network (European Network of National Information Centres on academic recognition and mobility) to include the Member States of the EU, the EEA and associated countries.

16 Approved in the 67th session of the WHO Regional Committee for Europe and stated in WHO Resolution EUR/RC67/R5, 13 September 2017.

17 World Health Assembly Resolution WHA69.19, Document A69/38.

18 A report of the United Nations High-Level Commission on Health Employment and Economic Growth.

19 By resilient I mean a workforce able to adjust and transform in the face of societal challenges such as an ageing population, technological innovation in medicine and health care, preparedness for critical events (i.e. natural disasters, armed conflict, pandemics, etc.).

20 Notwithstanding, its public relevance should not go unnoticed. Consider, for instance, the debate introduced by anti-European parties during the Brexit campaign around the National Health Service (NHS) and its supposed threats to its sustainability caused by the financial costs of the UK´s European Union membership.

References

ACSS. (2018). Relatório Social do Ministério da Saúde e do Serviço Nacional de Saúde.

Anderson, A. (2012). "Europe's care regimes and the role of migrant care workers within them". *Population Ageing*, 5, pp. 135–146.

Archer, M. S. (1982). "Morphogenesis versus structuration: on combining structure and action". *British Journal of Sociology*, 33:4, pp. 455–483.

Baganha, I. (1999). "Legal status and employment opportunities: immigrants in the Portuguese labour market". Oficina do CES, 139.

Baganha, I., J. Marques & P. Góis. (2004). "Novas Migrações, Novos Desafios: a imigração do leste europeu". *Revista Crítica de Ciências Sociais*, 69, pp. 95–115.

Bakewell, O. (2010). "Some reflections on structure and agency in migration theory". *Journal of Ethnic and Migration Studies*, 36, pp. 1689–1708.

Baldwin, R., C. Scott & C. Hood (eds.). (1998). *A Reader on Regulation*. Oxford: Oxford University Press.

Barad, K. (2007). *Meeting the Universe Halfway: Quantum Physics and the Entanglement of Matter and Meaning*. Durham, NC: Duke University Press.

Blok, A., M. Nakazora & B. R. Winthereik. (2016). "Infrastucturing environments". *Science as Culture*, 25:1, pp. 1–22.

Burkitt, I. (2016). "Relational agency: relational sociology, agency and interaction". *European Journal of Social Theory*, 19:3, pp. 322–339.

Castles, S., & M. J. Miller. (2003). *The Age of Migration: International Population Movements in the Modern World*. New York: The Guilford Press.

Chamberlain, J. M., M. Dent and M. Saks (eds.). (2018). *Professional Health Regulation in the Public Interest - International Perspectives*. Bristol: Policy Press.

Dépelteau, F. (2008). "Relational thinking: a critique of co-deterministic theories of structure and agency". *Sociological Theory*, 26:1, pp. 51–73.

Engbersen, G., A. Leerkes, P. Scholten & E. Snel. (2017). "The intra-EU mobility regime: differentiation, stratification and contradictions". *Migration Studies*, 5:3, pp. 337–355.

Esping-Andersen, G. (1990). *The Three Worlds of Welfare Capitalism*. Cambridge: Polity Press.

Fierke, K. M. (2010). "Critical theory, security and emancipation". In N. Sandal and R. Marlin-Bennett (eds.). *Oxford Research Encyclopedia*. Oxford: Oxford University Press.

Geddes, A., & O. Korneev. (2015). "The state and the regulation of migration". In S. McMahon and L. S. Talani (eds.). *Handbook of the International Political Economy of Migration*. Cheltenham, UK; Northampton, MA: Edward Elgar.

Giddens, A. (1984). *The Constitution of Society*. Cambridge: Polity Press.

Glick Schiller, N., & N. B. Salazar. (2013). "Regimes of mobility across the globe". *Journal of Ethnic and Migration Studies*, 39:2, pp. 183–200.

Granovetter, M. S. (1973). "The strength of weak ties". *American Journal of Sociology*, 78:6, pp. 1360–1380.

Groutsis, D., D. van den Broek & W. S. Harvey. (2015). "Transformations in network governance: the case of migration intermediaries". *Journal of Ethnic and Migration Studies*, 41:10, pp. 1558–1576.

Holland, D., & P. Paluchowski. (2013). *Geographical labour mobility in the context of the crisis. European Employment Observatory, Ad-hoc Request*. London: National Institute of Economic and Social Research.

Itzigsohn, J. (2000). "Immigration and the boundaries of citizenship: The institutions of immigrants`political transnationalism". *International Migration Review*, 34:4, pp. 1126–1154.

Korpela, M. (2016). "Infrastructure". In N. B. Salazar and K. Jayaram (eds.). *Keywords of Mobility: Critical Engagements*. Oxford: Berghahn.

Lutz, H. (2017). "Care as a fictitious commodity: reflections on the intersections of migration, gender and care regimes". *Migration Studies*, 5:3, pp. 356–368.

MacKenzie, R., & M. Lucio. (2005). "The realities of regulatory change: beyond the fetish of deregulation". *Sociology*, 39:3, pp. 499–517.

Mainwaring, C. (2016). "Migrant Agency: negotiating borders and migration controls". *Migration Studies*, 4:3, pp. 289–308.

Massey, D. S. (1990). "Social structure, household strategies and the cumulative causation of migration". *Population Index*, 56:1, pp. 3–26.

Meeus, B., K. Arnaut & B. van Heur (eds.). (2019). *Arrival Infrastructures: Migration and Urban Social Mobilities*. London: Springer.

Peixoto, J. (2007). "Dinâmicas e regimes migratórios: o caso das migrações internacionais em Portugal». *Análise Social*, 42 (183), pp. 445–469.

Peixoto, J., & C. Sabino. (2009). "Portugal: immigration, the labour market and policy in Portugal: trends and prospects". IDEA Working Papers, n° 6.

Ribeiro, J. S. (2018). "Being called 'skilled': a multi-scalar approach of migrant doctors`recognition". *Migration Letters*, 15:4, pp. 477–490.

Ribeiro, J. S. (2019). "From interculturalism to inter-recognition: towards an ethico-onto-epistemological approach in migration research". *Journal of Multicultural Discourses,* 14:1, pp. 46–60

Santos, B. S. (1995). *Toward a New Legal Common Sense: Law, Science and Politics in the Paradigmatic Transition.* New York: Routledge.

Salazar, N. B., & A. Smart (eds.). (2011). "Anthropological takes on (im)mobility". Special issue, *Identities: Global Studies in Culture and Power,* 18:6, pp. i-ix.

Sandoz, L. (2019). *Mobilities of the Highly Skilled towards Switzerland. The Role of Intermediaries in Defining "Wanted Immigrants"* (Springer IMISCOE Series). Springer Open.

Sauders, D. (2010). *Arrival City: How the largest migration in history is reshaping our work.* New York: Pantheon Books.

SEF/Departamento de Planeamento e Formação (Núcleo de Planeamento). (2019). "Relatório Imigração, Fronteiras e Asilo (RIFA) – 2018". Lisbon: SEF.

Sewell, W. H. (1992). "A theory of structure: duality, agency and transformation". *American Journal of Sociology,* 98:1, pp. 1–29.

Tissot, F. (2018). "A migration industry for skilled migrants: the case of relocation services". *Migration Letters,* 15:4, pp. 545–560.

Urry, J. (2008). "Moving on the mobility turn". In J. Urry (ed.). *Tracing Mobilities: Towards a Cosmopolitan Perspective in Mobility Research.* Aldershot: Ashgate.

van den Broek, D., W. S. Harvey & D. Groutsis. (2016). "Commercial migration intermediaries and the segmentation of skilled migrant employment". *Work, Employment and Society,* 30:3, pp. 523–534.

WHO. (2005). International Health Regulations. Geneva: World Health Organisation. Available from: http://apps.who.int/iris/bitstre am/10665/246107/1/9789241580496-eng.pdf. (1.06.2018).

Wismar, M., C. B. Maier, I. A. Glinos, G. Dussault & J. Figueras. (2011). *Health Professional Mobility and Health Systems: Evidence from 17 European Countries.* Copenhagen: World Health Organisation (on behalf of the European Observatory on Health Systems and Policies).

Xiang, B., & L. Lindquist. (2014). "Migration infrastructure". *International Migration Review,* 48:1, pp. 122–148.

Gendered labour migration in South Africa: A capability approach lens

Alice Ncube and Faith Mkwananzi

Introduction

The progression and variety of current international migration streams reveal clearly that migration can no longer be divorced from population and development policy agendas (Hugo, 2005). Although migration has always been part of societies, globalisation has intensified this phenomenon particularly in the twenty-first century where there are instabilities in most countries, particularly in the global South. Together with globalisation, migration is shaping the pace of modern-day developmental issues. The movement of people across continental, regional and national boundaries is becoming a daily occurrence, and in sub-Saharan Africa (SSA) especially the artificiality of the boundaries is being tested. Brown (2008) predicted a tenfold increase in the current number of international migrants and refugees by 2050. The Human Development Report (HDR, 2009) noted that the probability of migration increases for those with links to people already abroad was very high. Sometimes a culture of migration emerged in which international migration was associated with personal, social and material success, while staying home indicated failure. According to De Bruijn, Foeken and Van Dijk (2001), Africa has been a continent of people on the move with many individuals migrating within the continent for labour purposes.

In relation to women and migration, earlier literature on migration (for example, in the 1960s and 1970s) largely excluded the movement of women (Saggar, Somerville, Ford & Sobolewska, 2012). According to Boyd and Grieco

(2003), in the past migration generally referred to the migration of men, sometimes with "their families" referring to their wives and children, making the migration of women almost invisible. This assumption, of seeing the place of women to be the home, gradually changed as migration emancipated women from their gendered roles and responsibilities (Mkwananzi, 2019). It was only in the 1980s that the literature on migration became more visibly gendered (Stølen, 1991). For a long time, women have been migrating as single and married (Martin, 2004), uneducated and educated entities, dependently and independently, in search of better livelihoods in other countries. While female migration behaviour is no different from that of migrating men, it is influenced by the gendered nature of life. Some would even argue that coping and adaptation are dependent on the gender dynamics of the migration process (Piper, 2007). Boyd (2006) noted that migration is not gender-blind nor gender-neutral, but gender-sensitive. The socialisation and often patriarchal nature of migrants' countries of origin often create challenges for them to cope and adapt in the host country. According to a United Nations (UN) survey in 2006, unjust legislation and beliefs made it difficult for women to migrate. These laws and especially beliefs included those that denied women rights to be accompanied by their spouses and children. Women were subjected to pregnancy tests before being permitted to move and also could not consent to anything without their guardians who, in some cases, were the husbands (United Nations Department of Economic and Social Affairs, 2006). Such patriarchal arrangements may also be a hindrance to women's coping and adaptation, as men may not be willing to join their wives as dependents in host countries. According to Jolly, Reeves and Piper (2005), migration brings a window of opportunity for women to better their lives and break the glass ceiling imposed by the gendered nature of the society. Migration can also empower women economically and increase their independence, improve their self-esteem and their general well-being (Raimundo, 2009). The fact is that even specific forms of forced migration of women, for example, migration resulting from conflict, can lead to modifications in existing gender roles and duties to women's benefit (Wells et al., 2013). Conversely, migration can also embed traditional roles and disparities and expose women to new vulnerabilities as the result of precarious legal status, exclusion and segregation (Adepoju, 2006).

In terms of regional migration, migration to South Africa from surrounding countries and other countries within sub-Saharan Africa has been steadily growing over the years. For example, the 2014 United Nations High Commissioner for Refugees' (UNHCR) planning figures show that the total number of asylum-seeker applications in South Africa was estimated to be 350,000 in December 2014 compared to 300,600 in December 2013. This may be attributed to South Africa's economic stability and often flexible migrant and refugee self-settling policy, allowing migrants to participate in economic activities to sustain their livelihoods. Within this economic migration there has been limited research on its gendered nature and what this may mean for human development and the direction of gender discourse.

Levels of resilience in migration contexts vary from woman to woman due to their demographic, socio-economic characteristics, as well as their short- and long-term aspirations (Ncube, 2017; Mkwananzi, 2019). The adversity factors due to the gendered nature of migration can also be taken as a disempowering experience, which can result in a particular physical or social vulnerability for individual migrant women. For instance, factors such as educational level (Berry & Sam, 2006), language aptitude (Beiser & Hou, 2001) and host country residence status (Bollini & Siem, 1995) can be taken as significant contributing factors for women migrants' positive adjustment, while the lack thereof is a characteristic of women who do not adapt well to the host environment. It is yet to be seen how these negative factors are converted into what is valued by women migrants in host communities to enhance their resilience and their ability to cope and adapt.

This chapter's contribution is therefore grounded on the view that there is a significant number of women migrating globally; it is timely as discourses on gender equality are central to most development-focused debates and agenda. Grounded within the human development-informed capability approach (CA), we highlight how migration has allowed women to be agentic and interrupt ascribed traditional gendered roles and stereotypes. The CA allows us to understand how gender is reconstructing traditional structures that saw women as passive in development associated with labour migration. It does so by focusing on women's agency in pursuing what they deem valuable in their lives and the lives of those around them. We return to this later in the chapter. We further argue that modern-day human and economic development encompasses both males and females and require unified efforts for individuals to live the lives they value. We conclude by providing an assessment of what gendered migration may mean, contribute and challenge in relation to gender, the labour market and the human-development agendas. We draw on capability aspects of opportunities, agency and conversion factors to make an analysis of how migrant women manoeuvre in a foreign land.

The landscape of gender and migration

Migration is not gender-neutral, and the experience of migration is unquestionably gendered (Caritas Internationalis, 2004; Piper, 2007). In the last century and currently, migration has manifested itself in the following engendered forms from sub-Saharan Africa to South Africa in particular:

- Men and women migrate independently
- Migrants can be family accompanied
- Migrants have become permanent residents thanks to the post-apartheid policies
- Migrants are offered permanent jobs because of their skills (Adepoju, 2006)

In the 1980s very little was done to raise the barometer on women's migration except to emphasise the privileges women enjoyed as accompanying spouses; these allowed women to break away from the traditional gender roles in host countries (Ncube, 2017). This brings to the fore the misconception about the gender paradigm that highlights sexual differences and the societal expectations of men to be breadwinners (Haferkamp & Smelser, 1992). Women migrate for different economic reasons. Some women migrate as primary caregivers from single-parent homes, while other women migrate alone to gain personal autonomy and escape the traditional gender roles in their countries of origin. Other women follow their husbands to reunite as a family (Llácer, 2007; Di Belgiojoso & Terzera, 2018). Economic and social upheavals can drive women to migrate; for instance, educated women who experience discrimination in the home countries' work environment migrate to find better jobs in line with their education and skills (Njogu & Orchardson-Mazrui, 2008). Scrutiny by communities and masculine traditions can, however, deny women opportunities and freedom in the home country. Hence, women may decide to migrate to claim their deserved opportunities in host countries where social systems are non-prescriptive (Eisenstadt, 2002). Some women will migrate to escape abusive marriages, domestic violence and desire for equal opportunities with men (Dako-Gyeke, 2013). Socio-economic inequalities in home countries, such as discernment against particular groups of women like single mothers, single women and widows, lead women to migrate to new locations to start a new life without the usual community judging them based on their gender identities (Caritas Internationalis, 2004; Ncube, 2017). The other notable dynamic that has led woman to migrate is the issue of genital mutilation that is still actively practised in some countries. For instance, according to the Refugee Studies Centre (2015), in the first nine months of 2014 more than 25,000 women and girls from female genital mutilation-practising countries sought asylum in the European Union, of whom an estimated 71 per cent had already undergone female genital mutilation.

The gender-segregated job markets in some host countries influence women migrants' employment opportunities, earnings and threats of exploitation (Boyd, 2006). Gender is another aspect that enhances the integration of migrants in host countries. Migrant men and women integrate differently in host countries. While migration entails economic betterment for the individual concerned (both men and women), getting a job in the host country, earning a livelihood that can sustain one, may subject women to gender dynamics together with ethnic and racial discrimination in the host country; hence migrant women are triple-disadvantaged in the host country (Piper, 2006; Liebig & Tronstad, 2018). The triple disadvantages are being foreign, being a woman and (sometimes) being a woman of colour. It has been proved that women are more confident of their culture of origin and take more time to adjust to the host culture than men (Ting-Toomey, 1981; Ghaffarian, 1987; Harris & Verven, 1996).

In relation to South Africa there are vast amounts of literature documenting labour migration into the country (see Landau 2005; Trimikliniotis, Gordon & Zondo, 2009; De Haas, 2008). Various structural determinants of migration set the human mobility to South Africa in motion. For instance, the end of apartheid, the civil and ethnic wars, disasters and famines in Africa facilitated the migration of people to South Africa (Trimikliniotis et al., 2009). The historical bilateral relationships between South Africa and its neighbouring countries to share labour and provide employment to the populations had also become a window of opportunity for migrants to migrate to South Africa en masse and South Africa became a preferred destination (Crush & James, 1995). For example, since the late 1890s the mining industry had been recruiting heavily from countries within the region (Trimikliniotis et al., 2009; Wentzel & Tlabela, 2006) while, during the 1990s, some farmers relied on seasonal migrant labour (Ulicki & Crush, 2010). While the historical trends of migration were in male-dominated fields, there has been a significant increase in women's migration, particularly owing to the bilateral agreements allowing many women to take on domestic work in the country. Yet, within this literature very little attention has been paid to how this gendered nature of labour migration impacts on human development.

Capability approach (CA) and migration

Over the years, the impact of migration has been measured based on remittances, implying that migration's impact should be seen in economic terms. Arguably, a narrowed focus on migration has led some researchers to bemoan the absence of a comprehensive approach (for example, De Haas, 2008) that encompasses diverse aspects of development. While we do not disregard the impact of migration on the economy, our view is that the contribution of migration to development goes beyond economic measures, to focusing on individual wellbeing (see Mkwananzi, 2019). The human development-informed capability approach allows for addressing the complex and diverse nature of migration, cutting across political, economic, cultural and social spheres. Within these spheres, aspects such as capabilities and functionings, wellbeing, conversion factors, agency, as well as adaptive preferences become key assessment areas. Individual capabilities influence what each migrant may be capable of being and doing (Dubois & Trani, 2009) and these opportunities can be assessed by focusing on the functionings in existence. It is these individual functionings that provide a window into achieved wellbeing (Wilson-Strydom & Walker, 2015). Mkwananzi (2017) reiterates this notion by highlighting that, for assessment of the wellbeing of migrants, it would be important to look at the opportunities (capabilities) that migrants have to achieve what they value being and doing and the kind of life that they are living. However, before one can start assessing the wellbeing of migrants it is essential to consider the processes that influence the conversion of available opportunities, capabilities and resources into the desired functionings. These conversion factors may not be the same for all migrants as a result of personal and structural influences, one of these influences being gender. For example, gender socialisation may on its own be a hindrance to what women may or may not be able to do, whether they are able to migrate or not, and the role that they play within the family as a result of migration. Within asking questions of how migrants are faring in bringing about what they value, Sen (1999) highlights the importance of agency – the freedom to bring about one's valued achievements. In situations where agency may be low, individuals may adapt their preferences which, according to Sen (1985), results from negative circumstances and hardships that limit individual freedom, leading to acceptance of one's situation.

A capabilities viewpoint on gendered labour migration

A number of studies have used the CA to look at gender (see Unterhalter, 2007; Nussbaum, 2011; Loots & Walker, 2015; Cin, 2018) as well as migration (Gasper & Troung, 2010; Biggeri & Libanora, 2011; Mkwananzi, 2019). However, there have been very few studies that looked at gendered migration from the CA viewpoint. Using the CA to establish a basis for the assessment and analysis of migrant women, we advocate for the expansion of opportunities among women through education and economic empowerment, which may be instrumentally important for future prospects of countries (Loots & Walker, 2016). According to Sen (1999), the framework is concerned with the opportunities individuals have to be and do what they have reason to value. As Gasper & Truong, (2010) note, the significance of the CA in transnational accounts is that the approach emphasises multidimensional evaluation, taking into account the social (culture, norms, roles, expectations, customs) and political spaces (policies, markets) in which these women live and work. As a result, there is a link between women, labour migration and development, and this connection could offer a potential win-win scenario in which the sending country benefits from remittances that are repatriated, while the host country gains the skills and labour of these women.

We draw on three of the CA concepts; capabilities (opportunities), agency (for example, the action taken by women to survive in a foreign land) and conversion factors (personal, environmental and social conditions of each individual's existence). While the framework provides a space to view women as more than child bearers and individuals whose place is in the kitchen, it also views them as more than economic producers. In migration contexts, the role of women goes beyond remittances back home, but is also concerned about their own wellbeing and their living the lives they have reason to value in South Africa; for instance. Loots and Walker (2016, p. 262) note that the CA:

> [...] also includes possibilities for well-being, agency expansion and mobilization (enabling people to participate in their own development according to their own goals), and critically reflecting on one's own values and well-being (through inclusion in the development and policy process).

Thus, in essence, we reject both extremes, the traditional view that sees women as homemakers and the other view that sees women as economic providers who are overtaking men. The latter claim, although emerging in recent discourses, may, in comparison to historical labour segregation that saw men as sole providers, be a yardstick to women's involvement in labour activities. Yet an assessment of women's development or progressions should, in addition to being contextualised, take into account the opportunities that women have in making choices associated with these two views. We are careful not to be oblivious of the challenges that women are exposed to because of migration, and which in the process have a negative impact on their wellbeing.

Methods

An ethnographic case-study was used, focusing on sub-Saharan African migrant women in the South African metropolitan cities of Johannesburg, Pretoria, Ekurhuleni, Durban, Cape Town and Bloemfontein. The main focus was on the respondents' positive capabilities in the form of socio-economic demographic characteristics and the livelihood capitals they possess and had acquired in the host country. The opportunities available in South Africa to the migrant women could possibly enhance their wellbeing so they may live the lives they desire. As part of the ethnography, a semi-structured questionnaire was administered face to face to collect data from 332 migrant women from 23 of the 54 sub-Saharan African countries; although the Zimbabwean migrants dominated the study, the dynamics of these migrants are similar. The respondents were from Angola, Benin, Burundi, Cameroon, Congo-Brazzaville, DRC, Eritrea, Ethiopia, Ghana, Ivory Coast, Kenya, Lesotho, Malawi, Mauritius, Mozambique, Nigeria, Rwanda, Senegal, Somalia, Tanzania, Uganda, Zambia and Zimbabwe. Data were collected over two months between March and April 2016, though the information-gathering and acquisition had always been ongoing. Data were collected on the socio-economic characteristics of the migrant women such as their ages, marital status, education levels, primary position in the household and their occupations. The sustainable livelihood capitals, namely, human, economic, social, physical, cultural and political, adapted from the sustainable livelihood framework (United Kingdom, Department for International Development (DFID), 1999; Ncube, 2017) were the basis of the opportunities, freedom and challenges of the capabilities of the migrants' adaptation in South Africa. More than 80 per cent (268) of the respondents were in the 18 to 49 years age group. More than half of the respondents (193 out of 332) had a secondary education and 25 had certificates, 36 had diplomas, five had technikon[1] qualifications, 18 had university degrees, and 31 had postgraduate qualifications. There was one woman from the DRC who had no education at all.

Findings

In this chapter we report findings related to the labour- and job-market experiences of the women. Emerging from the data, in the midst of various challenges facing the heterogeneity group of women from different parts of sub-Saharan Africa, women possessed entrepreneurial skills that most of them were using to sustain their livelihoods. Migrant women from Mozambique, Angola and Lesotho were observed to be residing in the high-density suburbs in South Africa, usually termed black residential areas, where they had their own small businesses or were working in groups in hairdressing businesses (Ncube, 2017). Ethiopians, Somalis and Eritrean migrant women were observed to be mostly wives of wealthy businessmen from the same countries. Most of the women worked in their husbands' shops, with some also running their own small businesses. Most of the women from the DRC and Congo-Brazzaville in the study had hairdressing businesses, with some of them engaging in selling beauty products, which are in great demand among women in South Africa. Other migrant women from the Ivory Coast, Kenya, Burundi, Rwanda, Mauritius, Uganda and Benin were also working and trading in their own businesses (such as salons, retail shops, hospitality outlets like guesthouses and lodges) and some were formally employed in South Africa. In this discussion, we present the key themes related to the opportunities, agency, as well as conversion factors as experienced by the women.

Opportunities (capabilities)

Access to employment opportunities
The migrant women were asked to evaluate how they perceived the job market in South Africa; by focusing on the job market, the highest ranked was job availability, followed by skills transfer in the workplace, then ethnic preferences in the workplace, policies on getting jobs, chances of getting a job and getting a specific job. These opportunities were also constrained as noted below:

It's challenging for me because many South Africans are currently jobless, hence decreasing the possibility of me finding a job.

According to the women, while jobs were readily available in South Africa, the hindrances to getting a job were the skills necessary, the qualifications needed and the correct or legal documentation required by foreigners to be employed in a foreign country. As a result, while the opportunities to access employment may have been present, the women were at risk of being exploited, highlighting the number of vulnerabilities associated with gender and migration (e.g. Mbiyozo, 2018; Walker & Galvin, 2018).

There were some migrant women who indicated that they possessed the necessary qualifications and skills, but were struggling to get employment in South Africa; this emerged to be a result of challenges in proper documentation as noted below:

They only hire people with green identity document books and it is not fair.

If you have a permit, they will consider you as a third choice after they hire illiterate people with green books.

It is not easy for foreigners to get a job but there are jobs. The policies favour the locals. With the right papers, experience and skills you can get a job.

Despite these feelings of constraint some of the women had a positive experience:

Personally, I feel well accommodated at my work and it is very comfortable.

It's better here than Cameroon. There is job in South Africa as opposed to my country.

Life is much better here than Mozambique. There are jobs here in S.A. It's better than my home country.

I think the job environment is fair as long as you prove that you are able to do the job.

Since a work visa (in a few instances or an Asylum Seeker's Permit) is required for one to be employed, most did not have visas and it meant that it was not possible for them to even apply for specific jobs that were commensurate with their qualifications. From a CA perspective, the opportunities to live the lives they had reason to value, although present, had significant constraining factors. Furthermore, structural factors emerged as women noted that the laws and policies were too strict; hence they struggled to get employment. However, for those with the necessary documentation the chances of getting jobs in South Africa were available, provided the individual met all the legal requirements. Without the necessary documentation it was difficult for them to get the type of job that they were trained to do, and as a result they were prone to under employment. This was particularly true of those who indicated that they were trained nurses, accountants, biologists and business management professionals but noted that they were not doing the jobs that they were trained to do. Some who were already in employment reported other workplace challenges, as highlighted below:

> The cleaners stopped cleaning my office and desk, the messengers never collected any mail from my office and when serving tea to personnel they skipped my office, just because I am a foreigner. Even cleaners and messengers think that they are better than foreigners.

Some of the women indicated that they had stopped looking for jobs because of the discriminatory job market. Experiences of discrimination were, however, not common, as most of the women were self-employed. Despite the challenges, the migrant women indicated that jobs were available in South Africa, unlike in their home countries, and that South Africa has a conducive atmosphere for entrepreneurship, so creating jobs for themselves and others.

Entrepreneurial skills
With most of the women falling between the ages of 18 and 49, and this being the economically-active age group, entrepreneurial skills become essential in a country that is already strained in relation to employment, as asserted by Bongaarts (2001). However, South Africa is perceived as a rich country and full of opportunities. According to Gebre, Maharaj and Pillay (2011), South Africa was filled with promises and was a successful country offering opportunities for advancement. South Africa still had the best economic prospects to offer to

migrant women in the African continent (Adepoju, 2007). Entrepreneurship opportunities are highlighted below:

> We create jobs here for ourselves as foreigners. Most foreigners doing their own business. Most Ethiopians are into business. We are independent. We create jobs. I actually provide employment to my country's ladies and also a South African.

Unemployment is a challenge in South Africa with the majority of the unemployed being the youth; in 2016 the unemployment rate was 26.5 per cent (STATS SA, 2016; Census, 2011). There was, however, a high human capital of migrant women with relevant skills and qualifications who were in, and continued to arrive in, South Africa during the period in which this study was conducted. As noted, most women brought with them various skills, capabilities and capacities from their home countries. One of the respondents from Ghana explained that in her country the education system is such that it allows for entrepreneurs' skilling. According to Ashiboe-Mensah (2017), entrepreneurship education started at a Ghanaian college as far back as 1993. Through the informal interviews, women had informally to learn crafts such as hair plaiting, weaving and tailoring before they decided to migrate to South Africa. These created opportunities for them to survive in South Africa, a country perceived as full of hope but faced with socio-economic challenges such as unemployment and other governance issues. The entrepreneurial skills brought by women varied from woman to woman from hairdressing, weaving, knitting to general acumen for business such as general trading. Gries and Naude (2011), however, note that factors associated with entrepreneurship such as technological innovation, economic growth and improvements in productivity do not automatically translate into human development. Hence, entrepreneurship ought to be seen to expand one's capabilities through being both a resource and a process. Thus, women in this case provide us with a basis of thinking about the impact of entrepreneurship on human development, looking beyond only the economically thinking entrepreneurship.

Ability to adapt to new labour environment
While migrant women possessed various skills, they had to work in any job that was available at the time. Unemployment is very high in South Africa, standing at 29.1 per cent (STATSA, 2020). The probability of the respondents getting

jobs that they were qualified to do was low, and hence they made themselves available to work in any job, adjust to any conditions such as selling in the streets or even working in a salon in order to survive. According to Meraj (2015), highly qualified and skilled professionals in developed countries are often obliged to accept jobs below their educational rank after they migrate to those countries and may experience a downhill shift both in their careers and in their quality of life. This also applies in South Africa. They have no choice but to deskill themselves as a coping and adaptation mechanism (Ncube, 2017). The difficulty of finding employment is highlighted in the extract below:

> It's challenging for me because many South Africans are currently jobless, hence decreasing the possibility of me finding a job.

Over and above the self-settling policy that required them to integrate into society, thereby leaving them with no option but to be economically active, some of the women had responsibilities at home. For example, 122 respondents indicated that they were the heads of their households and also the sole breadwinners. As a result, migration was one of the few ways to help in fending for the family. While, according to the International Organisation of Migration (IOM), this may lead to greater independence and autonomy (IOM, 2003), from a capability perspective it highlights constrained opportunities as there are no options to choose from. Thus, the experiences of migration become multidimensional opportunities, but also mean constraint. Thus, when making such assessment, Sen (2009) call us to be critical about the social arrangements – in this case it is the environment in which the women experience their daily lives – and thus not just to take adaptation as a positive or negative value without critically considering other factors.

Conversion Factors

Gender
Asked whether being women hindered their chances of getting jobs or coping and adapting in South Africa, 130 of the respondents indicated that they were being affected and 198 indicated that they were not. The marital status of an individual migrant and the gender aspect could also create limitations on the chances of women getting jobs or devising coping and adaptation mechanisms. Since the

majority of the respondents indicated that their marital status had nothing to do with their getting jobs in the country, this meant that marriage had no significant influence on the getting of jobs. Other factors such as educational level, skills and networks had more influence than marital status, as illustrated below:

> I can't say because I have low education, never looked for a job.

> I never looked for a job, because I heard that even with a degree you cannot get a job as a foreigner. I didn't go to school so I cannot complain.

This finding paralleled with Goodman (2004) who indicated that young Sudanese refugees in Kenya prioritised education above getting married and that that allowed them to cope and adapt better than others. The positive policies in South Africa that promote gender equality could be useful for migrant women who are in South Africa to gain economic independence and to break the "glass ceiling" usually associated with being a woman in the work situation. Besides, policymakers should further enforce policies in pursuance of an inclusive approach, to nurture equality of all migrants, regardless of their marital status. In addition to this, there are social and cultural factors that influence the migrant women's faring in South Africa, as discussed in the next section.

Social factors
A number of social conversion factors influenced the women's experiences in South Africa. These included religion, family, friends, ethnicity, colleagues and neighbours. For instance, close family members, as well as husbands of the migrant women who were already in South Africa, contributed to their coping and adaptation in South Africa.

> The church is providing spiritual and emotional support. At times people from church give me food. They assist when I have problems. Some church members lend me money, and they help with referring me to places where I can get employment. I have managed to link up with a group from church to be able to buy goods in bulk so that we can sell at competitive prices. At times, when one moves to another town, church members connect you to the church members in a new town. There are always people ready to welcome you and make you feel at home.

My family is motivating me to work harder. My family from home sends me some money. Family – they keep me happy and motivate me to keep going. My family from home help me by sending money from home; my sister is always there providing me with food. My brother assisted when I came to South Africa, sent me to school and assisted me to start the salon business. My uncle assisted me with accommodation and basic things like food.

A number of salon owners indicated that they also employed local South Africans in their businesses and the professional relationship was based on trust and mutual support. A good rapport had been developed between migrants from various countries and with locals; this made coping and adaptation easier. However, there were some migrant women in Durban who said that they did not trust anyone and also felt alienated in South Africa. These same migrant women stated that they would be glad if they had the means to return to their home countries.

Cultural factors
The cultural factors included traditional beliefs, work ethics and respect for authority. Some of the migrant women had migrated to South Africa but maintained visible cultural markers such as their dress and their culinary habits, which made them acquire both positive and negative identities. The negative impact of the culture practised by the migrant women put them at risk of being the target of xenophobic attacks. On the other hand, as a conversion factor, the positive formation of identity led to a sense of belonging and easy integration into society. The freedom for migrants to maintain cultural practices highlights the importance of and relationship between culture and identity formation.

Although South Africa still experiences gender disparities in the workplace, some of the women applauded the initiatives and programmes that support women's empowerment in the country, unlike in their countries of origin. Some of those initiatives include Affirmation Action (AA) and Employment Equity (EE) in employment procedures that ensure that historically disadvantaged individuals (HDIs), including women and people living with disabilities, are given fair employment opportunities to redress past inequalities. One of the women noted, "There are policies governing the job environment in South Africa and they are fair".

The women stated that there was a lot of respect for women in South Africa compared to their countries of origin, especially by the South African policymakers. South Africa was also commended for its positive and progressive laws about respect for variety in cultural practices, values and norms in the country. The migrant women stated that there was professionalism and respect for authority in the workplace, shown by both the employer and employee.

However, most migrant women indicated that, within these progressive policies, local citizens had adopted eurocentrism in their conduct, rather than being Afrocentric as they were Africans. The cultural capital factors that emerged as valued by the migrant women were: firstly, respect for authority; secondly, gender issues; thirdly, work ethics; and, fourthly, traditional beliefs.

Agency

In addition to the above factors, our data show that migrant women are resilient, independent and can resist and withstand the challenges of migration and integration into society. We understand resilience according to the Human Development Report (HDR) which sees resilience as addressing the deterioration in wellbeing which is determined by people's ability to adjust and cope with these challenges (HDR, 2014). As migrant women experience various challenges in the endeavour to break into the market, through either employment or entrepreneurship, their choices and capabilities become limited. However, migrant women's resilience can reduce vulnerability and marginalisation by eliminating barriers that restrict their choices and capabilities (HDR, 2014). Thus, using their agency, the women negotiate social, economic and political challenges.

Discussion

We now return to our earlier assertion that the CA allows us to understand the opportunities, agency and factors that have an impact on the lives migrant women experience in a foreign land. The findings demonstrate that the women possess certain capabilities that allow them to function in a foreign land. Firstly, the opportunity to migrate may be seen as a capability that is available to the migrant women who, in turn, exercise their agency by taking action to move to South Africa. Recognising the capabilities that migrant women possess, particularly in the labour market, and advancing such capabilities through programmes that strengthen the skills that these women possess may result not only in an advanced labour market, but also in advancing the wellbeing of others. As studies show, women have also been found to be more willing to help family members, and their remittances are more consistent over time (Lopez-Ekra et al., 2011). These remittances, among other non-financial kinds of support, allow the migrant women to be active transnational actors – balancing their lives in both countries as they also take up responsibilities back home.

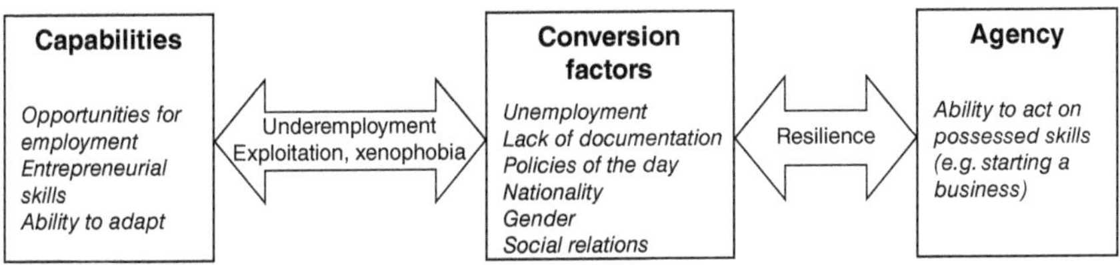

Figure 1: Capabilities interaction among labour migrant women

In Figure 1, capabilities such as opportunities for employment, possessed skills and the ability to adapt highlighted the capabilities environment for migrant women. Although these capabilities may have been present for them, there were factors that had a negative impact on those available capabilities and the factors include unemployment, lack of documentation, policies of the day, nationality and gender. As a result, the women in the study could not fully exercise their capabilities, making them prone to exploitation, underemployment and xenophobia.

We also take into account that each woman has a unique profile of conversion factors (Robeyns, 2011), for example, background, experiences, age and country of origin, making them both structural and personal. Personal conversion factors relate to language and level of education. Structural conversion factors relate to the current political situation, labour policies and unemployment. Some of the women were aware of the high unemployment rate in South Africa, which made it difficult for them to find employment. However, these opportunities were even more limited for migrant women, as most of them noted the lack of recognised documentation, which possibly limited job opportunities. Those limited opportunities could lead individuals to resort to low-paying jobs bearing the risk of labour exploitation in some cases.

Social relations were reported as having a positive impact on the women's experiences as they largely comprised support networks of friends, family and religion. Despite the negative impact of most of the conversion factors, the women exercised their agency, putting into use the entrepreneurial skills they possessed from home, thereby practising resilience, withstanding the negative impact of the challenges that came with being in foreign land, without appropriate work permits, among others. They ran small businesses like sewing, basketry, knitting, buying and selling, running vegetable stalls and opening street hair salons. All women valued the opportunity for income generation as they sent money back home with the hope that they would go back to their countries one day. The income also helped them to manage their day-to-day lives. The initiative taken by migrant women in starting their own businesses highlights levels of agency. This is in line with Ojong's (2002) observation that some African migrant women in South Africa possessed several acquired coping mechanisms from their home countries such as handiwork, professional skills and entrepreneurial skills, which – because of agency – enabled them to integrate fairly into the economic sector.

Resilience therefore becomes a necessary capability for survival among these women. The capability for resilience can be built into the presence of one or more of the following conversion factors: motivation, policies or support systems (emotional and material). Other studies have also found resilience to be greater in the presence of strong structures (these could include policies of the day), social support and feelings of security (Waller, 2001; Ahmed et al., 2004). Resilience may also be viewed as a conversion factor influencing other factors. For instance, resilience can influence agency, the kinds of action that the women take to lead decent lives.

Resilience is also visible among those women who have hope that life will change for the better in future. For broader, deliberate human development intentions, resilience as a capability can be built by putting in place structures that support the strengthening of this capability, such as accessing resources and short-term micro loans for those aspiring to be entrepreneurs. With such strategies in place, opportunities for employment and contribution to the labour market may be expanded. As a result, migrants (in this case, women) may contribute to the various aspects of development in South Africa, including to their own personal progression.

From a human development viewpoint, we draw from the findings that the decision to migrate leads to an "expansion of migrant women's opportunities to live their lives as they choose" (HDR, 2009). As all migrant women are economically active, it is safe to note that their migration addresses some key issues of concern to human development and, inter alia, eradicating poverty and hunger, and promoting gender equality and empowering women. According to the International Organisation for Migration, such increased independent migration of female breadwinners leads to greater independence and autonomy (IOM, 2003). Furthermore, the availability of such opportunities (capabilities), together with the women's agency, contributes to improved self-esteem associated with skills and knowledge that can make women powerful in their countries of origin. These opportunities for migrant women are also in line with the Sustainable Development Goals (SDGs):

Goal 5: Gender Equality
Goal 6: Decent work and economic growth, and
Goal 8: Reduced inequalities

In addressing gender inequalities, women's migration has the potential to eliminate certain forms of discrimination and violence against women, and this is evidenced by their involvement in economic activities and opportunities for decision-making without patriarchal influence. Such freedom in decision-making and participation in the labour market disrupts the traditional gendered stereotypes that view men as the sole breadwinners and women as home keepers. The activity of women in the labour market also addresses the need to increase decent employment and economic growth. Such opportunities increase women's chances of actively participating in opportunities for decent work across all sectors, including in entrepreneurship. Capability expansion can ultimately address the intersectional discriminatory social norms based on age, gender, language, ethnicity, poverty and other social norms, thereby reducing inequalities. As a result, while migrant women represent a high number of remittance senders in some countries (United Nations, 2006), this change in women's development should be considered beyond their economic contribution, to include the altering of social and cultural development spheres. Such a broad contribution may be seen to expand the wellbeing and flourishing of the women beyond economic value.

While significant contributions are made by women's migration to the empowerment and development of women, we are cognisant that the migration of women may, for some, result in constrained family relationships as migration may interrupt traditional family relations. However, what remains critical is that migrant women pursue the lives they deem as valuable to their flourishing and their wellbeing.

Conclusion

It emerges from the narratives in the study that as women take up the role of provider in their families, there is a gradual shift from the traditional expectations. The various capabilities, in the form of skills that the women bring with them, and their ability to act on those skills (agency) enable them to assimilate into the host communities, successfully navigating some of the conversion factors with negative effects.

In conclusion, the chance of actively participating in employment and other innovative activities to earn a living is enhanced by most of the migrants falling within 18 to 49 year age bracket. The high ratio of working-age people compared to the total respondents clearly impacted positively on the labour market, as most of the migrants were economically active. This productive age could be useful to South Africa as it would assist in growing the economy. As such, it would also be a worthy consideration for policymakers to try to tap into such a productive capacity, especially if the migrant women might have skills that would be required for a developing economy like South Africa. Returning to the SDGs, we see that women's labour migration has the potential to reduce poverty and improve wellbeing in both host and sending countries. It is within this understanding that the potential contribution of women to development ought to be recognised.

Note

1   Universities of Technology which offer vocational oriented diplomas and degrees.

References

Adepoju, A. (2006). "Recent trends in international migration in and from Africa". Human Resources Development Centre, Abuja, Nigeria.

Adepoju, A. (2007). *Creating a borderless West Africa: Constraints and prospects for intra-regional migration.* In A.Pécoud and P. de Guchteneire (eds.) *Migration without borders: Essays on the free movement of people* (pp. 161–174). New York and Oxford: Berghahn Books for UNESCO, UK.

Ahmed, R., M. Seedat, A. Van Niekerk & S. Bulbulia. (2004). "Discerning community resilience in disadvantaged communities in the context of violence and injury prevention". *South African Journal of Psychology*, 34:3, pp. 386–408.

Ashiboe-Mensah, K., (2017). "Ghanaian tertiary graduates' perception of entrepreneurship education on employment opportunities, Universities, Entrepreneurship and Enterprise Development in Africa". In J. Munyoki and J.Bode (eds.) *Universities, Entrepreneurship and Development in Africa - Conference Proceedings 2017*, Vol. 6, pp. 50–72.

Beiser, M., & F. Hou. (2001). "Language acquisition, unemployment and depressive disorder among Southeast Asian refugees: A 10-year study". *Social Science and Medicine*, 53:10, pp. 1321–1334.

Berry, J. W., & D. L. Sam. (2006). *The Cambridge handbook of acculturation psychology*. Cambridge: Cambridge University Press.

Biggeri, M., & R. Libanora. (2011). "From valuing to evaluating: Tools and procedures to operationalize the capability approach". In M. Biggeri, J. Ballet and F. Comim (eds.). *Children and the capability approach* (pp. 79–106). Basingstoke: Palgrave Macmillan.

Bollini, P., & H. Siem. (1995). "No real progress towards equity: Health of migrants and ethnic minorities on the eve of the year 2000". *Social Science and Medicine*, 41:6, pp. 819–828.

Bongaarts, J. (2001). "Dependency burdens in the developing world". In N. Birdsall, A. C. Kelley and S. W. Sinding (eds.). *Population matters: demographic change, economic growth, and poverty in developing world*. New York: Population Council.

Boyd, M. (2006). *Women in international migration: The context of exit and entry for empowerment and exploitation*. New York, United Nations.

Boyd, M., & G. Grieco. (2003). "Women and migration: Incorporating gender into international migration theory". Migration Policy Institute Article 6. Available at https://www.law.columbia.edu/sites/default/files/microsites/gender-sexuality/Gender_Justice_Fall_2018/boyd_migration_policy_institute_2003.pdf.

Brown, O. (2008). *Migration and climate change*. Geneva: International Organisation of Migration.

Caritas Internationalis. (2004). "The female face of migration: Advocacy and best practices for women who migrate and the families they leave behind". Caritas Internationalis Working Document. Available at http://www.caritas.org/includes/pdf/advocacy/FFMCaritasPolicyDoc.pdf.

Cin, F. M. (2018). *Youth, Gender and the Capabilities Approach to Development: Rethinking Opportunities and Agency from a Human Development Perspective*. London: Routledge.

Crush, J., & W. James. (1995). *Crossing Boundaries: Mining migrancy in a democratic South Africa*. Cape Town: Creda Press.

Dako-Gyeke, M. (2013). "Conceptualization of female migrants: Experiences across the lifespan". *Academic Journal of Interdisciplinary Studies*, 2:3, pp. 259–266.

De Bruijn, M., D. Foeken & R. Van Dijk. (2001). *Mobile Africa: An introduction. Changing patterns of movement in Africa and beyond*. Leiden: Brill.

De Haas, H. (2008). "Migration and development: A theoretical perspective". IMI Working Paper 9. Oxford: International Migration Institute.

DFID (United Kingdom. Department for International Development). (1999). "The sustainable livelihoods guidance sheets: Introduction – overview". London: Department of International Development. Available at http://files.ennonline.net/attachments/871/dfid-sustainable-livelihoods-guidance-sheet-section1.pdf.

Di Belgiojoso, E. B., & L. Terzera. (2018). „Family reunification – who, when, and how? Family trajectories among migrants in Italy". *Demographic Research*, 38:1, pp. 737–772.

Dubois, J. L., & J. F. Trani. (2009). "Extending the capability paradigm to address the complexity of disability". *ALTER-European Journal of Disability Research/Revue Européenne de Recherche sur le Handicap*, 3:3, pp. 192–218.

Eisenstadt, S. N. (2002). "The continual reconstruction of multiple modern civilizations and collective identities". In G. Preyer and XX. Bös (eds.). *Borderlines in a globalized world: New perspectives in a sociology of the world-system* (pp. 3–12). Dordrecht: Kluwer Academic Publishers.

Gasper, D., & T. D. Truong. (2010). "Development ethics through the lenses of caring, gender and human security". In S. Esquith and F. Gifford (eds). *Capabilities, Power and Institutions: Towards a More Critical Development Ethics* (pp. 58–95). Pittsburgh, PA: Pennsylvania State University Press.

Gebre, L.T., P. Maharaj & N. K. Pillay. (2011). "The experiences of immigrants in South Africa: A case study of Ethiopians in Durban, South Africa". *Urban Forum*, 22:1, pp. 23–35.

Ghaffarian, S. (1987). "The acculturation of Iranians in the United States". *Journal of Social Psychology*, 127:1, pp. 565–571.

Glick Schiller, N., L. Basch & C. S. Blanc. (1995). "From immigrant to transmigrant: Theorizing transnational migration". *Anthropological Quarterly*, 68:1, pp. 48–63.

Goodman, D. (2004). "Qinghai and the emergence of the west: Nationalities, communal interaction and national integration". *The China Quarterly*, 178:2, pp. 379–399.

Gries, T., & W. Naudé. (2011). "Entrepreneurship and human development: A capability approach". *Journal of Public Economics*, 95:3–4, pp. 216–224.

Haferkamp, H., & N. J. Smelser. (1992). *Social change and modernity*. Berkeley, CA: University of California Press.

Harris, A. C., & R. Verven. (1996). "The Greek-American acculturation scale: Development and validity". *Psychological Reports*, 78:2, pp. 599–610.

Hugo, G. (2005). *Migrants in society: Diversity and cohesion*. Geneva: Global Commission on International Migration.

Human Development Report. (2009). *Overcoming barriers: Human mobility and development*. New York: United Nations Development Programme.

Human Development Report. (2014). *Sustaining Human Progress: Reducing Vulnerabilities and building Resilience*. New York: United Nations Development Programme. Available at http://hdr.undp.org/sites/default/files/hdr14-report-en-1.pdf.

IOM (International Organisation of Migration). (2003). *World Migration 2003 – Managing Migration: Challenges and Responses for People on the Move*. Geneva: IOM World Migration Report Series, Volume 2.

Jolly, S., H. Reeves & N. Piper. (2005). "Gender and migration: Overview report". Institute of Development Studies. Available at http://www.bridge.ids.ac.uk/sites/bridge.ids.ac.uk/files/reports/CEP-Mig-OR.pdf.

Landau, L. (2005). "Migration, urbanization and sustainable livelihoods in South Africa". Migration Policy Brief No. 15. Cape Town: Southern African Migration Project.

Levitt, P. (2004). "Transnational Migrants: When 'Home' Means More Than One Country". Available at: http://www.migrationpolicy.org/article/transnational-migrants-when-home-means-more-one-country.

Liebig, T., & K. Tronstad. (2018). "Triple disadvantage?: a first overview of the integration of refugee women". OECD Social, Employment and Migration Working Papers, No. 216. Paris: OECD.

Llácer, A. Z. (2007). "The contribution of a gender perspective to the understanding of migrants' health". *Journal of Epidemiology and Community Health*, 61:2, pp. 4–10.

Loots, S., & M. Walker. (2015). "Shaping a Gender Equality Policy in Higher Education: Which Human Capabilities Matter?". *Gender and Education*, 27:4: pp. 361–375.

Loots, S., & M. Walker. (2016). "A capabilities-based gender equality policy for higher education: Conceptual and methodological considerations". *Journal of Human Development and Capabilities*, 17:2, pp. 260–277, DOI: 10.1080/19452829.2015.1076777.

Lopez-Ekra, S., C. Aghazarm, H. Kötter & B. Mollard. (2011). "The impact of remittances on gender roles and opportunities for children in recipient families: research from the International Organization for Migration". *Gender & Development*, 19:1, pp. 69–80, DOI: 10.1080/13552074.2011.554025.

Martin, S. F. (2004). "Women and migration". In United Nations, Division for the advancement of Women, *Consultative Meeting on Migration and Mobility and how this movement affects women*.2–4 December 2003. Malmö. Available at http://www.un.org/womenwatch/daw/meetings/consult/CM-Dec03-WP1.pdf.

Mbiyozo, A. N. (2018). *Gender and migration in South Africa: Talking to women migrants*, Pretoria: Institute for Security Studies. Available at: https://issafrica.s3.amazonaws.com/site/uploads/sar-16.pdf.

Meraj, N. (2015). "Settlement experiences of professional immigrant women in Canada, USA, UK and Australia". PhD thesis, The University of Western Ontario, Canada.

Mkwananzi, F. (2017). "Exploring the lives and educational aspirations of marginalised migrant youth: A case study in Johannesburg, South Africa". PhD thesis, Centre for Development Support, University of the Free State, Bloemfontein, South Africa.

Mkwananzi, F. (2019). *Higher Education, Youth and Migration in Contexts of Disadvantage: Understanding Aspirations and Capabilities*. London: Palgrave McMillan.

Ncube, A. (2017). "The Socio-economic coping and adaption mechanisms employed by African migrant women in South Africa". PhD Thesis, University of the Free State, Bloemfontein, South Africa.

Njogu, K., & E. Orchardson-Mazrui. (2008). *Gender inequality and women's rights in the Great Lakes: Can culture contribute to women's empowerment? Culture, performance and identity: Paths of communication in Kenya*. Nairobi: Twaweza Communications.

Nussbaum, M. C. (1997). "Kant and stoic cosmopolitanism". *Journal of Political Philosophy*, 5:1, pp. 1–25.

Nussbaum, M. C. (2011). *Creating Capabilities. The human development approach*. Cambridge, MA: Harvard University Press.

Ojong, V. B. A. (2002). "A study of idependent African migrant women in KwaZulu Natal (South Africa): Their lives and work experiences". Master's dissertation, University of Zululand. Available at http://uzspace.uzulu.ac.za/bitstream/handle/10530/934/A%20study%20of%20independant%20african%20migrant%20women%20in%20KZN.%20VBA%20Ojong.pdf?sequence=1.

Piper, N. (2006). "Gendering the politics of migration". *International Migration Review*, 40:1, pp. 133–164.

Piper, N. (2007). "Governance of migration and transnationalisation of migrants' rights". *International Migration Review*, 22:1, pp. 1–24.

Raimundo, I. M. (2009). "Gender, choice and migration". PhD thesis, University of the Witwatersrand, Johannesburg.

Refugee Studies Centre. (2015). "FGM and Asylum in Europe". *Forced Migration Review* 2, pp. 1–12. Available at http://www.refworld.org/docid/5566c7f74.html.

Robeyns, I. (2011). "The Capability Approach". In E.N. Zalta et al. (eds). *Stanford Encyclopedia of Philosophy*. Available at: http://plato.stanford.edu/entries/capability-approach/.

Saggar, S., W. Somerville, R. Ford & M. Sobolewska. (2012). "The impacts of migration on social cohesion and integration. Final report to the Migration Advisory Committee". London: Home Office.

Sen, A. (1985). *Commodities and Capabilities*. Amsterdam: North Holland.

Sen, A. (1999). *Development as Freedom*. Oxford: Oxford University Press.

Statistics South Africa. (2015). "Census 2011: Migration dynamics in South Africa". Available at 12 July 2018. http://www.statssa.gov.za/publications/Report-03-01-79/Report-03-01-792011.pdf.

Statistics South Africa. (2020). "Quarterly Labour Force Survey, 2019". Pretoria, businesstech.co.za > News > Government.

Stolen, K. A. (1991). "Introduction: Women, gender and social change". In K. A. Stølen and M. Vaa (eds.). *Gender and change in developing countries*. Oslo: Norwegian University Press.

Ting-Toomey, S. (1981). "Ethnic identity and close friendship in Chinese-American college students". *International Journal of Intercultural Relations*, 5:1, pp. 383–406.

Trimikliniotis, N., S. Gordon & B. Zondo. (2009). "Globalisation and migrant labour in a 'rainbow nation': A fortress South Africa?". In R. Munck (ed.). *Globalization and Migration: New Issues, New Politics* (pp. 95–111). London and New York: Routledge Taylor and Francis Group.

Ulicki, T., & J. Crush. (2010). "Poverty, gender and migrancy: Lesotho's migrant farmworkers in South Africa". In J. Crush and B. Frayne (eds). *Surviving on the Move: Migration, Poverty, and Development in Southern Africa* (pp. 164–182). Cape Town: Logo Print.

UN-DESA (United Nations Department of Economic and Social Affairs). (2006). *World survey on the role of women in development*. New York: United Nations.

United Nations. (2006). "Gender, migration, remittances and development". Available at: http://www.un.org/en/development/desa/population/migration/events/coordination/5/docs/P02_INSTRAW.pdf.

United Nations High Commission for Refugees (UNHCR). (2014). "Kenya Somali refugees: Refugee population in Kenya". Available at: http://data.unhcr.org/horn-of-africa/country.php?id=110.

Unterhalter, E. (2007). "Gender equality, education and the capability approach". In M. Walker and E. Unterhalter (eds.). *Sen's Capability Approach and Social Justice in Education* (pp. 87–107). London: Palgrave.

Walker, R., & T. Galvin. (2018). "Labels, victims, and insecurity: an exploration of the lived realities of migrant women who sell sex in South Africa". *Third World Thematics* 3:2, pp. 277–292. DOI: 10.1080/23802014.2018.1477526.

Waller, M. A. (2001). "Resilience in ecosystemic context: Evolution of the concept". *American Journal of Orthopsychiatry*, 71:3, pp. 290–297.

Wells, L., D. H. Antonio, V. Lation, R. C. Abbond, C. Claussen & L. Lorenzetti. (2013). "A context of domestic violence: Learnings for prevention from the Calgary Filipino community". *International Journal of Child, Youth and Family Studies*, 4:1, pp. 147–165.

Wentzel, M., & K. Tlabela. (2006). "Historical background to South African migration". In P. Kok., D. Gelderblom., J. O. Oucho & J. Van Zyl (eds.). *Migration in South and southern Africa: dynamics and determinants* (pp. 71–96). Cape Town: HSRC Press.

Wilson-Strydom, M., & M. Walker. (2015). "A capabilities-friendly conceptualisation of flourishing in and through education". *Journal of Moral Education*, 44:3, pp. 310–324.

"I am not moving life, but life moves me." Experiences of intra-EU (im)mobility among West African migrants

Mirjam Wajsberg

Introduction

The reinstatement of border controls within the Schengen area has, over the past years, been invoked as one of several ways to manage and halt migration between European countries. While the free movement of goods, services and capital in the European Single Market has been largely upheld, human mobility, specifically migration from the Global South to the Global North, has become the target of increased restrictions within the European Union (EU) (Andersson, 2016; Glick Schiller & Salazar, 2013; Schapendonk, 2017).

This ethnographic chapter explores West African migrants' diverse approaches to remaining mobile in the EU in the context of increasingly restrictive migration policies. I draw on recent scholarship that approaches mobility by focusing on migration trajectories (Schapendonk et al., 2018; Wissink et al., 2018; Khosravi, 2018) to illustrate that migrants employ a variety of navigational tactics[1] to resist the spatial and socio-economic immobility experienced through the European migration regime, while also actively challenging the migration regime itself to (re-)gain mobility. The chapter will highlight instances of frustration and precarity but also hope and contestation, when interlocutors move through the EU. Based on the empirical findings, I elucidate the multiple ways in which West African migrants assert agency while subjected to different constraints by European migration policies.

Framing intra-EU mobility trajectories

A growing body of literature (Mainwaring, 2016; Toma & Castagone, 2015; Schapendonk, 2012, 2017; Ahrens, 2013; Schuster, 2005) explores the migration trajectories, particularly of irregularised migrants towards and within the EU. This body of research investigates the effect and effectiveness of EU migration policies that assign migrants to legal categories and attempt to confine them spatially, but also addresses how migrants navigate these migration regimes.

Transnational migration theory has long embraced the idea that migration does not only occur between a country of origin and a country of destination, but also encompasses countries of transit. However, recent work in mobility and migration studies has added a new layer of analysis to transnational approaches by applying a trajectory methodology. This trajectory approach extends the transnational approach by addressing transit spaces as integral parts of the migration experience (Papadopoulou-Kourkoula, 2008; Collyer et al., 2012; Bredeloup, 2012). Informed by the recent attention on the fluidity of migration journeys, I focus on the role of trajectories in that they point to the importance of (im)mobilities in and of their own right, thereby problematising the presumption of linearity in migratory journeys (Schapendonk et al., 2018; Ahrens, 2013; Mainwaring, 2016). The focus on trajectories directs attention to the ways in which migration paths are continuously re-shaped and re-negotiated en route in relation to the regulations imposed by migration regimes as well as personal aspirations and circumstances. Thereby, moments of immobility become equally as important to the understanding of migration trajectories as periods of movement (Schapendonk et al., 2018; Schwarz, 2018).

Restrictive migration regimes in Europe make it particularly difficult for many people from sub-Saharan Africa to obtain visas to enter the EU through regular channels, leading people to seek out ever more dangerous routes to Europe via the infamous Mediterranean crossing and, since 2018, increasingly via the Strait of Gibraltar (Spiegel Online, 2018). Moreover, these policy restrictions continue to govern migrants' mobility within Europe (Ahrens, 2013; Lucht, 2012; Schapendonk, 2012, 2017; Vigh, 2009a; Toma & Castagnone, 2015). Schapendonk (2017) applies the concept "multiplicity of transit" to address the relationship between migrants' diverse mobilities and EU migration policies that bind them to a legal category, e.g. refugee, asylum seeker, rejected asylum seeker. This conceptualisation helps to expose "[...] the politics and human cost of migration management in the EU as well as of migrants' creativity to transgress the hindrances that the EU's migration management puts in place" (ibid, p. 210). The uncertainty experienced by migrants with precarious legal statuses can perpetuate the desire and need for continued mobility within Europe. This spatial mobility between countries is also reflected in "status mobility" (Schuster, 2005, p. 762): moving between different legal categories such as documented/ undocumented, asylum seeker, refugee, labour migrant and tourist. While legal categories are often presented in essentialised terms, scholarship in migration and border studies has demonstrated how "illegality" is socio-politically constructed (De Genova, 2002; Düvell, 2011). De Genova (2002), for example, explores how state displays of power at the US-Mexico border serve as spectacles intending further marginalisation of irregularised migrants so as to ensure a steady supply of cheap labour, i.e. impeding the granting of working rights, rather than actually halting migration. Kubal's (2013) conceptualisation of semi-legality further aids in deconstructing the binary representation of conceptualisations of "legal" and "illegal" by highlighting "the in-between statuses" (p. 555) encountered in migrants' everyday lives when manoeuvring national and supranational migration regimes. Semi-legality is a useful tool to explore the complexities involved in migrants' intra-EU mobility trajectories and challenges the idea of legal statuses as the predominant identifier of migrants' life situations, but instead allows for a more flexible and challenging framework that prompts the researcher to engage with migrants' narratives. Trajectory approaches to migration that focus on the journey in all its fragmentation and stagnation, therefore, allow for a critical questioning of categories such as legal/illegal by providing insight into how migrants experience and navigate between and across legal categories as well as national borders.

Methodological approach

This chapter is based on short-term ethnographic fieldwork carried out among West African migrants in Hamburg between April and May 2017. I conducted in-depth, semi-structured interviews with six men from West African countries. All interviews were held in either English or German.

I applied a biographical approach to the interviews, which pays attention to the processes of identity formation, whereby acts of migration become an important part in one's understanding of the past, present and future. Furthermore, this approach elucidates how one move may relate to following ones (Iosifies &

Sporton, 2009, p. 102). Informal conversations with interlocutors and participant observations, e.g. at a service at a Ghanaian church and during the annual Africa Day Festival, were useful to gain further insight into the interlocutors' everyday lives in Hamburg.

I analysed the empirical material through themes of (im)mobility and with attention to the navigational tactics applied by interlocutors to manoeuvre everyday life in the urban spaces of Hamburg. The empirical findings illustrate how mobility and immobility in migration trajectories can occur simultaneously and present two sides of the same coin.

Encountering involuntary immobility

Carling (2002) refers to "involuntary immobility" as the inability to migrate through formal channels as a result of limitations set by migration policies as well as structural constraints placed upon migrants even before their departure. This understanding of involuntary immobility was mirrored in the experiences narrated by interlocutors who were already in Europe, but were disciplined in their mobility either on or after arrival according to the legal status assigned to them, e.g. refugee, asylum seeker, tourist, rejected asylum seeker. This, however, also spurred continued movement, whereby immobility comes to inform mobility and vice versa (see also Salazar & Smart, 2011). This is also addressed by Schapendonk (2012, p. 578) who argues that "[...] statuses and feelings of immobility are vital to a better understanding of mobilities". However, while all interlocutors that I spoke with felt immobilised at some point during their migration trajectories, the conditions experienced as immobilising varied. Based on my material and the academic literature on migration trajectories, these different modes of immobility are identified as spatial immobility and socio-economic immobility (see also Schuster, 2005; Ahrens, 2013; Carling, 2002). This distinction allows to examine how immobility holds different meanings for the interlocutors and how these modes of immobility overlap and intersect. In other words, immobility occurs in several ways and the tactics employed to overcome it vary accordingly.

Spatial immobility

In the following, spatial immobility is understood as the experience of being forced to remain in one's position by structures set up by the national or supranational migration regimes. These are referred to as "internal externalities" (Schapendonk, 2017). Internal externalities typically describe institutions and practices such as detention centres and the asylum system more generally.

When I met Hamid[2] from Niger in Hamburg, he had refugee status and had lived in Germany for four years. As is the policy in Germany, people seeking asylum and refugees are assigned to the various Länder (federal states) according to a quota system. Hamid lived in an asylum centre in a city in Saxony Anhalt and was, according to German asylum regulations, obliged to remain in the municipality he was registered in. Yet, I met Hamid in Hamburg, several hundred kilometres away from his official place of residence. Hamid was unhappy at the asylum centre and decided to travel to Hamburg, where he had a friend. He hoped to find work in the informal labour market and make a livelihood. Hamid was frustrated with his housing situation in Saxony Anhalt. During our conversation, he described feeling isolated and confined in the centre itself as well as the near-by small town. His experiences at the asylum centre were in stark contrast to the life which he believed to take place in Hamburg and in which he wanted to partake. Hamid did not want to return to the asylum centre and would rather stay in Hamburg, even though this would be a breach of his residence terms and he would risk encountering problems with the authorities, potentially in the form of cuts to his subsidy payments.

The instance recounted above highlights how Hamid experienced spatial immobility by being unable to choose his own place of residence in Germany, feeling immobilised by having to reside in a town which he called "depressing". Yet, although the asylum policies affect spatial immobility and containment, Hamid challenged these restrictions by choosing to travel and move physically. He was planning to stay in Hamburg for a few weeks to see what his possibilities of finding work and housing were. This situation elucidates that feelings of being rendered spatially immobile and physical mobility can exist simultaneously, thereby illuminating the complex interplay between mobility and immobility in migration trajectories.

The feeling of constraint inflicted by the regulations imposed on refugees in Germany was also brought up by Ahmad during our conversations. He has lived in Germany for over 14 years, during which he shifted between different legal statuses and cities. In 2016, he received temporary residence as a refugee in Hamburg. Due to a physical disability, the municipality placed him in a care home for seniors and people with dementia. Being in his early forties, Ahmad was neither a senior nor did he have dementia. During our conversations, he expressed his frustration about his accommodation. He told me, "I am not like these other people here". Ahmad had asked the municipality to relocate him to an accessible apartment. However, at the time of our conversation these attempts had not been successful. The accommodation assigned to Ahmad increased his experience of being rendered spatially immobile by the German asylum system. The journey from Hamburg's city centre to the care home took almost an hour and involved multiple changes of transport. Yet, Ahmad travelled to the city almost daily to meet his friends and browse the African shops in Hamburg's city centre. During our conversations, he emphasised that he tried to spend as little time as possible at his assigned accommodation: "I only go to that place to sleep", he said.

Ahmad and Hamid's experiences highlight different instances of involuntary spatial immobility processes. They also show that experiences of spatial immobility are not limited to migration from the home countries, but also occur during along migrants' trajectories in Europe and despite having residence status in an EU country. The migration policies constrain migrants' mobility on multiple scales, from the urban environment to cross-border movement.

Socio-economic immobility

Spatial immobility is only one type of immobility that the interlocutors expressed during our conversations. Experiences of socio-economic immobility due to structural constraints were repeatedly voiced. Gabriel, for example, left his home in a West African country because he could not find a job despite his university education. His frustration with the labour market and political situation in his home country propelled him to pursue a Master's degree abroad. Gabriel expressed his disappointment about not being able to build the life he desired as follows:

> [...] when you finish university, jobs are not there. The governments are not opening jobs, nor are the companies. They keep on saying: go out and use your knowledge from the university, the colleges, to do something for

yourself. But they are forgetting that the system that they are running is not giving the opportunity to do something for yourself. For instance, you finish school, you have ideas, but even a small capital to start a business is hard to come by. You sit back home and somebody, excuse me to say, who was a school drop-out, maybe from the same community that you belong to, who was able to move into Europe, to work for maybe five years, six, seven years and those people come back and you compare you wasting your time, university time, you going to school to that level and so you won't be noticed within the community. But that person will be noticed because they have a lot to do business.

This impediment encountered on the journey towards adulthood and social mobility can lead to feelings of "social death" (Hage, 2003; Vigh, 2009a). Based on fieldwork conducted amongst young men from Guinea Bissau, Vigh (2009a, p. 96) found that:

> [...] for urban youth, life in Bissau is practically characterized by an inability to move along a positive social trajectory as the socio-economic environment seems frozen in perpetual motion without progress. [...] this category has come to equal "social death".

Similarly, Honwana (2012) uses the concept "waithood" to describe the period of immobility between childhood and adulthood, characterised by young people's difficulty in entering the labour market and becoming socially recognised as adults. Being confronted with community peers who returned from abroad with financial means to embark on their trajectories towards adulthood increased Gabriel's feeling of being stuck in his socio-economic position. He explained that these experiences motivated him to move abroad "to Europe or America" and pursue further education. Gabriel elaborates that "when people have a European or American certificate, they will get a job very fast". In 2015, he received a student visa to study in Russia, which was not his preferred destination but was affordable to him at the time. Moving to Russia to get a university degree was a deliberate decision taken by Gabriel to escape the experience of social death at home.

Having worked in Libya for several years Freddy, from Nigeria, fled the country in 2011 due to the war. He arrived in Lampedusa, Italy, and was granted humanitarian asylum on the basis of UN Resolution 1973 (United Nations Security Council, 2011). He soon moved to Florence, where he remained for almost two years. It was in Florence that he received his residence documents. Freddy explained that he quickly understood how the Italian system works. This included acknowledging the importance of remaining in one place while waiting to receive documents from the Italian authorities. His ability to decipher the Italian migration system was beneficial to Freddy. He told me that some of his acquaintances in Italy were not aware of the significance that remaining in one place held and instead kept moving around. Their continued mobility, he said, prevented them from receiving their documents. After getting his temporary residence, Freddy was unable to find a job in his learned profession. He expressed frustration about the lack of support he received from his case counsellor and the Italian asylum system more generally. Not being able to work and being in a situation of limbo wore him down: "[w]hen all you do is eat, sleep, wake, it kills someone". One morning in 2013, Freddy woke up and realised, as he said, that his life in Italy was passing by without him being able actively to shape it and partake in it. He decided to leave Italy without a specific idea of where he should go. Eventually, he travelled to Hamburg, where he had been living ever since.

Freddy's experience of being rendered socially immobile by the Italian asylum system differs from Ahmad's and Hamid's experiences in Germany. While Freddy did perceive the spatial immobility as restrictive, he also noted that staying in one particular place in Italy had been advantageous for him. Yet, the immobility he experienced affected his possibilities of attaining socio-economic mobility. His use of the phrase "it kills someone" points to the severity of this experience and mirrors Gabriel's social death narratives. Once people seeking asylum in Italy have been granted temporary residence, they "are considered to be able to support themselves independently. Consequently, there are only very limited accommodation facilities offered by the authorities" (Gunten et al., 2011, p. 7) and people received no more financial support from the state. As Freddy's situation exemplifies, many refugees in Italy struggled to gain access to the formal labour market and experience precarious living conditions often characterised by homelessness and poverty (Schuster, 2005; Lucht, 2012). Intra-EU mobility may then be employed as a tactic to overcome this immobility. The interlocutors adapted to changing situations and developed creative tactics to overcome situations of involuntary immobility, and in effect circumvented the restrictions of migration policies.

Intra-EU mobility as a navigational tactic

The navigational tactics employed by the interlocutors aimed to improve life conditions, including socio-economic situations. Social navigation refers to "a special form of movement [...] the way we move in a moving environment" (Vigh, 2009b, p. 420; see also Tuckett, 2015). Vigh's (2006; 2009a, b) conceptualisation of social navigations provides a fruitful approach when attempting to grasp the different modes and scales of mobility that migrants employ, as it "directs our attention to the interaction between a navigator, the process of navigation, and the environment or terrain being navigated" (Vigh, 2006, p. 36). Mobility as social navigation allows for a reading of migrants' tactics as fluid processes that are based upon reducing risks and adopting a trajectory (Carling, 2015, p. 3).

Moving country, moving status

When I met Gabriel, he had been living in Hamburg for a few months. Gabriel received a student visa to study in Moscow in 2015, where he lived for two years. Although his visa was valid at the time of our encounter, Gabriel decided that he would not return and continue his studies in Russia. He travelled to Hamburg as a tourist. While Gabriel told me that he had not planned to leave Russia for good, he also remarked that travelling with all his documents had become a habit of his:

> Anytime I am moving, anytime I am travelling, it's just part of me that I have my documents with me. I don't leave my documents behind. Because the way I am always thinking, I am always planning ahead. So, I took all my documents from the university, from the language course – I took it. I wanted a transcript from the university.

Although Gabriel's initial plan was to return and finish his studies in Russia, once in Hamburg he changed his plans. Moreover, his explanation on travelling with all his certificates and legal documents at all times highlights the importance of mobility as a (potential) navigational tactic.

What strikes me as interesting about this account is Gabriel's deliberate transition from a legal residence status as a student in Russia to living without the officially required documentation in Hamburg, thus putting him at risk of deportation and experiencing precarity in Germany. He was himself acutely aware of this risk:

> I came here, so now I am stranded. So right now, I am illegal, but someone who has papers from Italy, who is a refugee from Italy, he is in a better position. The one who passed through the desert and went through the refugee system. He is protected by the Italian government. If he will be deported, he will be deported back to Italy. Right now [...] if I am being deported, I will have to go back [to the home country].

Gabriel ranked refugee status higher than overstaying a tourist visa and moving into irregularity. However, financial difficulties in Russia as well as encounters with racism spurred his need to resume mobility as a navigational tactic, even though this came at the price of living irregularised and thereby increasing the risk of experiencing precarity and marginalisation in Germany. After arriving in Germany, Gabriel destroyed his passport to prevent deportation to his home country should he be confronted by the migration authorities. While, on one hand, this measure "strands" him in Germany, as Gabriel cannot travel through authorised channels without identification papers, the lack of papers, on the other, provides him with a certain degree of flexibility in terms of denying his national identity and assuming another.

Freddy's and David's experiences of moving between countries and statuses point to another navigational tactic utilised to attain spatial and socio-economic mobility: Both men fled Libya, where they had lived and worked for several years, and reached Lampedusa in Italy in 2011. After receiving asylum in Italy and confronted with unemployment, they continued their migration trajectories and have been living in Hamburg since 2013. However, both of their Italian residence permits were due to expire in the months after our encounter. Freddy and David contemplated travelling within that year back to Italy, where they would stay until their residence status was renewed. A return to Italy would create economic and practical difficulties for them, but navigating this migration regime was necessary for Freddy and David to maintain their rights to remain in Europe. By renewing their residence status in Italy, they would be able to live in Germany semi-legally, as Kubal describes it, thus reducing the risk of being deported back to their home countries and allowing them to travel in the Schengen area without, however, giving them rights to pursue formal work in any country other than Italy. Moving between different legal statuses can thus simultaneously create situations of precarity for migrants and allow for creative approaches to (re)gaining spatial and socio-economic mobility.

A thorough understanding of the Italian migration regime is, however, indispensable to successfully navigating the murky waters of legal categories. Tuckett (2015) shows how migrants in Italy apply a variety of tactics to attain and retain their legal status in Italy. Yet, while migrants' ability to operate within this system may present a viable short-term tactic for spatial and socio-economic mobility, it also bears the risk of reproducing "migrants' marginal and insecure status" rather than actively challenging it (Tuckett, 2015, p. 113). This is also reflected in David's and Freddy's situation. A renewal of their residence in Italy would provide them with a higher degree of flexibility in terms of regularly travelling within the EU. Yet, it also bears the risk of perpetuating experiences of marginalisation and insecurity by remaining in precarious, short-term legal statuses tied to residence in Italy. Moreover, David and Freddy would have temporarily to abandon their lives in Hamburg in the hopes of returning at a later point with their renewed Italian residence permits.

In many cases, moving from one EU member state to another results in a shift in the documentation and residence statuses of interlocutors. Frequently, these shifts are associated with changing from a "better" legal category, such as refugee status, to a loss of status or semi-legal status associated with precarity and marginalisation (Schuster, 2005; Kubal, 2013; Ahrens, 2013). All interlocutors I spoke with were aware of these transitions between legal categories and the associated downward mobility, yet some deliberately opted for this path. To shift between legal statuses may increase the risk of precariousness. However, it can (often simultaneously) provide a higher degree of flexibility, which may at times be advantageous, particularly to find paid work and/or live in an area considered to be more desirable due to location, social ties and employment opportunities. The supposed rigidity of legal categories is thus actively called into question by the in-betweenness of migrants' lived experiences.

The next country, the next city

Joseph had a temporary residence permit in Italy which enabled him to travel freely within the Schengen area. However, while he was allowed to travel from one country to another, he was not allowed to sojourn in another Schengen country for longer than three months and was not eligible to work. Yet, after over a year of living mostly in Northern Italy without being able to find a stable job, Joseph continued his migration trajectory leading him to different cities in Spain and France. Eventually, he travelled to Hamburg after "talking with a friend on the phone, who said I should come here". However, once Joseph arrived in Hamburg his friend stopped answering his calls and his hopes of finding housing and work through this friend were disappointed. When I met Joseph, he had been living in Hamburg for four months and was struggling to find employment. Joseph's navigational tactic can be understood as "trial-and-error" mobility (Schapendonk, 2017, p. 222), moving between European countries based on information received through acquaintances and hearsay. Although he was able to travel regularly, his temporary residence status in Italy prohibited Joseph from working outside the country. To resist the socio-economic immobility produced by unemployment, Joseph continued his migration journey in Europe. Joseph expressed frustration about not being able to work outside Italy:

> In Europe if you don't have the document, how are you going to live? If you don't have connections you can't make the life. Why can't I use my European document to work in Europe?

Moreover, Joseph's statement points to his frustration with the discrepancy between an imaginary of the EU as an integrated space on the one hand and a focus on national settlement and integration policies on the other. Yet, Joseph's navigational tactic of intra-EU mobility also kept him hopeful that the next country, the next city or the next encounter would improve his situation. He said, "Life is not easy for us, but I am hoping for success one day". Kleist and Thorsen (2016) emphasise the importance of paying attention to the role of hope in migratory journeys, as it "offers a particular take on uncertainty, one which emphasizes potentiality and anticipation rather than fear and doubt" (p. 2). As Freddy explained to me:

> It's only when you're dead that you've reached your final position, as long as you are alive you don't know where you are going to be or where you are going to stay. I am not moving life, but life moves me and it's about creating chances for myself in that kind of movement.

Similarly, Joseph's account of his migration trajectory as an interplay between hope and continued mobility suggests how hope rather than hopelessness can shape mobility trajectories. The intra-EU migration trajectories of the people interviewed here are characterised by processes of re-negotiation, tactical insight and pertinence to the goal of improving one's life situation despite restrictive migration policies and precarious legal statuses. In doing so, the interlocutors defied ideas of passivity in the face of immobility and actively employed navigational tactics to improve their situation.

Confronting the EU migration regime: Lampedusa in Hamburg's political activism

During my fieldwork, I encountered an additional approach to the migration regime, informed not only by navigational tactics aimed to circumvent spatial and socio-economic immobility, but also by active contestation of the system enforcing this immobility. While circumvention and contestation tactics differ with regard to their visibility and political framing, it is important to bear in mind that they are not mutually exclusive and some interlocutors adopted both approaches, sometimes simultaneously, to secure and improve their situation in Hamburg, Germany and the EU.

In 2013, a social movement by the name of Lampedusa in Hamburg[3] emerged in Germany. The group was formed by about 300 migrants from sub-Saharan Africa, many of whom had been working in Libya and fled to Lampedusa in 2011 during the Libyan Civil War. Many of them were granted asylum for humanitarian reasons in accordance with UN Resolution 1973. The Italian economic crisis, the lack of a coherent asylum system and support for refugees, however, made it difficult for many to sustain themselves in Italy, and some moved to other European countries (Odugbesan & Schwiertz, 2018; Tazzioli, 2015; Borgstede, 2017). On its website, LiHH (2017) states:

> In Italy, there is nothing for us, no work and no future. Only homelessness and misery awaits [*sic*] us and many other refugees in Italy.

In Hamburg, the LiHH activists demanded recognition of their Italian work and residence permits throughout the EU as they hold the EU collectively accountable for having to flee Libya (Lampedusa in Hamburg, 2017). Their claim is summed up as follows:

> We just want the right to stay and work here in Hamburg so that we can sustain ourselves and our families. We demand the europe-wide [*sic*] recognition of our Italian residence and working permits. Is Italy not a member of the European Union? Or don't the European rights apply for everyone? (Lampedusa in Hamburg, 2017)

This illustrates how LiHH members perceive the migration regime, and particularly the Dublin II Regulation which determines which European state is responsible for processing the asylum application, as inconsistent and unjust. While the European migration regime addresses migrant integration nationally, LiHH propose an understanding of the EU as an integrated space in which having residence and work permits in one country should not hinder them from living and working in another Member State. Additionally, LiHH argues that EU migration policies should jointly take responsibility for people displaced where there has been European intervention in conflicts. LiHH's goal to receive group asylum in accordance with Article 23 of the Residence Act (Federal Ministry of Justice and Consumer Protection, 2018), by which groups can receive asylum and work permits on humanitarian grounds. Hamburg's government has thus far refused this demand and granted only a temporary suspension of deportation to Italy for individuals of the group.

LiHH's case elucidates how migrants living between legal categories exert resistance to the migration regime in Europe by actively engaging with and challenging what they perceive as unjust. LiHH has been successful in garnering support from several socio-political organisations, such as other migrant rights organisations, labour organisations as well as anti-gentrification initiatives. It has established itself as an important movement among activist initiatives in Hamburg (Borgstede, 2017; Odugbesan & Schwiertz, 2018). During several conversations, interlocutors articulated feelings of group membership: "[w]hen we came with our own movement [LiHH] we challenged the system". However, being actively engaged with the LiHH movement is not required in order to utilise the LiHH information tent in Hamburg's city centre. Many (newly arrived) migrants frequent the tent as a place of first contact, to build social networks and to establish navigational tactics to manoeuvre everyday life in the city or beyond. Thus, LiHH's information tent has become an important point of contact for many migrants from different countries and with different legal statuses and a part of people's navigations in the city.

After years of waiting in Italy and as a result of homelessness and precarity experienced in Hamburg, the LiHH activists were "done with sitting around", as Freddy put it. David said, "We wanted to bring our voice to the authorities". Furthermore, LiHH has focused on the discussions surrounding EU responsibility for refugees in Europe. As a banner at an LiHH protest stated, "We did not survive the NATO war in Libya to die in the streets of Hamburg". Jørgensen (2016) has argued that lived precarity can become a basis for political struggle. The case of LiHH elucidates how migrant activism actively contests the EU's restrictive migration policies and the "exclusionary access to space" (Tazzioli, 2015, p. 5). By demanding to be heard and refusing to be invisible, LiHH navigates the political terrain and reshapes the social space of Hamburg (Odugbesan & Schwiertz, 2018). In this regard, this tactic differs from tactics evoked by other interlocutors, who attempted to avoid encounters with the EU migration regime to become and/or remain spatially and socio-economically mobile.

Conclusion

This chapter addressed intra-EU mobilities of migrants in Europe and the migration regime that governs them. It explored West African migrants' experiences of (im)mobility and the navigational tactics employed throughout their migration trajectories. Moving within Europe's exclusionary migration regime is a constant process of navigation. Irregularised people moving within this system thus adopt different tactics to remain mobile or in place.

Based on the analysis of the empirical material, I distinguish between two main tactics to navigate everyday lives in the EU: The first tactic was characterised by attempts to circumvent the restrictions on socio-economic and spatial mobility by counteracting both forms of immobilisation interdependently and/or separately. The second tactic was using social activism, such as through participating in the LiHH movement to contest the EU's migration regime. This tactic actively challenges the national migration regime by demanding group residence under Article 23 of the Residence Act in Germany. LiHH has been vocal in Hamburg for many years and its participants have decided to forego invisibility often associated with irregularisation and rather actively and visibly to claim rights from national authorities and the supranational EU migration regime. Yet, the distinction between the different tactics is often blurred as interlocutors shift between visibility and invisibility, movement and stasis in their migration trajectories in a process of continuous (re)negotiation.

The migration trajectory approach allows us to focus on the complex interplay between migrants' hopes, frustrations and aspirations during their journeys. The aspirations and goals that interlocutors seek to achieve through the numerous considerations and decisions they make are not unique to migration, but are ardently governed and closely policed by migration regimes. This chapter hopes to contribute to a nuanced understanding of the complexity of the (fragmented) migration trajectories and continuous navigation processes undertaken by irregularised migrants in the EU.

Notes

1   Drawing on the works of De Certeau (1984) and Vigh (2009b) tactics are here understood as means of the marginalised, whereas strategies are means of the powerful. De Certeau states, "The space of a tactic is the space of the other. Thus it must play on and with a terrain imposed on it and organized by the law of a foreign power" (p. 37).
2   All names and other personal data have been changed to ensure interlocutors' anonymity.
3   Hereafter referred to as LiHH.

References

Ahrens, J. (2013). "Suspended in Eurocrisis: new immobilities and semi-legal migrations amongst Nigerians living in Spain". *Journal of Mediterranean Studies*, 22:1, pp. 115–140.

Andersson, R. (2016). "Europe's failed 'fight' against irregular migration: ethnographic notes on a counterproductive industry". *Journal of Ethnic and Migration Studies*, 42:7, pp. 1055–1075. DOI:10.1080/1369183X.2016.1139446.

Borgstede, S. B. (2017). "'We are here to stay'. Reflections on the struggle of the refugee group "Lampedusa in Hamburg" and the Solidarity Campaign, 2013–2015". In P. M. S. Chattopadhyay (ed.), *Migration, Squatting and Radical Autonomy* (pp. 162–179). London and New York: Routledge.

Bredeloup, S. (2012). "Sahara transit: times, spaces, people". *Population, Space, and Place*, 18, 457–467. DOI:10.1002/psp.634.

Bundesministerium für Justiz und Verbraucherschutz. (2018). Gesetz über den Aufenthalt, die Erwerbstätigkeit und die Integration von Ausländern im Bundesgebiet (Aufenthaltsgesetz - AufenthG) § 23 Aufenthaltsgewährung durch die obersten Landesbehörden; Aufnahme bei besonders gelagerten politischen Interessen; Neuansiedlung von Schutzsuchenden). Retrieved from https://www.gesetze-im-internet.de/aufenthg_2004/__23.html.

Carling, J. (2002). "Migration in the age of involuntary immobility: Theoretical reflections and Cape Verdean experiences". *Journal of Ethnic and Migration Studies*, 28:1, pp. 5–42. DOI:10.1080/13691830120103912.

Carling, J. (2015). "Pathways out of waithood: Initial steps towards a conceptual framework". Paper presented at the 6th European Conference on African Studies, Paris.

Certeau, M. D. (1984). *The Practice of Everyday Life*. Berkeley and Los Angeles, CA: University of California Press.

Collyer, M., F. Düvell & H. d. Haas. (2012). "Critical approaches to transit migration". *Population, Space, and Place*, 18, 407–414. DOI:10.1002/psp.630.

Düvell, F. (2011). "Paths into irregularity: the legal and political construction of irregular migration". *European Journal of Migration and Law*, 13:3, pp. 275–295.

Genova, N. D. (2002). "Migrant 'illegality' and deportability in everyday life". *Annual Review of Anthropology*, 31, 419–447. DOI:https://doi.org/10.1146/annurev.anthro.31. 040402.085432.

Gunten, C. v., M. P. Jacobsen & I. Jordal. (2011). "Asylum procedure and reception conditions in Italy. Report on the situation of asylum seekers, refugees, and persons under subsidiary or humanitarian protection, with focus on Dublin returnees". Berne and Oslo: Swiss Refugee Council.

Hage, G. (2003). *Against paranoid nationalism, searching for hope in a shrinking society*. Annandale, NSW: Pluto Press.

Honwana, A. (2012). *The time of youth, work, social change, and politics in Africa*. Sterling: Kumarian Press.

Iosifides, T., & D. Sporton. (2009). "Editorial: Biographical methods in migration research". *Migration Letters*, 6:2, pp. 101 – 108.

Jørgensen, M. B. (2016). "Precariat – what it is and isn't – towards an understanding of what it does". *Critical Sociology*, 42:7–8, pp. 959–974. DOI:10.1177/0896920515608925.

Khosravi, S. (2018). "Afterword. Experiences and stories along the way". *Geoforum*. https:// doi.org/10.1016/j.geoforum.2018.05.021.

Kleist, N., & D. Thorsen. (2016). "Introduction". In N. Kleist and D. Thorsen (eds.). *Hope and Uncertainty in Contemporary African Migration*. New York; London: Taylor and Francis.

Kubal, A. (2013). "Conceptualizing semi-legality in migration research". *Law & Society Review*, 47:3, pp. 555–587. DOI:https://doi.org/10.1111/lasr.12031.

Lampedusa in Hamburg. (2017). "We demand the recognition of our Italian residence and working permit!" Lampedusa in Hamburg. Retrieved from http://lampedusa-hamburg. info/recognition-of-the-italian-residence-and-working-permit/.

Lucht, H. (2012). *Darkness before daybreak. African migrants living on the margins in southern Italy today*. Berkeley, CA: University of California Press.

Mainwaring, Ċ. (2016). "Migrant agency: Negotiating borders and migration controls". *Migration Studies*, 4:3, pp. 289–308. DOI:10.1093/migration/mnw013.

Odugbesan, A., & H. Schwiertz. (2018). "'We Are Here to Stay' – Refugee struggles in Germany between unity and division". In S. Rosenberger, N. Merhaut and V. Stern (eds.). *Protest Movements in Asylum and Deportation* (pp. 185–203). Cham: Springer Open.

Papadopoulou-Kourkoula, A. (2008). *Transit Migration. The Missing Link Between Emigration and Settlement*. Basingstoke: Palgrave Macmillan.

Salazar, N. B., & A. Smart. (2011). "Anthropological takes on (im)mobility". *Identities*, 18:6, pp. i–ix. DOI:10.1080/1070289X.2012.683674.

Schapendonk, J. (2012). "Turbulent trajectories: African migrants on their way to the European Union". *Societies*, 2, pp. 27–41. DOI:10.3390/soc2020027.

Schapendonk, J. (2017). "The multiplicity of transit: the waiting and onward mobility of African migrants in the European Union". *International Journal of Migration and Border Studies*, 3:2/3, pp. 208–227.

Schapendonk, J., I. v. Liempt, I. Schwarz & G. Steel. (2018). "Re-routing migration geographies: Migrants, trajectories and mobility regimes". *Geoforum*. https://doi.org/10.1016/j.geoforum.2018.06.007.

Schiller, N. G., & N. B. Salazar. (2013). "Regimes of mobility across the globe". *Journal of Ethnic and Migration Studies*, 39:2, pp. 183–200. DOI:10.1080/1369183X.2013.723253.

Schuster, L. (2005). "The continuing mobility of migrants in Italy: Shifting between places and statuses". *Journal of Ethnic and Migration Studies*, 31:4, pp. 757–774. DOI:10.1080/13691830500109993.

Schwarz, I. (2018). "Migrants moving through mobility regimes: The trajectory approach as a tool to reveal migratory processes". *Geoforum*. doi:https://doi.org/10.1016/j.geoforum.2018.03.007.

Spiegel Online. (2018). "Shifting overseas route. Spain becomes new target for migrants". Retrieved from http://www.spiegel.de/international/world/refugees-now-aim-for-spain-in-their-migration-route-a-1221537.html.

Tazzioli, M. (2015). "Which Europe? Migrants' uneven geographies and counter-mapping at the limits of representation. Movements". *Journal for Critical Migration and Border Regime Studies*, 1:2, pp. 1–20.

Toma, S., & E. Castagnone. (2015). "What drives onward mobility within Europe? The case of Senegalese migration between France, Italy and Spain". *Population*, 70:1, pp. 65–94.

Tuckett, A. (2015). "Strategies of navigation migrants' everyday encounters with Italian immigration bureaucracy". *The Cambridge Journal of Anthropology*, 33:1, pp. 113–128. DOI:10.3167/ca.2015.330109.

United Nations Security Council. (2011). Resolution 1973 (2011). Retrieved from http://www.un.org/ga/search/view_doc.asp?symbol=S/RES/1973%20%282011%29.

Vigh, H. (2006). *Navigating Terrains of War: Youth and Soldiering in Guinea-Bissau*. New York and Oxford: Berghahn Books.

Vigh, H. (2009a). "Wayward migration: On imagined futures and technological voids". *Ethnos*, 74:1, pp. 91–109. DOI:10.1080/00141840902751220.

Vigh, H. (2009b). "Motion squared. A second look at the concept of social navigation". *Anthropological Theory*, 9:4, pp. 419–438. DOI:10.1177/1463499609356044.

Wissink, M., F. Düvell & V. Mazzucatoa. (2017). "The evolution of migration trajectories of sub-Saharan African migrants in Turkey and Greece: The role of changing social networks and critical events". *Geoforum*. doi:https://doi.org/10.1016/j.geoforum.2017.12.004.

Part II:
Labour migration, imaginaries and aspirations

Balancing personal aspirations, family expectations and job matching: "migratory career" reconstruction among highly educated women in the Basque Country

Maria Luisa Di Martino, Concha Maiztegui and Iratxe Aristegui

Introduction

International migration is a complex phenomenon in which individuals face a decision-making process based on different determinants at personal, relational and professional levels. Aspirations are crucial in this process, but they cannot be separated from structural and relational factors, which produce different impacts and mark bifurcations for each person on the move (Bermúdez, 2014). Personal aspirations and professional expectations are crucial for shaping the migratory process. Scholars claim that migratory aspirations are linked not only to socio-economic and political factors related to the expectations of better life and job opportunities in the host country society, but geographical imaginaries linked to the place of immigration (Thompson, 2017; Timmerman, 2008; Timmerman & Wets, 2011). Among women, the sentimental imaginaries of their partners' countries of residence seem to play a key role (Riaño, 2016). In this respect, "migration, in the broadest sense, is much more than mere movement between places; it is always embedded in wider processes of meaning-making" (Salazar, 2010, p. 6). Therefore, professional expectations of job matching are also crucial in shaping highly educated women's migratory careers. Precisely for this reason, "the relationship between qualifications, policies and local labour market dynamics is thus central for defining the value of immigrants in this context" (Hercog & Sandoz, 2018, p. 455), which has generated the unsolved dilemma between highly skilled and highly educated conceptualisation and problematisation.

This chapter analyses the migratory careers of a group of highly educated[1] women in the Basque Country (Spain) by using, on the one hand, a qualitative approach through in-depth biographical interviews from the life-course perspective (Wingens, Windzio, de Valk, & Aybek, 2011) and, on the other hand, a multidimensional analytical perspective, at macro (structural), meso (relational) and micro (personal) levels. With this text we seek to contribute to the scientific knowledge on the fostering or hindering factors concerned in the international migrations of highly educated women by exploring, on the one hand, personal aspirations and professional expectations, shaping their migratory careers, and the coping strategies that have allowed them to achieve job matching; to overcome the structural/personal constraints encountered in the process; and to seize the evolving opportunities in the host country (Mahieu, Timmerman & Heyse, 2015). On the other hand, we seek to advance the understanding of the interplay between the macro, meso and micro determinants that influence highly educated women's migration experience which, while occurring under privileged conditions, also entails experiences of vulnerability and weakness in the context of the host country.

The concept of migratory career is the lens that allows us to advance beyond personal aspirations as motors of the mobility process in order to understand the invisible dynamics in a process of constant evolution among highly educated women in the transit from home to host country (Martiniello & Rea, 2014). Actually, it offers an inspiring tool for the reconstruction of respondents' experiences in different domains such as the personal, family and professional. Migratory career conceptualisation has been used in previous studies of migrant women occupied in low qualified sectors (Godin, Freitas & Rea, 2015; Poncelet & Martiniello, 2015), but has rarely been applied to highly skilled women's mobility. The literature on highly educated women, from a macro and micro analytical perspective, argues that over-qualification and deskilling are the main problems in the professional career building process due to structural constraints in the host country (Liversage, 2009; Kofman, 2013; Raghuram & Kofman, 2004).

Nevertheless, deskilling is also linked to family obligations (Meares, 2010; Roca, 2016; Timmerman, Martiniello, Rea & Wets, 2015). In Spain, some of the best-known cases are the downward occupational mobility of women from Latin America (Aysa-Lastra & Cachón, 2015; Oso & Parella, 2012; Parella & Cavalcanti, 2010; Roca, 2016). The main research question we address in this paper are the following: what is the interplay between personal aspirations and strategies (micro level), structural constraints and opportunities (macro level) and relational chances (meso level) that explains job matching and work-life balance in highly educated migrant women from two different geographical areas of origin (extra-European and intra-European) in the Basque Country?

Literature on highly skilled migrant women is quite new compared with studies focused on migrant women employed in highly feminised and lower skilled reproductive sectors (Kofman, 2000). Moreover, it has been recognised that the international movement of highly skilled professionals is also a gendered phenomenon (Docquier, Marfouk, Salomone & Sekkat, 2011), and migration may be a loophole for overcoming gender-based discrimination (Ruyssen & Salomone, 2018). A number of studies have documented women's difficulties in entering the high-level labour markets in many countries, such as Denmark (Liversage, 2009); the UK (Kofman & Raghuram, 2004); between Germany and the UK (Föbker & Imani, 2017); México (Ramírez & Tigau, 2018; Ramos, 2018); New Zealand (Meares, 2010); Switzerland (Riaño & Baghadi, 2007; Riaño, 2016); and Spain (Fernández & Parra, 2013; Riaño, 2014; Roca, 2016; Shershneva & Fernández, 2018). Studies show that the intersection of gender/ethnicity is another constraint (Grigoleit-Richter, 2017; Killian & Manohar, 2015; Triandafyllidou & Isaakyan, 2016). This body of work often suggests that migration has a negative impact on women's professional careers, indicating the deskilling process as one of the biggest risks they take (Raghuram & Kofman, 2004). Furthermore, studies which explore highly educated migrant women's and men's social and occupational integration, such as that of Sandoz (2019) in Switzerland, show that the interplay between structures and agency shapes different settings related to different opportunities and constrains for each migrant situation.

Another topic of the research has been the concomitant intensification of their work at home (Liversage, 2009; Meares, 2010; Roca, 2016). Riaño (2016) described the paradox of job-education mismatch and proposes the term 'marginalised elites' (p. 1) to express the imbalance of women's pre-migratory expectations and the post-migratory reality. This chapter builds on this body of literature to focus on the experiences of women who have achieved a job suited to their level of studies. In the process, we contribute to the discussion on highly educated migrant women and the analysis of the process towards job matching. The empirical analysis is based on a qualitative study of 36 in-depth interviews conducted with respondents from Latin America (18) and Europe (18). Their backgrounds are in different sociopolitical contexts, and restrictive non-gender-sensitive European labour migration policies affect them in different manners. However, regularisation seems insufficient to understand different dynamics for labour integration (Shershneva & Fernández, 2018). By providing in-depth insights into the selected groups, the migratory career perspective helps us to understand how their experiences could be affected by structural or personal factors. This study emphasised that there is not a univocal career, but heterogeneous experiences emerging from the intersection of multiple elements in migrant women's biographies.

The present chapter is structured as follows: the first section examines the theoretical and methodological importance acquired by the analysis of migratory careers due to the great heterogeneity and variability of migration paths. The second section describes the research methods. The third section is based on our findings, analysing highly educated migrant women's biographies from the life-course perspective.

Migratory careers and migrant women

Martiniello and Rea (2014) have developed an analytical tool which allows us to integrate "structures of opportunities, individual characteristics and networks to make sense of the migratory experience" (p. 1079). In doing so, it provides a holistic perspective on the migration process that includes, simultaneously, objective dimensions (legal-institutional structures) and the subjective perspective related to the migrant's personal assessment of their migratory trajectory from a retrospective angle (Mahieu et al., 2015, p. 19). This approach is valuable for understanding the logics that accompany the mobility process and the meaning the employment strategy acquires for migrants within the framework of their life trajectories. The migration career framework has been applied to gender studies.

Among the various studies it is worth mentioning the FEMIGRIM collective research "Factors and dynamics affecting and explaining female migration in Belgian society" (Timmerman et al., 2015). This project proposed a gender sensitive framework for research on women which includes a longitudinal perspective based on the macro, meso and micro levels. FEMIGRIM's fieldwork carried out five case-studies based on the careers of migrant women of different nationalities (Zibouh & Martiniello, 2015; Poncelet & Martiniello, 2015; Godin et al., 2015; Mahieu et al., 2015). Those cases in Belgium point to women's agency as a key element in the interplay between macro, meso and micro dimensions. According to Godin et al. (2015), "women place their expectations, aspirations and projects at the very core of their migratory careers, which are [...] shaped by existing structures of opportunities and constraints" (p. 129). The migratory career analytical framework is suitable for analysing the changes and bifurcations in migrant women's trajectories (Bermudez, 2014; Freitas & Godin, 2013; Poncelet & Martiniello, 2015; Ramos, 2018). Either way, far from being linear, migratory careers are subject to bifurcations as a result of changes linked to sociopolitical opportunities, the ability to mobilise financial resources following the acquisition of new capital and individual trajectories, responding to new frameworks of mobility. According to Martiniello and Rea (2014), these paths are not always rationally planned, but built by people in the interplay between structural opportunities and challenges and personal coping strategies. Observing the careers of migrant women reveals the confrontation between initial expectations and the realities experienced through the migratory experience. Local context has an impact on this process.

In contrast to the traditional analyses of migration, mobility focused on the structural dimensions (macro), "political-economic process by which people are bounded" (Salazar, 2018, p. 157). The studies carried out in Spain on women's immigration and their patterns of incorporation into the labour market highlight that Spanish migration policies favour the concentration of women in the care and domestic work sectors (Parella, 2003). Most foreign women are in a situation of labour market and social vulnerability, related to patterns of employment characterised by the concentration of these workers in jobs linked to social reproduction (cleaning, caring) (Oso & Parella, 2012). This is due to the dynamic of commercialisation of care responsibilities in an insufficiently developed welfare state that lacks an adequate design of social services for people and families of universal character. It corresponds to a "regime of care" that distributes the responsibility for care and assistance between the state, the family and the market (Lutz, 2008). These conditions also present a serious worsening as a result of the economic crisis for women of Latin American origin in particular (Aysa-Lastra & Cachón, 2015).

In the Basque Country, according to Shershneva and Fernández (2018), 48.1 per cent of foreign women perceive an over-qualification in their work compared to 36.7 per cent of men. The origins of most women (54%) affected by this phenomenon (above the average of the Basque Country) are Latin American (especially those of recent settlement) and eastern European. The lower percentage of women does not have a dependent family in the home country, reducing slightly the pressure on them, as they can prioritise qualified job search

(Shershneva & Fernández, 2018). In addition, the stable legal situation allows for formal contracting and the possibility of broadening the job search in sectors according to the training received. Other factors are the recognition of the degree obtained in the home country and the time of residence. Four years is considered as the first step in the "stability continuum" (Moreno & Aierdi, 2008, p. 11) for securing residence and work permits.

Methodological aspects and profiles of respondents

We adopted an interpretative approach to enable a deeper understanding of the interplay between personal aspirations and strategies with the structural constraints and opportunities of the women interviewed, to understand their way of balancing initial aspirations and desires with the reality faced in the host country. Data from field work were collected in the Basque Country throughout 2016. In total, 36 in-depth interviews were held with respondents from six European[2] and nine Latin American countries. Women interviewed from those two areas were considered for this research study based on their different migration patterns: South-North and North-North (or intra-European) migration in the Basque Country. The interviewees were contacted within personal networks and by the snowball sampling technique, based on the following selection criteria: a) high educational level (university degree, master's, PhD); b) job-education matching; c) a minimum of three years of professional experience; and d) a minimum of four years of continuous residence in the Basque Country (after the first step in the regularisation process for Latin-American and European women). The sample provides a picture of different occupational sectors (Table 1). Among the women interviewed, eight are self-employed and freelancers (four from intra-European mobility and four from Latin America). The respondents' average age is 40 and the average time of permanent residence in the Basque Country is 12 years.

The main interview approach for the examination of the career path reconstruction process in different mobility regimes was the life-course perspective. The term "regime" suggests how national administrations affect individual mobility (Glick Schiller & Salazar 2013). Firstly, nationality is a key variable that establishes who is entitled to what type of mobility. In addition, the possibilities granted to certain nationality-holders depend on their economic power or class position. In the case of the people interviewed, it can be seen that the variety of circumstances in which they arrive in the Basque Country depends

Table 1   Respondents' Occupation Sectors in the Basque Country labour market

Occupational Sectors		European	Latin American	Total
Transversal Sectors Technicians (gender, culture, environment, cooperation, international relations)		6	6	12
Education & Research		5	2	7
Music		4	1	5
Health	**Medicine & Nursing**	0	3	3
	Psychology	0	3	3
Translation		1	0	1
Communication, Journalism, Marketing		1	2	3
Fashion Style		1	1	2
Total		*18*	*18*	*36*

not only on their origin, but also on the opportunities derived from their legal situation. Having a native couple or an employment contract prior to their arrival opens the door to possibilities that other women of the same nationality cannot obtain.

Open-ended questions related to the motivations for migrating, past and current employment, families and expectations. Interviews were recorded and transcribed verbatim. The data were analysed thematically, based on the interplay of: a) constraints; b) opportunities; and c) coping strategies. They were organised in macro, meso and micro dimensions (Table 2).

Searching for balance in a migratory career: opportunities, constraints and strategies

We used the aspirations for emigration criteria, because women's "aspirations can be considered as a crucial step towards actual migratory behaviour" (Van Mol et al., 2018, p. 1), and identified three main behaviours among the set of nationalities.

(1) Women who moved for sentimental reasons. They are mainly European with partners from the Basque Country. In this group women face periods of initial job mismatch; their main strategy for labour market integration passes

through upskilling and/or reskilling as a main post-migratory strategy for better job opportunities.

(2) Women who moved for professional reasons (single or with a partner). They had a pre-existing employment contract before moving. This group is characterised by matching opportunities raised from the intersection of pre-migration professional aspirations and job opportunities in the host country, like the musicians from both Latin-American and European countries.

(3) Women whose strongest reason for migration was breaking structural violence and oppression in their home country, most of whom came from Latin American countries. For this group migration seems have had a real "instrumental value" (Carling, 2014, p. 2) related to an intrinsic imaginary of constructing a better future, planned through their migratory careers.

These circuits reflect the diversity of migratory itineraries. All three groups share aspirations to achieve job matching. Other characteristics these women share is the lack of support networks. They view their migration as an individual project. Some of them claim to have had satisfying socio-economic conditions before migration; others claim to have used the opportunity to get a scholarship to start migration. Based on the narratives of the interviewees, Table 2 presents the constraints, opportunities and strategies in the migratory careers of a group of highly educated women in this study.

Legal status of entry is one of the factors that determines job placement (Bermudez, 2014). In Spain residence status is conditional upon a work contract, an internship or study enrolment. Women who came with a "sentimental regime" had an easier entry compared with other groups. Most of them were considered to be movers in the multisite landscapes of their migratory careers, which may start with an "Erasmus" experience in the case of European mobility, or studying for a Master's degree abroad and taking a job in another country. In one of these several experiences in a "pit-stop country modality" they meet their sentimental Basque partner and decide to start a family. In the case of a European woman from France:

> I was studying in the United States to improve my English; I decided to attend a master's in a feminist environment, which was an innovative subject in the 80s. After that, I couldn't stay in the US without a job, I was searching on the internet, and it was amazing in those times [...]. I applied for a job in London, and they hired me. So, I was working there in a great job for 5 years [...]. There I met my husband; he is Basque, that's why we moved

Table 2 Opportunities, Constraints and Strategies of Highly Skilled Women in the Basque Country

	Opportunities & Constraints		Migrant Women's Strategies	
Structural Dimension (macro)	**Opportunities**	Education: Grant policies	Apply for a grant.	
		Labour market: Fixed contract	Submit the CV; Skype interviews.	
	Constraints	Residence & work permits	Student visa; Naturalisation; Marriage.	Migratory Career towards job matching
		No homologation studies; No validation of previous work experience; Temporal de-skilling	(Partial) homologation; Reskilling; Upskilling.	
		Temporal Immobility	"Bridge-works"; Multitasking; Moonlighting; Volunteering.	
		Languages	Reorientation of career toward international sectors.	
Relational Dimension (meso)	**Opportunities**	Sentimental couple & family project	Attempt matching interests/ opportunities & family/work balance.	

	Opportunities & Constraints		Migrant Women's Strategies
Relational Dimension (meso)	**Constraints**	Limited Networks	Participation in non-profit organisations; Relationship with native partner's groups of reference (friends, family).
		Immobility as product of family & maternity	Native husbands' temporary support based on his better job conditions; Self-employment.
Personal Dimension (micro)	**Opportunities**	New perceptions of personal experience	Change desires/ aspirations; Lower expectations; Redefinition of ladder of priorities and road maps.
	Constraints	Frustrated aspirations of self-realisation	Resilience & flexibility; Redefinition of the professional profiles (horizontal mobility).

here. (EU17, France. Gender Expert, 50 years old, 30 years in the Basque Country).

Another group of European women migrants moved upon being hired, as it is the case for musicians. Musicians are part of a steadier professional career group, but that does not mean that their migratory process was also linear. On the contrary, they were part of the cosmopolitan culture "marked by diversity rather than homogeneity" (Glick Schiller & Salazar, 2013, p. 186) and experienced upskilling in different European countries before getting a steady contract in Bilbao. In the case of a musician from Albania with French heritage:

> I was studying my master's in Rome and after that I prepared several auditions for different orchestras. Finally, I was hired in the *Bilbao Orkestra Sinfonika*. (EU3, Albania. Musician, 38 years old, ten years in the Basque Country).

The third group of women corresponds to the type of "migrant students" (Bermúdez, 2014) who have completed their schooling and apply – especially in the case of Latin American women – for student visas. Later they start procedures to acquire an NIE (National Identification Number for foreigners). Some of the respondents found an opportunity through a grant in the host country, and once arrived they applied other coping strategies to start new lives in the Basque Country. Hence, they opt for personal development, aimed towards upskilling linked to better future job expectations with an open perspective on the destination where they will settle down. In the case of a Paraguayan woman's decision to migrate:

> I married an Argentinean to escape my family's gender-based violence. I divorced and I came back home. But, I could no longer abide so much narrow-mindedness and structural violence in my country's society [...]. I had a friend in Malaga, so I decided to come to Spain to finish my thesis. Once here, I chose to remain, because there were better opportunities for my life, after all. (AL9, Paraguay. Psychologist, 42 years old, 11 years in Spain, five years in the Basque Country).

According to Salazar (2010), "the link with imaginaries is established through the recognition of possibilities, of alternative constructions of future lives in other places" (pp. 9–10). In the migratory careers of migrant women with high levels of education migration has an instrumental value (Carling, 2014), with the main aim of changing their lives and achieving better jobs, in equality of conditions, with better salaries, according to their high level of qualifications.

> I was tired of the glass ceiling under which I lived in Venezuela. So I decided to move to the Basque Country [...]. But, everybody told me that I would have had to wait for everything: for title recognition, for job access, for work permits, for opportunities [...]. I had no idea about the euskera; I had to work in home care sector; I had to wait and I said to myself "resist, resist". Anybody told me the truth about migration and anybody told me about all the false myths about Spain! (AL4, Venezuela. Freelance in cooperation issues, 40 years old, ten years in the Basque Country).

Related to this, although migration could often be the outcome of a social network, in this research with highly educated women some of the interviewees do not seem to follow a network model in their migratory processes. There is an exception to the trend of women as agents of their migratory careers. In the case of a Peruvian woman, emigration is a family decision with a long-term strategy for settlement in a better country, whose family migratory imaginary established the United States as the first choice for a better standard of living.

> I was tired of the gender inequality, prejudice and stereotypes, and also of the bad political and economic situation in my country. I thought that the better option was to go to the United States. But I didn't know English, so the other option was Spain. I was desperately looking for a grant. I emailed hundreds of universities [...]. Finally, I was offered a half grant from the University of the Basque County [...]. Once my situation was regularized [five years at least] I started the family reunification process and I brought my grandparents and my brother too. (AL3, Peru, Psychologist, 50 years old, 18 years in the Basque Country).

Educational credentials could be predictive of labour market success. However, additional mechanisms seem to reduce the effect of education on newcomers (Kogan, Kalter, Liebau & Cohen, 2011, p. 76). In Spain, restrictions on the homologation and validation of diplomas, as well as delays in procedures, are obstacles to the labour mobility of qualified women (Parella & Cavalcanti, 2010). Among Latin American respondents the main tendency was to complete a partial homologation process as a pre-migration strategy. Later, they had to take new examinations within the Basque Country system at a post-migration stage. This is the case for respondents working in the area of healthcare. They knew how easy it was to find jobs if they provided the academic certificates:

I tried to homologate my nursing studies from Venezuela, and I had to be examined again on some subjects [...]. (AL15, Venezuela. Nurse, 36 years old, eight years in the Basque Country).

Other women, for whom it seems less clear that they can use their professional qualifications to get jobs, opt for non-homologation or partial homologation. They apply upskilling and/or reskilling strategies in order to neutralise partial gaps in the host country. The academic literature on skilled women migrants with their families describes an entrenching of domestic roles related to their difficulties in entering the labour market (Meares, 2010; Riaño, 2014; Roca, 2016). Our interviewees reveal that this process was also shared by women who arrived for sentimental reasons. When they experienced difficulties in overcoming constraints related to homologation they opted for different strategies (upskilling or reskilling) to increase future job opportunities. Similar findings were found by Liversage (2009) when analysing professional trajectories in highly skilled women in Denmark.

In terms of family life, the impact ranges from increased household and/ or childcare responsibilities to complete immersion in the domestic sphere (Meares, 2010). The redomestication process (Yeoh & Willis, 2005) drives the transformation of a professional woman into a housewife (Riaño & Baghadi, 2007; Roca, 2016). The main strategies for fitting family conciliation and professional aspirations are part-time jobs, self-employment of the women and/ or a partner with more flexibility. Those options are based on their personal aspirations as professionals, while at the same time they require family support strategies. A doctor from Costa Rica explains that the role her partner plays allowed her to combine their professional and family responsibilities during her first steps in her working life:

We have three children and I was working night shifts at the beginning. In the evenings and nights my husband was in charge of childcare [with a flexible job]. (AL12, Costa Rica. Doctor, aged 55, 25 years in the Basque Country)

Language seems to be a crucial aspect of the choice of labour integration strategies. Our interviewees reported some limitations associated with the official nature of the Basque language when joining the local labour market, due to its prescriptive use in specific working environments (such as education) in both public and private sectors. A woman from Latin America says:

> The linguistic policy is an unknown obstacle for migrants who come to the Basque Country; it clashes with our aspirations as it is very difficult to learn. (AL4, Venezuela. Freelance in cooperation issues, 40 years old, ten years in the Basque Country).

To overcome language constraints, previous studies highlighted that skills related to language knowledge have been used as an opportunity when they are convertible into economic capital (Föbker & Imani, 2017). Among the women interviewed, we identified three strategies related to language skills. First, some of the women decided to move towards an international work environment where those capabilities are valued, such as technicians or researchers. Second, some women were able to enter into the education field as teachers specialising in their mother tongue (French, English). The third group combines this tactic with reskilling. This is the case of the German interviewed, who chose reskilling convinced that the new professional profile as translator would be helpful for work-life balance and childcare:

> I was studying a master's in translation online while I was employed in a company. I wanted to start my own professional project and be able to balance my family life and childcare [three children] with my professional aspirations. (EU7, Germany. Translator, age 38, 13 years in the Basque Country).

At a personal level (micro), the main constraints in both groups are frustrated aspirations linked to the temporary initial immobility in the local labour market. Moreover, women often cite the pain and sadness of leaving their country (Roca, 2016). Our results suggest that, whether married or not, with or without a job, the experience of solitude is quite common. Whereas some initiated strategies to construct networks (meso level) through contacting intercultural or migrant women's associations, our respondents explained that they distinguish themselves from women with other regimes of mobility which forced them to accept more precarious jobs in order to help their families. For this reason, even if they feel partially identified, they do not manage to create bonds of friendship.

Respondents confirm that migratory processes independent from companies or states require great initiative and investment (Kofman & Raghuram, 2004). Women who have had less difficulty finding jobs due to labour shortages in certain fields (health, music) confirm that once this goal is achieved their careers tend to stabilise. On the other hand, when some women are asked about why the mobility experience became static when they got their permanent employment contracts, they explain that they have adapted to this life and have not risked moving to progress professionally, even if they desire to move on:

I thought I was going to be somewhere else, but then it happens that you lower your expectations completely, and, to tell you the truth, I didn't take much risk [...] because I also wanted to build my family project [...]. (EU9, Poland. International Relations, aged 32, eight years in the Basque Country)

From an intersectional perspective it is interesting to note that personal and family factors can be, at the same time, constraints or opportunities, depending on the case analysed and migratory career evolution. The music composer from Latin America said:

Maternity has delayed all my plans for my professional career, it was a big sacrifice at the same time that it was the most inspiring phase of my life, and a big resistance-building too. (AL18, Argentina. Musician, aged 59, 14 years in the Basque County)

In line with previous analysis (Liversage, 2009; Zibouh & Martiniello, 2015) our findings show that women have an active role in achieving their aspirations. At the same time, the data show a contradictory situation with the reproduction of gender roles at times exacerbated by loneliness and isolation in migration. Both the women who have come to create a family and those who form a family in the host country affirm that they made decisions to relegate their projects to a second level. It seems that affective relationships and the family take precedence over paid work, although they were able to maintain job matching. There has been a change in priorities, and in more extreme cases a process has been noted that could affect their autonomy:

I continue to reproduce traditional family roles, as woman responsible for the home. I must admit it: the mistake was mine. Out of the house? When I got here I felt like a "fish out of water". I went with a "bodyguard" everywhere. I always move with my husband, but with the years I am becoming more autonomous. (EU5, Italy. Lecturer, aged 55, 25 years in the Basque Country).

Conclusion

In this chapter we have focused on the coping strategies that highly educated women from Latin America and Europe have activated for overcoming structural and personal constraints through the renegotiation process of their personal aspirations and professional expectations in order to achieve job matching and work-life balance. The analysis of their migratory careers allows us to explore how initial aspirations, expectations and desires that women had when they arrived have been adapted, to a certain extent, to the circumstances encountered. There is a common characteristic of all the women interviewed: none of them has abandoned her professional expectations which, finally, have allowed her to achieve a job suited to her level of studies. In some cases, it has been a long process based on different professional strategies, such as retraining, bridging jobs or family support. During the meaning-making process, personal aspirations have also evolved, redefining their scales of priorities. For example, in the case of women with families, the professional goals have been temporarily relegated.

The fieldwork confirms that there are no univocal careers, but heterogeneous experiences related not only to the reasons for migrating and settling, but also to different migrants' situations (Sandoz, 2020). Despite the fact that all the women interviewed fulfilled the requirements established a priori (higher education studies, embedded work, length of stay), in the analysis we have confirmed that their country of origin is not a main variable for identifying the processes associated with their migratory careers. On the one hand, aspirations among the women interviewed are adapted to their particular social contexts. Thus, there is an interconnection between the personal and relational dimensions. Among the women whose migratory process is initiated by an affective relationship, the imaginaries about the country of destination are not always fulfilled since they observe difficulties, personal and professional, which they had not thought of. On the other hand, the women interviewed who have fled from situations of structural violence and the women whose migratory process is based on a professional project also modify their imaginaries. The feeling of loneliness and the difficulty in finding affective relations and friendship, suppose the main difficulties of personal nature, beyond the structural difficulties related to access to the labour market.

As previous research showed (Bermúdez, 2014; Godin et al., 2015; Liversage, 2009; Timmerman et al., 2015), the findings illustrate that migratory career evolution is not linear, but depends on the interplay of different structural and personal/family factors which hinder or foster women's goals and aspirations. Moreover, fundamental variables such as age, the presence or absence of children, the years of residence and the direction and duration of mobility should be considered, as they influence migratory careers in various ways.

One of the main conclusions of this study is that the diversity of careers seems to be related to the different regimes of mobility. These regimes seem to be a more powerful factor than nationality in understanding the process of integration and mobility in the labour market. In particular the diversity is reflected in two turning points: sentimental and professional. Both seem to be deep-rooted motives that provoke processes of subjective immobility, modifying the work expectations of women who, until then, had stood out for their ambition and agency capacity.

One of the limitations of this study is the heterogeneity of nationalities and regimes of mobilities selected. For future research it would be interesting to focus on a deeper analysis of migratory careers in specific professional groups; specific mobility regimes; or length of stay, in order to understand more particular dynamics linked to specific profiles.

Our focus has been on the work experience and work-life balance of our protagonists. The findings are partially consistent with what other authors have pointed out about the determination to maintain skills or even upskill. For this reason, we highlight how women's agency has a key role in the achievement of this matching by activating coping strategies to overcome barriers (both in home and host country) and find the best way for their self-realisation. Agency, as a main finding, is also present in Sandoz's (2020) study related to different highly skilled migrants' situations moving in different migration channels.

The main strategies found in the respondents' narrative analysis are the following: first, the use of their personal "toolkits" based on international competences (transversal and intercultural skills; multilingual skills; international degrees; international job experience); second, flexibility in the management of the life-work balance (assumed by respondents to be a projection towards an international setting of work and life); third, taking the path of self-employment as a good option for matching aspirations and work-life balance.

Finally, findings also suggest that social networks are not identified by our respondents as a resource for looking for either jobs or social relationships. It seems remarkable that most women in the "sentimental regime" seem not to value these networks, instead relying on their households and partners. Women who arrive for structural reasons also do not seem to value these networks. On the other hand, it is true that some women mention having approached women's associations as a way out of immobility, but it does not seem that they have had a relevant role in their migratory processes and job matching.

Notes

1 In this chapter with the term "highly educated" we refer to migrant women with tertiary-level education, such as a university degree, PhD or post-doctoral studies. This stream of migration is often associated by scholars with the terms "skilled" or "highly skilled", which have implications for the problem of definitions. On the one hand, the indiscriminate use of these terms has generated the unsolved dilemma between skilled and highly skilled migrants and professionals on the move, as the standards of qualifications are based on different ways of measuring depending on the criteria of classifications adopted and applied in each country of immigration. On the other hand, it is stressed that "skill recognition policies belong to the realm of migration selection because they contribute to defining more or less wanted categories of immigrants" (Hercog & Sandoz, 2018, p.455).

2 France, Germany, Italy, Moldova, Serbia and the United Kingdom.

References

Aysa-Lastra, M., & L. Cachón. (2015). *Immigrant Vulnerability and Resilience. International Perspective on Migration*. Cham: Springer.

Bermúdez, R. (2014). "Trayectorias laborales de migrantes calificadas por razones de estudio". *EstudiosDemográficosUrbanos*, 29:86, pp. 257–299.

Carling, J. (2014). "The role of aspirations in migration",,Determinants of International Migration, International Migration Institute, Sept. 23–25. Oxford, University of Oxford https://jorgencarling.org/2014/09/23/the-role-of-aspirations-in-migration/(accessed12–12–2018).

Docquier, F., A. Marfouk, S. Salomone & K. Sekkat. (2011). "Are skilled women more migratory than skilled men?". *World Development*, 40:2, pp. 251–265.

Fernández, M., & C. Parra. (2013). *Integration of skilled third country nationals in Europe: a new proposal for circular talent management*. Salamanca: Kadmos.

Freitas, M., & M. Godin. (2013). "Carrièresmigratoires des femmes latino-américainesdans le secteur de la domesticité à Bruxelles". *Revue Europeenne des Migrations Internationales, REM*, 29:2, pp. 37–55.

Föbker, S., & D. Imani. (2017). "The role of language skills in the settling-in-process: Experiences of highly skilled migrants' accompanying partners in Germany and the UK". *Journal of Ethic and Migrations Studies*, 43:16, pp. 2720–2737.

Glick Schiller, N., & N. B. Salazar. (2013). "Regimes of mobility across the globe". *Journal of Ethnic and Migration Studies*, 39:2, pp. 183–200.

Godin, M., A. Freitas & A. Rea. (2015). "Gender and Latin American migration to Belgium". In C. Timmerman, M. Martiniello, A. Rea and J. Wets (eds.). *New Dynamics in Female Migration and Integration* (pp. 125–156). New York: Routledge.

Grigoleit-Richter, G. (2017). "Highly skilled and highly mobile? Examining gendered and ethnicised labour market conditions for migrant women in STEM-professions in Germany". *Journal of Ethnic and Migration Studies*, 43:16, pp. 2738–2755.

Hercog, M., & J. Sandoz. (2018). "Highly skilled or highly wanted migrants? Conceptualizations, policy designs, and implementations of highly-skilled migration policies". *Migration Letters*, 15:4, pp. 453–460.

International Organisation for Migrations, OIM. (2015). *Estudio sobre la situación laboral de la Mujer Inmigrante en España*. Madrid: OIM.

Killian, C., & N. N. Manohar. (2016). "Highly skilled immigrant women's labor market access: A comparison of Indians in the United States and North Africans in France". *Social Currents*, 3:2, pp. 138–159.

Kofman, E. (2000). "The invisibility of skilled female migrants and gender relations in studies of skilled migration in Europe". *International Journal of Population Geography*, 6:1, pp. 45–59.

Kofman, E. (2013). "Toward a gendered evaluation of (highly) skilled immigration policies in Europe". *International Migration*, 53:3, pp. 116–128.

Kofman, E., & P. Raghuram. (2004). "Gender and skilled migrant: into and beyond the workplace". *Geoforum*, 36:2, pp. 149–154.

Kogan, I., F. Kalter, E. Liebau & Y. Cohen. (2011). "Individual resources and structural constraints in immigrants' labour market integration". In M. Wingens, M. Windzio, H. de Valk and C. Aybek (eds.). *A Life-Course Perspective on Migration and Integration* (pp. 75–100). Dordrecht: Springer.

Liversage, A. (2009). "Vital conjuncture, shifting horizons: highly skilled female immigrants looking for work". *Work, Employment and Society*, 23:1, pp. 120–141.

Lutz, H. (2008). *Migration and Domestic Work: a European Perspective on a Global Theme*. Aldershot: Ashgate Publishing.

Mahieu, R., C. Timmerman & P. Heyse. (2015). "Gender-sensitive migration research: theory, concepts and methods". In C. Timmerman, M. Martiniello, A. Rea & J. Wets (eds.). *New Dynamics in Female Migration and Integration* (pp. 9–25). London: Routledge.

Martiniello, M., & A. Rea. (2014). "The concept of migratory careers: Elements for a new theoretical perspective of contemporary human mobility". *Current Sociology*, 62:7, pp. 1079–1096.

Meares, C. (2010). "A fine balance: women, work and skilled migration". *Women's Studies International Forum*, 33:5, pp. 473–481.

Moreno, G., & X. Aierdi. (2008). "Inmigración y servicios sociales: ¿Última red o primer trampolín". *Zerbitzuan*, 44, pp. 7–18.

Oso, L., & S. Parella. (2012). "Inmigración, género y mercado de trabajo: Una panorámica de la investigación sobre la inserción laboral de las mujeres inmigrantes en España". *Cuadernos De Relaciones Laborales*, 30:1, pp. 11–44.

Parella, S. (2003). *Mujer, inmigrante y trabajadora, la triple discriminación*. Barcelona: Anthropos.

Parella, S., & L. Cavalcanti. (2010). "La movilidad laboral de las mujeres brasileñas en España". *Sociedad y Economía*, 19, pp. 11–32.

Poncelet, A., & M. Martiniello. (2015). "Migration of Romanian women to Belgium: strategies and dynamics of the migration process". In C. Timmerman, M. Martiniello, A. Rea & J. Wets (eds.). *New Dynamics in Female Migration and Integration* (pp. 157–184). New York: Routledge.

Raghuram, P., & E. Kofman. (2004). "Out of Asia: skilling, re-skilling and deskilling of female migrants". *Women's Studies International Forum*, 27:2, pp. 95–100.

Ramírez, T., & C. Tigau. (2018). "Mujeres mexicanas altamente calificadas en el mercado laboral estadounidense". *Sociedad y Economía*, 34, pp. 75–101.

Ramos, C. (2018). "Onward migration from Spain to London in times of crisis: the importance of life-course junctures in secondary migrations". *Journal of Ethnic and Migration Studies*, 44:11, pp. 1841–1857.

Riaño, Y., & N. Baghdadi. (2007). "Understanding the labour market participation of skilled immigrant women in Switzerland: the interplay of class, ethnicity and gender". *Journal of International Migration and Integration*, 8:2, pp. 163–183.

Riaño, Y. (2014). "Highly skilled migrant women: dual career, households, family consideration and gender roles". In editors, *Harnessing Knowledge on the Migration of Highly Skilled Women*. Geneva: OIM, OECD and DEV Centre.

Riaño, Y. (2016). "Minga biographic workshop with highly skilled migrant women: enhacing spaces of inclusion". *Qualitative Research*, 16:3, pp. 267–279.

Roca, J. (2016). "De Sur a Norte, de Norte a Sur: el balance laboral de mujeres cualificadas migrantes por amor". *Revista Andaluza de Antropología, Trabajo y Culturas del Trabajo en la Globalidad Hegemónica*, 11, pp. 92–120.

Ruyssen, I., & S. Salomone. (2018). "Female migration: a way out of discrimination?". *Journal of Development Economics*, 130:C, pp. 224–241.

Ryan, L., & J. Mulholland. (2014). "Trading places: French highly skilled migrants negotiating mobility and emplacement in London". *Journal of Ethnic and Migration Studies*, 40:4, pp. 584–600.

Salazar, N. B. (2010). "Towards an anthropology of cultural mobilities". *Crossings: Journal of Migration and Culture*, 1:1, pp. 53–68.

Salazar, N. (2018). "Theorizing mobility through concepts and figures". *Tempo Social.Revista de Sociología da USP*, 30:2, pp. 153–168.

Sandoz, L. (2020). "Understanding access to the labour market through migration channels". *Journal of Ethnic and Migration Studies*, 46:1, pp. 222–241, DOI: 10.1080/1369183X.2018.1502657.

Shershneva, J., & I. Fernández. (2018). "Factores explicativos de la sobrecualificación de las mujeres inmigrantes: El caso vasco". *Revista Española de Sociología*, 27:1, pp. 43–66.

Timmerman, C. (2008). "Marriage in a 'Culture of migration'. Emirdag marrying into Flanders". *European Review*, 16:4, pp. 585–594.

Timmerman, C., & J. Wets. (2011). "Marriage migration and the labour market: the case of migrants of Turkish descent in Belgium". *Nordic Journal of Migration Research*, 1:2, pp. 69–79.

Timmerman, C., M. Martiniello, A. Rea & J. Wets. (2015). *New dynamics in female migration and integration*. London: Routledge.

Triandafyllidou, A., & I. Isaakyan. (2016). "Re-thinking the gender dimension of high-skill migration". In A. Triandafyllidou and I. Isaakyan. *High-Skill Migration and Recession. Migration, Diasporas and Citizenship* (pp. 3–21). London: Palgrave Macmillan.

Van Mol, C., E. Snel, K. Hemmerechts & C. Timmerman. (2018). "Migration aspiration and migration culture. A case-study of Ukranian migration towards the European Union". *Population, Space and Place*, 24:5, pp. 1–11.

Wingens, M., M. Windzio, H. de Valk & C. Aybek. (2011). *A Life-Course Perspective on Migration and Integration*. Dordrecht: Springer.

Yeoh, B., & K. Willis. (2005). "Singaporean and British transmigrants in China and the cultural politics of 'contact zones'". *Journal of Ethnic and Migration Studies*, 31:2, pp. 269–285.

Zibouh, F., & M. Martiniello. (2015). "The migration of Nigerian women to Belgium: qualitative analysis of trends and dynamics". In C. Timmerman, M. Martiniello, A. Rea & J. Wets (eds.), *New Dynamics in Female Migration and Integration* (pp. 185–206). London: Routledge.

"Working there is amazing, but life here is better": Imaginaries of onward migration destinations among Albanian migrant construction workers in Italy and Greece

Iraklis Dimitriadis

Introduction

Research on the effects of the 2008 financial crisis on migrant population in Southern European countries has largely focused on migrants' practices to cope with unemployment and deteriorating living and working conditions. Recent evidence has shown that many immigrants stayed put in the receiving country, or re-emigrated to a new EU country (Dimitriadis, 2017; Esteves, Fonseca & Malheiros, 2017; Gemi, 2016; Mas Giralt, 2017; Ramos, 2017).

Immigrants' relocation to a new destination country has thus gained attention among scholars who often used the term "onward migration" when referring to this migration pattern (Ahrens, Kelly & Van Liempt, 2016; Della Puppa & King, 2019; Della Puppa & Sredanovic, 2017; Esteves et al., 2017; Mas Giralt, 2017; McIlwaine, 2012; Ramos, 2017). Although putting much emphasis on the motivations underlying the onward move, these studies have overshadowed the prominence of imaginaries of the new destination (Salazar, 2011). One exception is the studies of Della Puppa and colleagues (2017; 2018) with Bangladeshi onward migrants, which showed how imaginaries of life in London and the UK induced new migration. However, they did not deal with how (negative) shared representations of the preferred destination may also be linked with decisions of foregoing onward migration and how these are constructed.

Earlier research on different types of migration (labour migration, life-style migration) and tourism has revealed that culturally and socially constructed representations inform decisions to move and settle (Appadurai, 1996; Paul, 2011; Salazar, 2011; Sayad, 2004). Individuals' orientations and motivations for migration are mediated by imaginaries of other places and people's lives, which are constructed through interaction with other migrants or people returning, and empowered by popular media (Coletto & Fullin, 2019; Dimitriadis, Fullin & Fischer-Souan, 2019). Yet little is known about imaginaries of onward migration, and how they can be associated with intentions of moving (or not) to a new destination.

In suggesting that imaginaries may orient onward migration, this chapter explores work- and life-related subjective representations that may inform desires to leave the initial destination, or decisions for staying put. Empirical evidence comes from a qualitative study on Albanian migrant construction workers who resided in Milan and Athens during the crisis. Focusing on labour migrants in Italy and Greece, the study confirms that subjective representations provide a useful tool for understanding drivers for re-emigration, and claims that the analysis of imaginaries may contribute to the debate on motivations for onward migration. This does not imply that onward migration (or not) can be driven only by imaginaries, but it is argued that socially and culturally constructed representations may inform migrants' decisions.

The chapter starts with a brief review of the existing literature on the motivations for onward migration and follows the concept of imaginaries (Salazar, 2011). Then, after providing some information on the methods and contexts of this study, it presents the analysis of the participants' narratives of onward migration and finally offers some conclusive considerations.

Literature review and concepts

Looking at recent studies conducted with onward migrants, motivations for a new move are in the centre of the analysis. These are multiple and related to migrants' experiences in the first destination, their aspirations for the future and desires (Graw & Scielke, 2012). With regard to onward migration from Southern European countries, Latin American immigrants are motivated to leave Spain due to the lack of job and career opportunities; to access a better educational system (for themselves as students, or with regard to the life-chances of their offspring); to escape discrimination and racism; to join larger co-ethnic communities (Mas Giralt, 2017; Ramos, 2017). Onward migration has been seen as a reactionary practice also in the case of onward migrants from Portugal, in the sense that individuals opted to move to overcome economic constraints. At the same time, they were driven by aspirations for new employment opportunities, better-paid jobs, and career advancement (Esteves et al., 2017). Unlike these contributions, Della Puppa and King (2019) stated that Bangladeshis' decisions to move to London have not been conditioned by the effects of the economic crisis, but have rather been shaped by concerns over their children's academic futures, the desire to join the largest Bangladeshi diasporic community and experiences of racism in Italian society and discrimination at work. When it comes to racism, hence, onward migration may be seen as involuntarily, while the same is true in the case of onward migrants who identify with the country they leave in order to cope with economic hurdles (Mas Giralt, 2017).

Regardless of being voluntary or involuntary, few of these works shed light on the imaginaries that lie behind these motivations and desire to re-emigrate. Exceptionally, Della Puppa and colleagues (2017; 2018) argue that collective visions of life in London inform Bangladeshis' decisions to move to the UK during the crisis. In other words, their onward migration is not due to unemployment, but because they regard London (and the UK) as a place where they will not suffer discrimination and can access better employment and career opportunities, and a generous welfare system. However, in these works the authors look only at the positive social representations associated with life in the new destination and not at the negative ones that probably could provide a useful tool to explain one's decision to stay put (Salazar, 2014).

Imaginaries have been defined as "socially shared and transmitted (both within and between cultures) representational assemblages that interact with people's personal imaginings" (Salazar, 2011, p. 576). Social actors use their imagination as a device to give meaning to their or others' acts; to form ideas about people and places. Immigration scholars have used this "meaning-making and world-shaping" device to demonstrate how (im)mobility and migration are influenced by the recounts of those who have already migrated (Appadurai, 1996; Salazar, 2011; Sayad, 2004) and how potential migrants may opt for one country or another, based on an imagined hierarchy of destination countries (Pajo, 2008; Paul, 2011). Imagination as a driving force (Salazar, 2018) for mobility and migration has been largely suggested by studies on life-style migration (Benson & Osbaldiston, 2014), labour migration (Appadurai, 1996) and tourism (Salazar, 2011), but not so much in recent research on onward migration.

Methods and contexts

The empirical material for this study consists of 61 in-depth interviews with Albanian migrant construction workers in Italy and in Greece: 29 were interviewed in Milan and 32 in Athens. All interviewees except one were settled migrants (most of them emigrated at least ten years ago) and have regular status. Fieldwork research was conducted from March 2015 to August 2016. Respondents were accessed through cultural associations, community events, trade unionists and personal contacts, and by "snowballing". Interviews were conducted face-to-face in Italian and Greek. Quotations used in the findings were translated into English. All interviews were with male migrants whose ages ranged widely, from 27 to 63 years, with the majority of them being 35- to 44-year-olds, married with two or three children. Although there are limitations emerging from a gender perspective, I remain sensitive to gender dynamics in my analysis.

Reflecting on some methodological challenges, it should be mentioned that there was a major difficulty in recruiting participants, and it is mainly due to three factors. First, it is the nature of their job, in the sense that, on the one hand, (migrant) builders often work in an informal way and may be reluctant to talk about irregular economic activities, and, on the other, they have to move across building sites which makes organising appointments with any researcher difficult. Similarly, the second challenge concerned another (transnational) spatial dimension, as many of my participants moved across countries to grasp casual working opportunities. Third, economic hardships faced by many migrant workers during the crisis could be a deterrent, as it is supposed that unemployed people would not be eager to talk about unpleasant experiences.

All respondents had contemplated onward migration regardless of their economic situation during the crisis. I collected their narratives by asking them "how did you cope with the crisis?", "have you ever thought of moving to another country? If yes, where?". Through naturally expressed opinions and representations of working conditions and life in Italy and Greece compared with what happens in other EU countries, imaginaries of the situation outside their current place of residence often emerged without elicitation. Although these imaginaries may inform plans for onward migration or staying put, I consider that there are also other factors explaining their decisions to relocate or not.

Contexts

Significant numbers of Albanians migrated to other countries in Europe after the collapse of Hohxa's regime in the early 1990s. Apart from a limited number of those who sought asylum for political reasons in Germany, France, or Italy, the majority of the first migrants settled and worked irregularly in Greece and Italy, taking advantage of the widespread informal economy (Reyneri, 1998; Ambrosini, 2018). Migration flows persisted due to the economic crisis in Albania in 1997 and the Kosovo war in 1998. Many citizens of the Albanian state mixed with Kosovan (Albanian) asylum seekers, and were granted asylum in various European countries. Nowadays, the biggest part of the Albanian diaspora resides in Italy and Greece (almost 75 per cent of Albanian emigrants – more than one million people). Germany and Switzerland also host a large number of Albanian immigrants (300,000 and 100,000 respectively). Although being non-EU migrants, Albanians have had the right to travel and stay within the Schengen area for up to three months since 2011. Recent research suggests that numerous Albanian migrants in Italy (Danaj & Caro, 2016) and fewer in Greece (Karamoschou, 2018) acquired Italian or Greek citizenship, and were thus able to enjoy EU citizenship rights of movement and work in the Union. For these new EU citizens, or even for long-term EU stay permit holders, onward migration has constituted a coping practice during the crisis, although Gemi (2016) claims that many Albanian migrants have not been able to stabilise their regular status due to the lack of formal contracts.

The Greek financial crisis began in 2009, and it "soon turned into a sovereign debt crisis", opening up a long and deep recession period (Matsaganis, 2013, p. 152). After that, Greece was in recession for a number of years, and Greek construction has been the sector that suffered by far the worst crisis effects. Thousands of Albanian construction workers became unemployed during the crisis or suffered under-employment, bad working conditions and cuts in salaries and welfare provisions (Maroukis, 2013).

The recent global financial crisis had negative effects also on the Italian economy, although it did not contract it as dramatically as the Greek (Di Quirico, 2010). From 2008 to 2014, the Italian Gross Domestic Product reduced in five years out of seven. The crisis particularly touched the banking system and, in this context, the national governments opted to shield the economy by supporting Italian banks and, thus, cutting public spending. However, it has to be highlighted that the crisis hit the Northern and Southern Italian regions disproportionately, predominantly affecting the South of Italy.

Imaginaries informing the desire for onward migration

The Greek and Italian economic and financial crisis affected the construction industry disproportionately compared to other economic sectors and, as a result, migrant workers who were concentrated in construction suffered from job losses and under-employment (Maroukis, 2013; Bonifazi & Marini, 2014). Unable to sustain their households, many respondents wanted to leave the first destination and move to another European country. In other words, onward migration constituted a coping strategy for an unexpected event (Martiniello & Rea, 2014), such as the economic recession.

However, not only is the lack of jobs in the Greek or Italian economies the driver for onward migration, but it seems that Albanian builders may opt to leave their first destination due to experiences of poor working conditions. Empirical evidence coming from interviews in both countries indicates that migrant construction workers contemplate onward migration because of dissatisfaction with their working conditions. Informants reveal that working conditions have worsened during and since the crisis. Salary cuts, unpaid overtime and de-skilling have been accentuated due to economic recession.

By contrast, research participants who develop plans for onward migration represent working conditions in other European countries as ideal. In other words, the idea that a move to a new destination can improve their working lives is associated with images of well-functioning labour markets in northern European countries. On being asked where they would like to re-emigrate, nearly all interviewees refer to Germany, and some of them also to Belgium, the UK, Sweden and Austria. These countries are represented as destinations where construction workers enjoy excellent working conditions. Most respondents tend to idealise the job situation in the construction sector in those countries, and these imaginaries generate the desire for onward migration. There their colleagues are not engaged in informal working practices, are not requested to work long hours and do not suffer stressful working conditions as happens in Italy and Greece. Some of my respondents recount:

[...] in Austria, let's say you are to work for 10 days [as a declared worker] [...] when you have to work one more day, the employers go to declare you [register with the authorities]; they are concerned about your security first of all! (Adnan, aged 40, Greece)

I am thinking of going to Germany [...] When I get there, I will work for 8-10 hours, and then go home. The work is pleasure [there] (Fatlum, aged 35, Greece)

[In Germany] it is said that if you are ok with your stay permit and you find a job, you are not stressed (Besian, aged 44, Italy)

The ubiquity of mentions of the optimum working conditions in terms of hours, occupational health and safety and the depiction of employers as sensible individuals who take care of their employees in other EU countries indicate the hurdles that Albanian builders have traditionally faced in Greece and Italy. These entail poor employment conditions and safety measures, and the prevalence of informal work (Dimitriadis, 2017; Maroukis, 2009; Perrotta, 2011; Reyneri, 1998). The absence of formal employment relations, in particular, has constantly put at risk the legal status of those with temporary stay permits (and consequently their migration experience) due to the rigid link between formal job contracts and regular status (Dimitriadis, 2018; Triandafyllidou & Ambrosini, 2011). On the other hand, imaginaries of ideal employment conditions in other European destinations may shape their aspirations to undertake onward migration.

Several interviewees also argued that they feel unprotected from unscrupulous employers in Italy and Greece who do not respect (oral or written) contractual agreements. At the same time, their rights are not sufficiently secured by institutional actors such as trade unions or work inspectorates. Describing his experiences as a builder in Italy, Enver is contemplating onward migration to Germany or Switzerland, although he was never unemployed during the crisis and had an open-ended contract with a prestigious construction firm.

There are no controls here (at building sites). They [employers] decide upon prices [salaries] as they want. There is no one to control them[...] and when they [authorities] make inspections, they do not care at all. It's a chain of bastards who take advantage of it (they are corrupted). Why don't they control my professional card to see that I'm paid below my qualifications? (Enver, aged 29, Italy)

Unlike in the situation in Greece and Italy, my participants often portray images of institutional actors who keep a constant watch on respect for labour rights in other EU countries. Enver, after criticising the weak position of migrant workers in the Italian construction sector, extolls the working conditions in the German construction sector, as well as the centrality of the state and its labour inspection authorities to protect labour rights. Images and discourses of efficient states that guarantee the rights of construction workers and take care of them seem to shape aspirations for onward migration. Imagined protection of migrant workers' rights also couple with imaginaries of meritocratic labour markets where workers are paid what they deserve to be. In his words:

In Germany, you receive the money you deserve through the State [by bank payment], and it monitors whether you get paid or not. [If not] the State twists the employer's ears [reprimand] and tells him 'come here, why did not you give the money to that guy [worker]? ... That guy did not receive his money, it's one day has already passed, and he has not been paid yet. What happened? You have to pay him immediately!'... Every month the State controls you [construction company]! ...If you are a builder [in Germany], you start [earn] with 3,000 euros a month; the lowest [minimum wage]. In Switzerland too. [...] I have recently been to Germany and I have been told that, according to the law, [workers] are paid 18 euros per hour; it does not exist below [this amount] [beating his punch on the table], it is obligatory! Otherwise, the State can destroy you [construction company]. First, they [employers] are given a fine of 100 thousand euros, and second [they go to] the jail. The municipality calls you and asks: 'Enver, is there any problem?' This is the State! This is democracy! (Enver, aged 29, Italy)

Although imaginaries can be seen as forces that trigger onward migration (Della Puppa & King, 2019), the narratives of my participants may also be considered a way to justify their difficulty in continuing to be the main breadwinners as happened before the crisis (Dimitriadis, 2017). Recurrent references to the importance of finding a job in European construction where competent workers can earn good money may be seen as a way to heal their wounded masculinities (Van Boeschoten, 2015). In addition, as Albanian migration has traditionally been a male pattern, onward migration may be represented as such in order to confirm males' prominent role in the household economy.

Collective or individual representations of efficient labour markets may also attract those who aspire to advance their careers. Self-employed workers and entrepreneurs of my sample often complained about the troubles that they had to face as construction firm owners. Difficulties in accessing credit, high taxation, late payments and complex bureaucratic procedures were common when describing the "problematic Italian and Greek economies". At the same time, many respondents considered that labour market regulation in the new destination would permit them to improve their careers in the construction sector. Fatlum narrates:

> In Greece, there is problem with the payments… if I go to Germany, everything is simpler. I know some people who work there and said me that I could make big money as sub-contractor! (Fatlum, aged 35, Greece)

Although the favourite destination of potential onward migration of Albanians both in Greece and Italy was Germany, it was not uncommon that Albanians in Greece also regarded Italy as a place where construction migrant workers are protected and enjoy welfare benefits. This confirms Pajo's (2008, p. 10) argument about migrants' imaginary world of hierarchy. In his work, the author suggests that potential migrants perceive some countries as being higher in the global hierarchy, since they "territorialize different degrees of fulfillment and of morality and allow for different degrees of individual achievement". The following quotation is a typical expression of this idea.

> My brother is in Italy. It is difficult to find a job, but as long as you get it, you become permanent (worker). You'll have your health insurance, you'll have everything! (Armend, aged 43, Greece)

Imaginaries of ideal labour markets have been gleaned from their family members or friends by word of mouth. Fellow countrymen and family share narratives of how the construction sector operates abroad, and these become social representations that may trigger onward migration. It is worth adding here that representations are spread not just by word of mouth, but onward migration may be also subject to images circulating through social media and smartphones. The following quotation shows how imaginaries come about:

> I am always talking via Skype or Viber [VoiP/IM software application] with my brother-in-law who lives in Switzerland. He works for a company and sends me photos. They [workers] have a kitchen to go to eat [at the workplace]! Here, it does not exist. Not even at the best company in Greece exists! Forget it! (Avni, aged 34, Athens)

Although imaginaries created by word of mouth or single images may inform onward migration plans, they are able also to deter immigrants from relocation. In the next section I argue that imaginaries may also shape one's decision to stay put.

Imaginaries of onward migration that shape decisions to stay put

Apart from certain structural factors that constrain onward migration (e.g. the lack of means or legal status to move onward and work in another EU country, material investments in the first destination), some respondents who would be able and aspire to onward-migrate decided not to do so. Delving into my participants' narratives, it can be argued that imaginaries of life abroad may inform decisions for non-migration.

In immigration studies, non-migration (defined also as immobility: Carling, 2002) refers to both those who voluntarily prefer to stay put and not migrate and those who lack the ability to do so. Rather than being involuntary (Babar, Ewers & Khattab, 2018), I argue here that non-re-emigration of low-skilled migrant workers may be voluntary and shaped by social imaginaries, and thus not be associated with incapacity to relocate. Hence, imaginaries of places may both orient onward migrants (Della Puppa & Sredanovic, 2017; Della Puppa & King, 2019) and discourage settled migrants from onward-migrating.

On the face of it, many respondents imagine life in other destinations as being arduous and monotonous. Although Northern European countries were represented as contexts in which there are more economic opportunities and workers are better off, onward movement entails change in the way of living which may inform Albanian migrants' decisions to onward-migrate. During our interview, Edward describes what relocation to Germany implies. Even if he became unemployed many times during the crisis and had to do other jobs to get by, he cannot imagine himself being satisfied with his life in Germany; something very different from what he has in Greece:

> I was thinking of it (migrate to a new destination), but there's nowhere like Greece! One cousin of mine who lives in Germany tells me that [in Germany] you cannot live the life you live in Greece. You can't! Here we work eight hours, from 7 am to 3 pm. Then, you can go home, you have lunch, you ride the car and you reach the beach in half an hour. You lie on the beach and have bath until 8 pm. Then, you can go out at any time [...] it does make the difference. (Edward, aged 32, Greece)

The quest for a "good life" and cultural consumption of this sort are often drivers for migration for so-called "lifestyle migrants" (Griffiths & Maile, 2014). In their work on Britons who live in Berlin, these authors suggest that such imaginaries inform the migration plans of well-off individuals. Here, it can be argued that negative images of quality-of-life aspects in Northern European countries may shape non-migration. This finding was more recurrent among my respondents in Athens. Images of uncomfortable work schedules and narrowing social life outside Greece that circulate among migrants seem to be a deterrent to onward migration. The difference between respondents in Athens and those in Milan might be due to the characteristics of Milan as a global city (Andreotti, 2006; 2019) in which life would be more similar to that in other European capitals or big cities.

Imaginaries of a better social life and leisure interests in a new destination also concern Albanian migrants' children. In their narratives, my participants recounted that life in Greece and Italy is "better" for their children than it would be in other EU countries. For those with families, onward migration is often seen as an obstacle to their children's well-being, not only due to a series of objective difficulties that they could face (e.g. learning a new language, adaptation in a new context), but also from a lifestyle point of view. In particular, some of my respondents represent new EU destinations as places where their children would suffer; the saying that children "grow up in a better way" in Greece and Italy was often repeated:

> If there is the opportunity in the future, maybe I'll do it alone, in the sense that I will go there for some years and I will return to Athens. I don't think about staying permanently there. I will save money and I will buy a house here [Athens]. The children and my wife will stay here. The life is better here also for them. (Gjin, aged 34, Greece)

This finding is in contrast with what has been claimed about onward migrants who leave their first destination to offer better future opportunities for their children; in places that are higher "in the global hierarchical order" (Pajo, 2008, p. 10). Looking at recent research on onward migrants who move from Italy to the UK, Bangladeshis represent London as "the global, multicultural, cosmopolitan city" where there are plenty of "opportunities which allows people from every country in the world to enhance their capabilities and potential" (Della Puppa & King, 2019, p. 1943). Motives concerning children's future are claimed in my case-studies as well, but these are of a different nature. Such differences might be due to a sense of cultural proximity between Albanians and Greeks or Italians or identification with the country of destination they live in (Karamoschou, 2018; Mas Giralt, 2018), a discussion that goes beyond the scope of this chapter.

As argued before, onward migration is represented as a male pattern. In my participants' narratives, plans for onward migration lack references about women's role in the new destination. Rather, women's contribution might be only bringing up children, even though during the crisis Albanian women's employment has been the key to coping with unemployment and poverty (Gemi, 2016; Dimitriadis, 2017).

Last but not least, for my participants a new movement implies new experiences of racism. Imaginaries of eventual experiences of discrimination in the new destinations were widespread among participants. They imagine that they will feel discriminated against as new migrants in the second destination. They do not want to feel "migrants" again as they said:

> Don't think that there is no racism in Germany or in Sweden. [Once we arrive] there, we will be once again migrants! (Valon, aged 44, Greece)

It is well documented that Albanian immigration into Greece and Italy has been accompanied by discrimination and stigmatisation, mainly during the first two decades of their migration experience (King & Mai, 2009; Kokkali, 2011). In both countries, media and public discourse have reproduced stereotypes of Albanians as criminals and uncivilised. Nowadays, although their economic integration has been severely challenged by the recent crisis, their socio-cultural integration is considered quite successful in Italy and Greece (Gemi, 2016). Hence, imaginaries of a problematic integration in the new receiving society, including expected hostility in various European countries against newly arrived migrants due to the recent so-called "refugee crisis", can deter them from deciding on onward migration. The same can also be true for migrants' children, in the sense that the parents imagine that their children may experience discrimination, and that that would be undesirable.

Conclusion

This chapter focused on the imaginaries of re-migration among Albanian migrant construction workers in Italy and Greece, thus contributing to an emergent literature on onward migration. It confirmed what has been argued about the role of socially constructed representations that may inform motives for relocation (Della Puppa & Sredanovic, 2017; Della Puppa & King, 2019), shedding light on motivations for onward migration. Delving into potential onward migrants' narrative though, it adds that imaginaries might also be at the roots of non-migration, suggesting an interrelationship between imaginaries and non-migration too, that is rarely investigated in studies about onward migrants. Although it is not suggested that imaginaries are in themselves sufficient to explain onward migration or non-migration, it underlines their importance in comprehending how they may inform migrants' decision-making, highlighting the dialectical nature of imaginaries and structures.

On the one hand, positive imaginaries of onward migration are associated with migration experiences, and in particular with the difficulties that Albanian migrants have traditionally faced in the Italian and Greek labour markets. These have been accentuated during the crisis period and include low payments, unpaid labour, informal work, and generally trampling on labour rights and a lack of protection by state authorities. Hence, migrants tend to idealise work environments in other EU countries where they would like to onward-migrate, and imaginaries reveal the desire to improve their employment (and economic) situation.

On the other hand, imaginaries may inform decisions for non-relocation, which means staying put in the first destination. Here it has been argued that onward migration cannot be driven only by the possibility of improving one's economic situation. Rather, more immaterial considerations seem to inform migrants, such as imaginaries of narrowing life in the new country of destination. Thus, it is shown that lifestyle considerations concern not only high-skilled and well-off migrants (Babar et al., 2018) but also low-skilled ones. In addition, new imagined experiences of racism against them and their children may inform their decision not to onward-migrate in order to maintain what they enjoy in the current destination country, even if it may entail their demoting better opportunities in the new destination for them and their offspring to second place.

Drawing on both literature on lifestyle migration and lived experiences among low-skilled migrant workers, another contribution concerns the idea of a hierarchy between countries at a global scale. Instead of economic prosperity and favourable conditions for individual achievement being the criteria assessing imagined ranking, the chapter shows the importance of social, cultural and geographical elements in appraising a country in which to migrate or live.

Looking at both positive and negative social representations of the new destination, it can be argued that the boundaries between voluntary and involuntary migration should be considered rather blurred. The desires for either onward-migration or staying put are intertwined, and motivations for engaging in or foregoing re-migration may be contradicting. This shows the complexity of the decision-making process for relocation, and that imaginaries may serve as needed devices to justify one's choice whether or not to relocate.

References

Ahrens, J., M. Kelly & I. van Liempt. (2016). "Free movement? The onward migration of EU citizens born in Somalia, Iran, and Nigeria". *Population, Space and Place*, 22, pp. 84–98. DOI: 10.1002/psp.

Ambrosini, M. (2018). *Irregular Immigration in Southern Europe Actors, Dynamics and Governance*. Basingstoke: Palgrave Macmillan. https://doi.org/10.1007/978-3-319-70518-7

Andreotti, A. (2006). "Coping strategies in a wealthy city of northern Italy". *International Journal of Urban and Regional Research*, 30:2, pp. 328–345.

Andreotti, A. (ed.). (2019). *Governare Milano nel nuovo millennio*. Milan: Il Mulino.

Appadurai, A. (1996). *Modernity at Large: Cultural Dimensions of Globalization*. Minneapolis, MN: University of Minnesota Press.

Babar, Z., M. Ewers & N. Khattab. (2018). "Im/mobile highly skilled migrants in Qatar". *Journal of Ethnic and Migration Studies*, 45:9, pp. 1553–1570. DOI: 10.1080/1369183X.2018.1492372.

Benson, M., & N. Osbaldiston (eds.). (2014). *Understanding Lifestyle Migration. Theoretical Approaches to Migration and the Quest for a Better Way of Life*. Basingstoke: Palgrave Macmillan.

Carling, J. (2002). "Migration in the age of involuntary immobility: Theoretical reflections and Cape Verdean experiences". *Journal of Ethnic and Migration Studies*, 28:1, pp. 5–42. DOI: 10.1080/13691830120103912.

Coletto, D., & G. Fullin. (2019). "Before landing: how do New European emigrants prepare their departure and imagine their destinations?". *Social Inclusion*, 7:4, pp. 39–48.

Danaj, S., & E. Çaro. (2016). "Becoming an EU citizen through Italy: the experience of Albanian immigrants". *Mondi Migranti*, 3, pp. 95–108. DOI: 10.3280/MM2016-003007.

Della Puppa, F., & R. King. (2019). "The new 'twice migrants': motivations, experiences and disillusionments of Italian-Bangladeshis relocating to London". *Journal of Ethnic and Migration Studies*, 45:11, pp. 1936–1952. DOI: 10.1080/1369183X.2018.1438251.

Della Puppa, F., & D. Sredanovic. (2017). "Citizen to stay or citizen to go? Naturalization, security, and mobility of migrants in Italy". *Journal of Immigrant & Refugee Studies*, 15:4, pp. 366–383. DOI: 10.1080/15562948.2016.1208316.

Di Quirico, R. (2010). "Italy and the global economic crisis". *Bulletin of Italian Politics*, 2:2, pp. 3–19.

Dimitriadis, I. (2017). "Migrant construction workers' tactics to cope with unemployment during the crisis. Case study on Albanian immigrants in Milan and Athens". Unpublished PhD thesis, University of Torino - University of Milan, Italy.

Dimitriadis, I. (2018). "'Asking around': Immigrants' counterstrategies to renew their residence permit in times of economic crisis in Italy". *Journal of Immigrant & Refugee Studies*, 16:3, pp. 275–292. DOI: 10.1080/15562948.2016.1273433.

Dimitriadis, I., G. Fullin & M. Fischer-Souan. (2019). "Great expectations? Young Southern Europeans emigrating in times of crisis". *Mondi Migranti*, 3, pp. 137–162. DOI:10.3280/MM2019-003007

Esteves, A., M. L. Fonseca & J. Malheiros. (2017). "Labour market integration of immigrants in Portugal in times of austerity: resilience, in situ responses and re-emigration". *Journal of Ethnic and Migration Studies*, 44:14, pp. 2375–2391. DOI: 10.1080/1369183X.2017.1346040.

Gemi, E. (2016). "Integration and transnational mobility in time of crisis: the case of Albanians in Greece and Italy". *Studi Emigrazione*, LIII:202, pp. 237–255.

Graw, K., & J. S. Schielke (eds.). (2012). *The Global horizon: Expectations of migration in Africa and the Middle East*. Leuven: Leuven University Press.

Griffiths, D., & S. Maile. (2014). "Britons in Berlin: imagined cityscapes, affective encounters and the cultivation of the self". In M. Benson and N. Osbaldiston (eds.). *Understanding Lifestyle Migration: Theoretical Approaches to Migration and the Quest for a Better Way of Life* (pp. 139–159). Basingstoke: Palgrave MacMillan.

Karamoschou, C. (2018). "The Albanian second migration: Albanians fleeing the Greek crisis and onward migrating to the UK". Working Paper No. 93, Sussex Centre for Migration Research, University of Sussex.

King, R., & N. Mai. (2009). "Italophilia meets albanophobia: paradoxes of asymmetric assimilation and identity processes among Albanian immigrants in Italy". *Ethnic and Racial Studies*, 32:1, pp. 117–138.

Kokkali, I. (2011). "From scapegoats to 'good' immigrants?: Albanians' supposedly 'successful' integration to Greece". *Quaderni del Circolo Rosselli*, 3, pp. 161–173.

Maroukis, T. (2013). "Economic crisis and migrants' employment: a view from Greece in comparative perspective". *Policy Studies*, 34:2, pp. 221–237. DOI: 10.1080/01442872. 2013.767589.

Martiniello, M., & A. Rea. (2014). "The concept of migratory careers: Elements for a new theoretical perspective of contemporary human mobility". *Current Sociology*, 62:7, pp. 1079–1096. DOI: 10.1177/0011392114553386.

Mas Giralt, R. (2017). "Onward migration as a coping strategy? Latin Americans moving from Spain to the UK post-2008". *Population, Space and Place*, 23, pp. 1–12. DOI: 10.1002/psp.2017.

Matsaganis, M. (2013). "The crisis and the welfare state in Greece: a complex relationship". In A. Triandafyllidou, R. Gropas and H. Kouki (eds.). *The Greek Crisis and European Modernity* (pp. 152–177). Basingstoke: Palgrave Macmillan.

McIlwaine, C. (2012). "Constructing transnational social spaces among Latin American migrants in Europe: Perspectives from the UK". *Cambridge Journal of Regions, Economy and Society*, 5:2, pp. 289–303. DOI: 10.1093/cjres/rsr041.

Pajo, E. (2008). *International migration, social demotion, and imagined advancement*. New York: Springer.

Paul, A. M. (2011). "Stepwise international migration: a multistage migration pattern for the aspiring migrant". *American Journal of Sociology*, 116:6, pp. 1842–1886. DOI: 10.1086/659641.

Perrotta, D. (2011). *Vite in cantiere: migrazione e lavoro dei rumeni in Italia*. Milan: Il Mulino.

Ramos, C. (2017). "Onward migration from Spain to London in times of crisis: the importance of life-course junctures in secondary migrations". *Journal of Ethnic and Migration Studies*, online first, pp. 1–17. DOI: 10.1080/1369183X.2017.1368372.

Reyneri, E. (1998). "The role of the underground economy in irregular migration to Italy: Cause or effect?". *Journal of Ethnic and Migration Studies*, 24:2, pp. 313–331. DOI: 10.1080/1369183X.1998.9976635.

Salazar, N. B. (2011). "The power of imagination in transnational mobilities". *Identities*, 18:6, pp. 576–598.

Salazar, N. B. (2014). "Migrating imaginaries of a better life... until paradise finds you". In M. Benson and N. Osbaldiston (eds.). *Understanding lifestyle migration: Theoretical approaches to migration and the quest for a better way of life* (pp. 119–38). Basingstoke: Palgrave.

Salazar, N. B. (2018). *Momentous mobilities: Anthropological musings on the meanings of travel.* Oxford: Berghahn.

Sayad, A. (2004). *The suffering of the immigrant.* Cambridge: Polity.

Triandafyllidou, A., & M. Ambrosini. (2011). "Irregular immigration control in Italy and Greece: strong fencing and weak gate-keeping serving the labour market". *European Journal of Migration and Law*, 13, pp. 251–273.

Van Boeschoten, R. (2015). "Transnational mobility and the renegotiation of gender identities: Albanian and Bulgarian migrants in Greece". In H. Vermeulen, M. Baldwin-Edwards & R. Van Boeschoten (eds.). *Migration in the Southern Balkans: From Ottoman Territory to Globalized Nation States* (pp. 161–182). Cham: Springer Open.

'Welcome to my waiting room! Please, take a seat!': On future imaginaries being shattered and postponed

Christine Moderbacher

Introduction: "Where could I be, I have nowhere to go!"

"Are we done now, Christine?" 55-year old Hamuda asked me during our last recording session at the end of my field research in Brussels. Back at my University desk in Aberdeen, Scotland, I was struggling to find an answer to his question. But the more I listened to his stories, the more I felt our work really could come to closure, at least for a while, not only because Hamuda and I had more or less gone through most of the stories he wanted to share, but also because Hamuda's life seemed to be "moving on" rather well. He had "better things to do now", as he told me once laughingly on the phone. A couple of months after we had finished our training, he had found a job in the countryside outside Brussels as a handyman at a large sports hotel, where he was able to continue using his carpentry skills, furnishing and maintaining the entire plot. He was busy not only with his new job but also with increasing orders from hotel guests who wanted small fitted furniture or repairs to their houses. He was proud that with his new salary he could fly twice a year back and forth to Tunisia, his birth country which he had left 20 years before. But while Hamuda's life seemed to follow the path he had imagined during the time we were crafting furniture together, it was Cise, one of the other carpentry apprentices, who left me wondering whether my fieldwork was really done.

I had met Hamuda and Cise – also in his mid-50s, and born in Guinea – in a carpentry training centre where I did a one-year apprenticeship in a life-long-learning programme for my PhD thesis entitled "Crafting Lives in Brussels. Making and Mobility on the Margins" during the previous year.[1] While my original intention in starting the woodworking apprenticeship was to examine skills acquisition, my research moved further and further away from the physical act of craftwork towards the individual life stories of artisans, whose voices tend to be left out of academic writing. Drawing on the argument that the history of western education in modernity has narrowly focused on conceptual thinking that led to a marginalisation of the body (Marchand, 2008), research on craft often focuses on the merely sensorial act of craftwork. The "craft world" in these accounts seems, in Adamson's terms, like a "ghetto of technique" (Adamson, 2007, p. 2). With this focus, an implicit reversal of the Cartesian dualism takes place: the body, not the mind, is elevated to a status worthy of investigation (Odland Portisch, 2010, p. 63). As a consequence, however, the "maker" himself remains silent.[2] It is this description of the silent maker that enforced my decision to extend my research focus through the use of life storytelling. Through this, Cise and Hamuda's own words stood at the centre of an "ongoing collaboration between interviewer and interviewee, instead of working from the conventional formula in which an outside investigation initiates and controls the research" (Cruikshank, 1990, p. 1).[3] Working with this method sheds light on the dialogical nature of bringing out stories and provides an understanding of the contexts that have shaped and influenced their lives. It demanded personal involvement and a willingness to share one's life with others. Cise, Hamuda and I spent many hours together, talking, walking round town, sitting on benches, where we shared our lunch in silence, when we needed a break from the constant drone of the machines. But regardless of the deep relationship Hamuda, Cise and I had established through our many hours of storytelling, I did not hear much from Cise after the carpentry training ended and I returned to Aberdeen. My numerous efforts to reach him via Facebook or phone were unsuccessful. I learned from Hamuda that Cise had not yet found work. Only once, when back in Brussels a couple of months later, did I finally manage to get Cise on the phone. It was around lunchtime and I noticed immediately that I had awakened him. Happy to have at least reached him, I kept asking him questions: "[h]ow are you? It has been so long! How are you spending your time? Are you at home?" He was a bit stunned by my sudden reappearance in his life, as he told me later on, and answered a bit reluctantly:

Of course I'm at home. Where *would* I be, I have nowhere to go!

The following day I was on my way to see Cise. As I opened the grey door to his house in suburban Overijse, I had to make an effort not to show my concern for how he looked. He had lost a lot of weight, seemed small and frail, and moved around his kitchen even more slowly than usual. Almost two years after I had first entered his home, Cise did not greet me with "Welcome to Cise-City!" but sat down in his room, looked at me and said, "Welcome to my Waiting Room! Please take a seat!".[4]

In what follows I will argue that, rather than equipping Cise with tools to help him move on with his life, the carpentry training was generating exactly the opposite: after all the years of imagining something better, he found himself once again stuck in a "waiting room" that was, as Jovanovic (2015) has likewise observed in a similar context, crafted alongside the crafting of furniture. By exploring how patient waiting was taught and encouraged within a training course, I will shed light on how the course I participated in mirrored a larger structure of governmental strategies that manipulate people's time in order to make them "patients of the state" (Auyero, 2012). This, in turn, saps people's capacity to continue imagining a better life and makes them almost incapable of moving on at all. But the focus of this article is less to relate the particulars of Cise's situation to larger structures of migrant imaginaries and their destruction and more, to say it with Jackson (2008, p. 58), to carve out "the empirical details of a particular person at a particular moment in time". Though this emphasis, to refer to Jackson again, might at first seem to compromise the idea of knowledge contribution within anthropology, I believe that only by highlighting in detail what was and is at stake for Cise during and after his training can we gain a profound understand of the damaging consequences of future-imaginaries time and again being shattered through recurrent waiting periods.[5]

Moving forward and stepping back

But to come back to where we are, together with Cise in his "Waiting Room", let me briefly explain what I understand by the notion of "imaginaries" and how Cise's feeling of being stuck is closely linked to the constant destruction and delaying of precisely these imaginaries of a better future. As Salazar (2010; 2011; 2012) and Strauss (2006) have summarised, studying collective imaginaries as well as individual, personal imagination is not an easy endeavour, because these notions have become widely used as well as approached from a wide range of disciplines, albeit rarely defined. For the purpose of this article, then, I must emphasise my interest in personal imaginaries that relate "to the ways in which people picture a world different from that which they actually experience" (Beidelman, 1986, p. 1). While imaginaries in the context of migration are often thought of and established "through the recognition of possibilities, of alternative constructions of future lives in other places" (Salazar, 2011, p. 676) this chapter is concerned with the consequences of shattered imaginaries of alternative constructions of future lives in the very same place one tries to build a life in. Of course, Cise was never immune to collective imaginaries of the "good life" linked to particular migration, movement and mobility in some African countries (Sanders, 2001).[6] But, as he told me himself, he neither wanted to leave his birthplace, Guinea, nor did he expect paradise when he came to Europe.[7] Cise was fleeing overnight due to political persecution. In addition, he was well aware of the difficulties that flight entails. He expected poverty, hardship and difficult working conditions. But what he did not expect were the many years of waiting, hoping, while all he felt was being stuck:

> Doing nothing, moving nowhere, is the most difficult thing, more difficult than leaving your family, more difficult than being alone. It's like observing your life oozing away from you while you are left behind.

In many other circumstances, Cise described the waiting periods – and along with them, the unrealised imaginaries of an alternative life – as among the most difficult things to endure. Cise's unfulfilled reveries of a better future had started long before I arrived at the carpentry centre with my anthropological questions and needs of analysis. It started when Cise came from Guinea to Belgium more than 20 years ago, remaining undocumented for 11 years, as he told me during one of our first storytelling sessions:

> Cise Ibrahima came to Europe like all the other immigrants. He goes somewhere to seek out a living. Somewhere, anywhere, really. He presents himself with a smile, because that is what people told him to do. He follows all the procedures and ends up living as an illegal alien, hidden, without rights, waiting for 11 years.

During the course of his life in Brussels, Cise waited many years for his right to remain legally in Belgium, waiting more than a decade for his sons to join him, waiting for a chance to start working.[8] Of course, it was not all about waiting and hardship. There were better times, such as when he finally received Belgian citizenship, which provided him with a minimum state security income and thus the chance to rent his own place and once again to travel legally across borders. Times were better when three out of his six children joined him in Belgium and gave him busy years of bringing up the boys on his own, or when he got intermittent work, or training stints similar to, but shorter than, the one we conducted together. But time and again there were setbacks. Yearnings, as Jansen says (2014: 78), have histories and frustrations. And there were many that accumulated for Cise: when he realised that finding work was harder than he thought, since all the years of living as an undocumented migrant had left a "long gap" in his CV: when he had to give up his small business of selling African masks at markets because he did not sell enough to make it worthwhile, when his sons grew up, started their own lives and were busy with their own struggles, and when he noticed that all the little training stints he had done were not showing any results. In spite of this, Cise continued to strive, keeping up a certain mobility of spirit. Cise's ability to start again many times brought home to me Arendt's observation that human capacity for new beginnings is "the one miracle-working faculty of man" (Arendt, 1998, p. 246). One of these new beginnings in Cise's life was the carpentry training course where we met and got to know each other.

From excitement to disillusionment: The participation in carpentry training

Since its creation in the 1960s, the life-long learning centre where I did my fieldwork has organised activities to facilitate the reintegration of the city's marginalised population. It is one of the life-long-learning organisations, of the many operating in the Brussels region, that aim to support people with migrant backgrounds, because of the very high unemployment rate of people of non-European origin (Garnier & Piva, 2019).[9] This of course has to be placed in the context of Belgium's being one of the most multicultural countries of the European Union, as stated by the sociologist and political scientist Martiniello (2003: 225), who addresses some of the key issues in Belgian immigration and integration policies today. More than 30 per cent of the inhabitants of Brussels are of foreign nationality, which has led to a widespread form of integration policy which, as in the case of the training course I participated in, is involved in granting or denying, amongst other things, economic rights. Regular participation was therefore required to continue receiving unemployment benefits. The activities offered are supported by the National Ministry of Culture as well as the European Union. To be able to participate in the training course a person must be registered at an employment agency, which often also refers participants for training. In Belgium's complex institutional landscape the regions are responsible for employment integration; in Brussels this takes place through "Actiris", in Wallonia through "Le Formen" and in Flanders through the "VDAB" (Garnier & Piva, 2019, p. 2). Because of the difficulties of recognising skills and qualifications obtained abroad, people who already have obtained degrees in their birth countries frequently find themselves doing another one in Brussels, as was the case for some of the 11 participants who started the carpentry course with me. Most of them did not want to appear with their real names in my work and remained "curiously distant" from "the anthropologist" interested in carpentry. As I mentioned before, I am interested in Cise's individual imaginaries rather than the collective ones of an entire group. But it should be mentioned that for most of the participants, the carpentry workshop initially triggered imaginaries for a better future in Europe's capital. This translates to the fact that the most important reason for taking the training course was not a passion for wood but to find decent work afterwards, allowing for the opportunity to move forward in life by moving socially upwards. "For imagination to become 'effective'", writes Salazar, "it has to relate closely to reality" (2011, p. 675). And indeed, in the case of Cise and many others, imaginaries of a better future did seem quite tangible at the beginning. Many daily discussions were linked to the economic advantages that the course might provide, such as being able to move out of Molenbeek and into better areas of this seemingly vast, bustling city, as I will describe in detail later on. Stories about former apprentices opening their own businesses circulated during the lunch breaks. Dreams and imaginaries of a good life ahead were not limited just to the near future in Brussels but also included retirement plans to rebuild places in the participants' home countries, such as Turkey or Morocco or, as in the case of Hamuda, Tunisia.

Initiating this new start was therefore linked to a general anticipation of finally "going somewhere", "doing things again". But then the days quickly became monotonous and increasingly and undifferentiatedly tiresome for everyone. Weekdays were structured by a rigid work schedule from 8.30 a.m. to 5 p.m. In retrospect, the many hours in the studio are blurred into memories of trying to cut along the thin pencilled lines the teacher had marked for us on wooden poles, accompanied by the grating sound of handsaw teeth. Alongside the weariness that woodworking entails, doubts slowly surfaced about whether what we were learning was actually useful for our respectively desired futures. Uncertainty was mostly addressed around the fact that what we were making was old-fashioned, largely "out of style" and hand-made, not incorporating enough industrial means in our handcraft. Cise once whispered to me while looking at a piece of furniture he had been working on for about two weeks, "This doesn't fit in today's world, or in today's homes!" Tarek, another apprentice, simply blurted out in his own manner, "What a waste of time!"

More frequently, the teachers at the centre (which also offers training in other trades) would refer to their courses as occupational therapy rather than actual pathways to, or preparation for, working life. While at first the carpentry training led to "new stimuli for the imagination" (Salazar, 2011, p. 683), what increasingly surfaced in the lunchtime talks was the reluctance of participants to invest time and energy in activities that possibly did not serve their desired futures. Despite their occasional attempts to suggest new ideas for the outdated curriculum, our teacher – of migrant background himself – preferred producing mostly hand-made furniture as he had learnt to do it from his father in Morocco many decades ago. Caught in his own childhood nostalgia about doing carpentry in his birthplace, Tangier, his attitude mirrored a larger problem of prioritising hand-craft over industrial means in vocational training.

In her research on the attractions and limitations of NGO gender development approaches in Bosnia Herzegovina, Pupavac (2010, p. 490), for example, has identified a similar "return to an idealized past". The NGO approaches that were examined address "Western consumer society's post-romantic yearnings" (ibid.) rather than ordinary Bosnians' economic needs and aspirations. As a consequence, she points out, the participants are offered non-industrial means of creating a sustainable living. Although it was not "Western sponsorship" that failed to provide the necessary material/industrial means in the training course I participated in, but rather the teacher's own romantic yearning for an idealised past, the focus on hand-craft had similar consequences: with the course failing to answer the participants' expectations of moving forward in life, there increasingly surfaced a demotivation to create things other than what the teacher demanded of them. The increasing complaints during lunch breaks showed how failed expectations illustrate the contingent nature of imaginaries "as socially transmitted representational assemblages that interact with people's personal imaginings" (Salazar, 2012, p. 864). Slowly, expectations were disappointed not only on an individual level but systematically after the training period, as we will see further on. Although some of the participants, like Cise, at first used their breaks to try out little designs that could render woodworking lucrative, after some months of training no one attempted any longer to do anything additional or outside the curriculum. Their successful completion of the course after all hinged on the teacher's judgment of their behaviour and work, and thus created a power relationship of dependency. The course organisers could not only provide the participants with a diploma for their future, but also decide whether or not to extend their state benefits in the immediate present. To receive such benefits of roughly 800 euros a month, their approval was necessary. Thus the relationship with the teacher became more and more ambivalent: while his knowledge and help were widely appreciated, some participants started to resent the power he held over them, which the trainees felt as an obstacle to their long-desired "mobility" in life. Mobility, as Marzloff (2005) has observed, refers to much more then sheer physical motion. Here I am referring to mobility as "a sense that one is 'going somewhere'", as Hage has pointed out, describing a "form of imaginary mobility" that every "viable life presupposes" (Hage, 2009, p. 97). Coined as "existential mobility", he refers to a kind of "imagined/felt movement" that describes the human need to feel that we are moving well in our lives (ibid, p. 98). These imaginaries of a better future to come that surfaced strongly during the start of the training period have to be read against the backdrop of a constant circulation of all kinds of imaginaries of mobility present in a city that has become a symbol of a modern metropolitan society. The EU quarter, a stepping-stone for international careers with direct public transport access to other European capitals, is one vivid example. A statistic showing Brussels to be currently the world's second most cosmopolitan city, after Dubai, has recently circulated on the Internet (Le Soir, 2016). Brussels, for some, is indeed an example of a place where transport systems "span the globe in a vast network of destination-to-destination connections" (Ingold, 2011, p. 152). In Europe's capital people come and go, make connections and travel in, out and "up" the social ladder. Hence imaginaries of a better future, of other possibilities ahead are closely linked to expectations of entering this stream of people constantly on the move towards a better life, living in better areas, circulating within the atmosphere of this seemingly vast, bustling city. But while the training at the beginning was perceived as "a stepping-stone" (Venkatesan, 2010, p. 171) for precisely this mobility to come, the motivation of the participants was more and more overtaken by an aversion to investing their time in something that seemed to have no profitable outcome. The continual struggle to make ends meet did not make things any easier. Most of the participants were financially stressed throughout the second half of each month, as I could repeatedly observe. Packed lunches became increasingly smaller and less varied until the next benefit payment arrived.

Cise was one of the few participants who kept his motivation going over many months. His previous experiences of waiting seemed to serve him well. Although he did stop his attempts to engage in "out of curriculum efforts" during working hours, he tinkered at home and on weekends, made chessboards out of wooden plates and recycled bottle caps, dreamt about manufacturing and selling wooden penholders, frequently visited flea markets to "hunt for" cheap tools, and continued imagining possible futures. His imaginaries of a future life that would enable him to finally move forward were apparent in our talks. Opening a little carpentry studio with Hamuda and myself in Molenbeek was one of his preferred scenarios. But I increasingly noticed a certain disillusionment in Cise's attitude and wording. Two months before the end of our training period, the rusty tools that he had carefully collected ended up, soaked in turpentine boxes, at the back of his cupboard.

This transformation expressed itself most demonstratively one morning when Cise handed me my coffee upon arrival, as he usually did. When I asked him the daily "*Ça va?*" he answered, "*Ça doit aller!*" And repeated, when seeing my surprised face, "*Ça doit aller, non?*" Cise's answering my rather commonplace question of "How is it going?" with "It has to go" was precisely what he meant. As Hage has suggested, to equate wellbeing with a sense of mobility is not simply a metaphor but is present in everyday life and language (Hage, 2009, p. 98). Similar to Cise's expression, Hage points out that in Lebanese dialect one asks "*Keef el haal?*" which literally means "How is the state of your being?". And the common reply is "*Mehsheh'l haal*" which literally means "The state of my being is walking". In German, we ask "*Wie geht's?*" which literally means "How is it going?" "*Es geht gut!*" – "It is going well" is the usual answer. But Cise, I argue, slowly came to realise that, once again, he was not going anywhere. Constructing tenon and mortise joints – one of the main types needed for wood constructions – at first had raised his hopes for the long desired future movement, but Cise slowly became aware that "stuckedness" was circumvented only temporarily and had once again caught up with him. His turn of speech not only reflected an increasing feeling of going nowhere but also mirrored an attitude that developed through the training, of encouraging "a mode of restraint, self-control and self-government", as Hage has argued (2009, p. 102). Come what may, "it has to go" anyway, as Cise pointed out. Marked by an uncertain present and an uncertain future, his words point to a larger phenomenon, namely that what we had learned alongside furniture making was patiently waiting to receive what is desperately needed to survive. What mattered was stoically accepting the apparent inevitability of hardship and its patient endurance. In the following section I will turn to exactly these processes that rob people of the capacity to continue imagining a better life through and while creating a "waiting room" that makes it impossible to move forward at all.

Crafting furniture and waiting rooms

Through informal discussions with people who work for similar organisations in the life-long-learning sector, I have come to know that what happened to the participants throughout the year is not at all unique to the course I attended. Participating in a wool-felting course for women in eastern Serbia, Jovanovic similarly argues that, rather than equipping the women with tools that help them to get back on the market more easily, it made older women even more dependent on the state (Jovanovic, 2015). Describing with her course organiser situations like the one I encountered, she points out that an unequal power relationship was maintained during the course. While the women were crafting felted objects, a "waiting room" was simultaneously crafted, and with it women's dependency (Ibid, 2015). Building on Auyero and Jovanovic, I argue that the production of the kind of waiting room that Cise found himself in is part of a larger "governmental technique" that makes people wait as "patients of the state" (Auyero, 2011; 2012). This does not mean that clients are passive, nor do I argue against state support of people in need. What I point out is what Auyero, following Bourdieu (1998), called the "doxa" of welfare: a "basic compliance with the fundamental presuppositions of welfare distribution: show patience, wait, and you might obtain benefits from the state" (Auyero, 2011, p. 23). Following this perspective, the example of the carpentry training course figures as only an extension of a larger system of power that does not end with training.

In the first months after the apprenticeship, Cise's life was largely structured by predetermined appointments in places that Jansen had so pointedly described as "zones of humiliating entrapment through documentary requirements" (Jansen, 2009, p. 815). The employment office that had sent him to the training centeer in the first place argued later that, given his age, a one-year course in carpentry without any previous experience in woodwork was maybe not the best idea. "Come back next week, come back in a couple of weeks, we will call you when we find something for you" were the promises he heard. "And what am I supposed to do?", Cise said to me much later in his own waiting room. "After all, I need the money. All I can do is wait!"

By analysing the sociocultural dynamics of waiting, Auyero's research on poor people's waiting in a welfare office in Buenos Aires shows how his research participants experience their waiting as what he calls "the patient model":

> To be an actual or potential welfare recipient is to be subordinated to the will of others. This subordination is created and re-created through innumerable acts of waiting. [...] In those recurring encounters at the welfare office, poor people learn that, despite endless delays and random changes, they must comply with the requirements of agents and their machines. (Auyero, 2011, p. 24)

Nuijten, who offers an interesting addition to the topic by exploring the life world of the state agencies that deal with the demands, shows that Mexican bureaucracy functions as a "hope-generating machine" that continually projects the message that things are still possible. While constantly creating expectations, many promises are never fulfilled, and rather than following a certain coherence, the bureaucratic machine insists on generating hope, fear and expectations (Nuijten, 2003, p. 16). Following these perspectives, the carpentry training course and its follow-up taught Cise the opposite of engagement for a better future. Cise learned to comply with the requirements, obeying the teachers' demands during lessons, and following the interview schedule he received after training. One of the few things he actually was rewarded for, albeit with only a small amount of money to keep going, was patiently waiting. And like the good citizen he was, Cise kept waiting, regardless of the outcome. But the condition of ongoing crisis and precarity, marked by many moments of stuckedness, led to an extreme sense of immobility, of "pattering in place", as Jansen's research participants in the outskirts of Sarajevo would describe it (Jansen, 2014, p. 79).[10] If, to refer back to Arendt again, human capacity for new beginnings is indeed "the one miracle-working faculty of man" (Arendt, 1998, p. 246), the question needs to be raised about what happens when the new beginnings never lead to any long-term outcome? What happens when all the imaginary lives are constantly postponed in real life; and what is the breaking point for an individual beyond which imaginaries are entirely abandoned? This is exactly what brings us back to where we left Cise at the beginning of this chapter: sitting in his waiting room, having nowhere to go, caught in a feeling of hopelessness, daunted, dependant on state benefits, without any concrete end in sight.

To be outside the world

The distress Cise experienced almost a year after the carpentry training had ended expressed itself strongly in the way he talked: slowly, often not finding the right words, telling me in random order about many different situations in which he was forced to wait without much outcome. While listening to him, I became convinced that he had not spoken to anybody for quite a while. In contradiction to what I have read in other accounts of waiting rooms in government institutions (Auyero, 2012; Jansen, 2009), waiting with and amongst others made Cise feel more alone in his struggle. "In many parts of the world", as Salazar has pointed out, "mobility is an important way of belonging to today's society" (2018, p. 154). Consequently, with the increasing feeling of "not belonging" to a world around him that he perceived as being in constant movement, Cise experienced a great loss of community feeling and a resulting loneliness that seemed to render this period especially difficult. Feeling disconnected, removed from time and place, it seemed as if Cise had crossed a threshold into a "non-place of existential waiting" (Dwyer, 2009, p. 25). He slept most of the day, lost track of time and more frequently asked his neighbour, one of the few people he was still in contact with, to deliver his food to him. Cise, to borrow Al-Mohammad's phrase, "disentangled himself" (2013, p. 228) more and more from the world around him:

> "Outside these walls", he told me hesitantly, crumpled in his chair, "everything seems to move. Only I don't. At a certain point, it becomes unbearable. And then I start thinking and thinking and it destroys me. I would need a general to buoy up my spirits, because in certain moments I just feel exhausted. It's like I don't feel the ground under me anymore. So, I'd better stay at home. I'd go crazy otherwise."

Cise's experience of stuckedness and waiting over a long period of time triggered a general reluctance to be part of the world surrounding him; and along with this reluctance Cise lost his capacity to imagine any other future: "[a]ll the doors we constructed didn't open many doors for me yet, no?", he asked me, referring to all the destroyed imaginaries that never materialised into real possibilities. "Now, I'm just waiting for whatever will come", was his answer to my question about his plans for the coming months. The anthropologist Weiss has observed that for young Tanzanian men "imaginaries of the 'good life' serve as an essential creative act that facilitates their ability to move beyond existing structural imbalances of power and economic constraints" (Weiss, 2002 in Salazar, 2011, p. 683). But, in Cise's case, the ability to imagine a better future was lost with the creation of a waiting room he felt more and more stuck in. Hence the training then not only "encourage[d] a mode of restraint, self-control and self-government" (Hage, 2009) but also discouraged Cise's power to hold onto one of the few things that could sustain some feeling of control over his life: imaginaries for something better to come. And exactly here, the interrelation between the production of a waiting room and the simultaneous destruction of imaginaries comes into effect in a person's life. In a city where everything was imaginable for Cise during every new beginning, the future became unimaginable for him. Through the governmental strategies that played out during and after the training, Cise had given up imagining – and so fighting for   a better life. "When the world refuses our efforts to interact with it on social and reciprocal terms", says Jackson, "it becomes, in our imaginations, a locus of minatory power that, from the perspective of a state, are better to be hindered" (Jackson, 2008, p. 70).

Remote horizons. Concluding remarks

As I mentioned at the outset, this article focuses mainly on the effects of future imaginaries being continually unmet and destroyed, in the case of one person. It needs to be stated, however, that Cise is by far not the only one who started the training course as a means of potentially overcoming marginalisation, while ending up with very limited abilities to go on. There were other participants who told me about their feeling of disillusionment, describing, when we occasionally met for a coffee after the training course had finished, how they suffered from becoming "hostages of a very complicated system" (Xhardez, 2016, p. 10).[11] Cise's story shows how structures that are disabling people also destroy their ability to imagine future horizons while at the same time producing a waiting room that turns people into "patients of the state" (Auyero, 2011; 2012). Despite the endurance Cise showed in countering negative circumstances during and after training, the continual, systematic failure of expectations led to his personal breaking point that made it impossible for him to move forward, whether in his real life or, at the absolute minimum, in his imaginary worlds. Trying to understand Cise's reluctance to be part of this world a year after the promising training course had ended not only suggests a less romantic reading of participation in vocational training courses and apprenticeships, as is so often represented in anthropological writing, but also sheds light on the damaging effects of being stuck in a seemingly endless waiting room where future imaginaries are time and again shattered and postponed. In Cise's case, this not only encompassed his increasing psychological ill-being, but also took its toll on his health.[12] Two months before we saw each other again, Cise's neighbour had found him unconscious in his flat. He was suffering a heart attack due to a blockage of the cardiac artery. After a successful operation, the doctors told him that he had to cut down the stress in his life, since his physical tests did not point to any risk factors. "I was laughing at the doctor", Cise said when retelling me the story. "How to not have stress when you are at war. *À la guerre comme à la guerre*, no ?".[13] While observing Cise showing me his medicine and telling me about his decreasing appetite, I was thinking about the many times he had used this French proverb, "*À la guerre comme à la guerre !*", literally meaning "At war as at war" since I had known him. Almost three decades had elapsed since he had fled war and came to Europe, yet he was still continually thrown back to the starting point: fighting for a decent life.

This article was developed in the framework of the ERC "Knowing from the Inside (KFI): Anthropology, Art, Architecture and Design" research project at the University of Aberdeen.

Notes

1 Due to the "sensibility" of the topic, in consideration of current "political" tendencies that are sweeping across Europe, no names of organisations are given. The question of research ethics in an apprenticeship setting is discussed in detail in Moderbacher 2019.

2 Also see Moderbacher 2018.

3 I reflect on my decision to work with life storytelling as well as its methodological challenges in more detail in Moderbacher 2018 and 2019.

4 Originally in French: "Asseyez-vous, Madame! Bienvenue dans ma salle d'attente!", translation by the author.

5   Strauss (2006) gives a detailed overview of "The Imaginary" within anthropological knowledge and specifically refers to Anderson's and Taylor's application of the imaginary as potentially valuable if person-centred methods are prioritised. Also see Weiss 2002.

6   On many occasions during our shared year in the carpentry class, Cise and other participants told me about their individual "contributions" to the creation of collective imaginaries of the "good life" in Europe. During one conversation, one trainee, for example, said, "It's all fucked up! When we arrive here we live a shitty life during the week and work like dogs without rights. Then, on Sunday, we dress up, drive to the Atomium [one of Brussels' most important sightseeing monuments] and take a picture in front of the most beautiful car we can find; and then we send it home with best greetings from our perfect life!"

7   Cise's story stands in contrast to common popular discourses suggesting that many refugees and migrants would rather migrate to Europe than continue living in their birth country. He often described himself as part of a Guinean generation that shared an eagerness to rebuild the country after its independence in 1958. This results from the countries' particular history (Gerdes 2009): As the only French colony, Guinea refused to be included in the "Communauté Français" and insisted on immediate independence in 1958. Guinea's "No!" to Charles de Gaulle's offer remained not only an important symbol throughout the (ongoing) post-colonial struggle (Lewin 2005) but encouraged a national pride in being able to lead the country to a better future without the "help" of the colonial rulers (Moderbacher 2019).

8   Between 1988 and 1999, the rate of acceptance as a refugee, as defined by the Geneva Convention, rarely exceeded 5 – 10% in Belgium. The examination of these applications was extremely slow, with a waiting period of, at times, up to seven years (Martiniello, 2003, 228).

9   According to a comparative analysis of migration policies in Europe conducted in 2014, Belgium has the highest unemployment rate of foreign-born people in Europe (17.4 % compared to 6.9 % "native-born"), followed by Sweden and France (Patay, 2017, p.147).

10 Jansen's research participants mean "going nowhere" by the expression "pattering in place" (2014: 79).

11 As mentioned previously, most of the participants did not want to appear under their real names in my work and preferred to keep our relationship on the level of superficial encounters, albeit knowing about my research and laughing about my sometimes seemingly spontaneous note-taking.

12 With his felt "immobility" influencing his health, Cise's story stands in harsh contrast to the current popular discourse of mobility and movement as part of a healthy lifestyle.

13 Literally translated as "in war as in war", often meaning "to make do with what one has".

References

Adamson, G. (2007). *Thinking through craft*. Oxford and New York: Berg.

Al-Mohammad, H. (2013). "Ravelling/unravelling: being-in-the-world and falling-out-of-the-world". In T. Ingold and G. Palsson (eds.), *Biosocial Becomings* (pp. 211–228). Cambridge: Cambridge University Press.

Arendt, H. (1998). The Human Condition, *second edition*. Chicago, IL, and London: The University of Chicago Press.

Auyero, J. (2011). "Patients of the state. An ethnographic account of poor people's waiting". *Latin American Research Review*, 46:1, pp. 5–29.

Auyero, J. (2012). *Patients of the State: The Politics of Waiting in Argentina*. Durham, NC: Duke University Press.

Beidelman, T.O. (1986). *Moral Imagination in Kaguru modes of thought*. Washington, DC: Smithsonian Institution Press.

Bourdieu, P. (1998). *Practical Reason. On the Theory of Action*. Stanford, CA: Stanford University Press.

Cruikshank, J. (1990). *Life Lived Like a Story: Life Stories of Three Yukon Native Elders (in collaboration with Angela Sidney, Kitty Smith and Annie Ned)*. Lincoln, NE: University of Nebraska Press.

Dwyer, P. (2009). "Worlds of waiting". In G. Hage (ed.), *Waiting* (pp. 15–27). Melbourne: Melbourne University Press.

Garnier, A., & A. Piva. (2019). "Labour market participation of refugees and asylum seekers in Brussels: innovation and institutional complementarity". Translated by J. Corrigan. In *Brussels studies. The e-journal for academic research on Brussels*. Brussels: ISRIB. Online: www.brusselsstudies.be [accessed December 2019].

Gerdes, F. (2009). "Militärputsch in Guinea. Hintergründe der aktuellen Entwicklungen". *AKUF Analysen*, 3, pp. 1–8.

Hage, G. (2009). "Waiting out the crisis: on stuckedness and governmentality". In G. Hage (ed.), *Waiting* (pp. 97–106). Melbourne: Melbourne University Press.

Ingold, T. (2011). *Being Alive. Essays on Movement, Knowledge and Description*. New York: Routledge.

Jackson, M. (2008). "The shock of the new: on migrant imaginaries and critical transitions". *Ethnos*, 73:1, pp. 57–72.

Jansen, S. (2009). "After the red passport: towards an anthropology of the everyday geopolitics of entrapment in the EU's immediate outside". *Journal of the Royal Anthropological Institute*, 15:4, pp. 815–832.

Jansen, S. (2014). "On not moving well enough: temporal reasoning in Sarajevo yearnings for 'normal Lives'". *Current Anthropology*, 55:9, pp. 74–84.

Jovanovic, D. (2015). "Ambivalence and the work of hope: anticipating futures in a Serbian industrial town". PhD thesis. Manchester: University of Manchester.

Le Soir. (2016). "Top 14 des villes les plus cosmopolites au monde". Online: https://infogr.am/top_15_des_villes_les_plus_cosmopolites [accessed January 2016].

Lewin, A. (2005). "Sékou Touré's 'No'". *African Geopolitics* 17, pp. 179–191.

Marchand, T.H.J. (2008). "Muscles, morals and mind: craft apprenticeship and the formation of person". *Journal of Educational Studies*, 56:3, pp. 245–271.

Martiniello, M. (2003). "Belgium's immigration policy". *The International Migration Review*, 37:1, pp. 225–232.

Marzloff, B. (2005). *Mobilités, trajectoires fluides*. La Tour d'Aigues: Editions de l'Aube.

Moderbacher, C. (2018). "Hamuda, the wood and I". *Etnofoor*, 30:1, pp. 77–95.

Moderbacher, C. (2019). "Crafting lives in Brussels: making and mobility on the margins". PhD thesis. Aberdeen: Aberdeen University.

Nuijten, M. (2003). *Power, community and the state: the political anthropology of organisation in Mexico*. London: Pluto Press.

Odland Portisch, A. (2010). "The craft of skillful learning: Kazakh women's everyday practices in western Mongolia". *Journal of the Royal Anthropological Institute*, 16, pp. 62–79.

Patay, T. (2017). "A comparative analysis of migration policies: (best) practices from Europe". *Acta Universitatis Sapientiae, Economics and Business*, 5:1, pp. 139–154.

Pupavac, V. (2010). "Weaving postwar reconstruction in Bosnia? The attractions and limitations of NGO gender development approaches". *Journal of Intervention and Statebuilding*, 4:4, pp. 475–493.

Salazar, N.B. (2010). *Envisioning Eden: Mobilizing imaginaries in tourism and beyond*. Oxford: Berghahn.

Salazar, N.B. (2011). "Tanzanian migration imaginaries". In R. Cohen and G. Jónsson (eds.). *Migration and culture* (pp. 673–683). Cheltenham: Edward Elgar.

Salazar, N.B. (2012). "Tourism imaginaries: a conceptual approach". *Annals of Tourism Research*, 39:2, pp. 863–882.

Salazar, N. B. (2018). "Theorizing mobility through concepts and figures". *Tempo Social, revista de sociologia da USP*, 30:2, pp. 153–168.

Sanders, T. (2001). "Territorial and magical migrations in Tanzania". In M. de Bruijn, R. van Dijk and D. Foeken (eds.). *Mobile Africa: Changing patterns of movement in Africa and beyond* (pp. 27–46). Leiden: Brill.

Strauss, C. (2006). "The imaginary". *Anthropological Theory*, 6:3, pp. 322–344.

Venkatesan, S. (2010). "Learning to weave; weaving to learn... what?". *Journal of the Royal Anthropological Institute*, 16:1, pp. 158–175.

Weiss, B. (2002). "Thug realism: inhabiting fantasy in urban Tanzania". *Cultural Anthropology*, 17:1, pp. 93–124.

Xhardez, C. (2016). "The integration of new immigrants in Brussels: an institutional and political puzzle". Translated by J. Corrigan.In *Brussels studies. The e-journal for academic research on Brussels*. Brussels: ISRIB. Online: www.brusselsstudies.be [accessed December 2019].

Found a nanny and lived happily ever after: The representations of Filipino nannies on human resources agency websites in Turkey

Deniz Berfin Ayaydin

Introduction

"Wouldn't you like your domestic worker to be energetic, clean, positive and able to take care of details that even you do not realize? Then Filipina helpers are the right choice for you."[1]

The above quotation is taken from a human resource consultancy website that matches Filipina nanny[2] candidates with potential employers, i.e. families in Turkey. Since the early 2010s, there has been an increase in the number of human resource consultancies that work on the placement of Filipina nannies. The websites of these agencies provide comprehensive lists of reasons to employ Filipina nannies rather than nannies from other nationalities and they provide ranges of wages for Filipinas.

A report by the International Labour Organisation published in 2018 (Addati, Cattaneo, Esquivel & Valarino, 2018) points to the wage differentials between local and migrant domestic workers, as well as between migrant domestic workers coming from different nationalities, noting that they cannot be explained by the differences in education or work experience. This leads to the question: what contributes to the differences in wages,[3] if not credentials? While Filipinas' knowledge of English makes them highly sought-after employees, this alone fails to explain why their salaries tend to be higher than those of other migrant women working as nannies for families in Turkey. In this chapter I attempt to tie representations of Filipina women to their imaginaries and their mobility and I argue that representations of Filipina women construct them as ideal nannies and pricier global commodities that act as status symbols for transnational, aspirant middle classes, and locate them higher in the domestic labour market hierarchy. Moreover, I suggest that imaginaries of Filipina women help structural forces such as gender, race and global capitalism to operate.

Migratory movements always involve the "process of cultural meaning-making" (Salazar, 2010, p. 2) and push-pull theories fall short of offering intelligibility of such dimensions (Salazar, 2011). To move beyond structuralist approaches that regard migration as a discrete event marked by movement, we require a broader and more complex understanding that values "imaginary and discursive dimensions" (Frello in Salazar, 2010, p. 6). Here, the notion of social imaginaries becomes crucial because it challenges the understanding that material realities are the sole driving force of migratory movements, and it encapsulates the symbolic dimensions that contribute to migration (Camacho, 2008, p. 5). With this understanding, not only places of deprivations and opportunities but also migrant imaginaries of what lies ahead and "regimes of mobility" (Glick Schiller & Salazar, 2013) co-produce migratory flows. Furthermore, imaginaries held by prospective employers about alleged qualities of migrant workers frequently translate into preferences in employing people of certain nationalities. Thus, imaginaries offer glimpses into how migration is pictured and how various anticipations play a role in the unfolding of migratory projects. Looking at imaginaries also sheds light on the power relations that are formed through migratory movements in the sense of how and to whom privileges are granted, and whom constraints are placed upon in relation to mobility.

Media play a central role in the development of migrant imaginaries and, reversing the gaze, imaginaries of migrants. Russell and Wood (2013, pp. 1–2) argue that "media may intervene in the migration process" in three principal ways: by feeding into images of destination countries, into representations of migrants in the destination country, and by facilitating transnational ties via "media originating from the migration sending country". All three types of links between media and migration are critical in how migration is imagined, dealt with and experienced, and therefore make mediated depictions of migrants central in the exploration of attitudes towards nannies from the Philippines in Turkey.

With the aim of contributing to the body of scholarly work regarding imaginaries, migration and media, this chapter looks at how Filipina nannies are portrayed on the human resource agency websites in Turkey. Gaonkar (2002, p. 4) suggests that social imaginaries are "embedded in the habitus of a population" and circulated through "images, stories, legends, and modes of address" (p. 10). He argues that social imaginaries exist "by virtue of representations or implicit understandings" (p. 10). Given this "fluid middle ground between embodied practices and explicit doctrines" (ibid.), the human resource agency websites provide a repository of such representations[4] refracted through lenses of race and gender that feed into social imaginaries and are fed by them and contribute to material realities for Filipina women in Turkey. Before examining such representations in more detail, this chapter starts with a brief overview of migration and division of domestic labour in Turkey.

Turkey: Migration and the Domestic Services Sector

In the last decade, Turkey has transformed from a major migrant-sending country to a major migrant-receiving country. The migration flows took an upward turn starting from the late 1970s when the political turmoil, "draconian politics" and humanitarian insecurity pushed people within and beyond the region to seek asylum in Turkey (Icduygu, 2014). Moreover, the country has been imagined to provide "a gateway to a new job, a new life, and a stepping stone to employment in the West" (Icduygu, 2009 in Kaya, 2016) and sometimes a new love (Bloch, 2011) for immigrants from Eastern European and former Soviet Union countries. More recently this came to include countries like the Philippines, Indonesia, Sri Lanka, Nepal and Tunisia. Together with favourable visa regimes, "Turkey's new liberal market economy characterized by informality" (İcduygu, 2014) has been instrumental in attracting migrants. As a result, Turkey witnessed immigration flows from four different categories: (1) irregular labour migrants; (2) transit migrants; (3) asylum seekers and refugees and (4) regular migrants (İçduygu, 2014).

Moreover, the Justice and Development Party's immigration policies and neo-Ottoman discourse played a critical role in the migration inflows. An example of such rhetoric is demonstrated in ex-President Abdullah Gül's address to a conference on migration, Islam and multiculturalism in Europe in Ankara on 11 April 2013:

Turkey is changing. Turkey is a country that has accepted migrants and is used as a transit point for migration to Europe. Not only are people from our neighbouring countries arriving in Turkey, but also people from other parts of the world are coming to our country. As Turkey is enjoying successful economic development, the country is becoming a country of immigration... We used to send our citizens to other countries [...] to Germany [...] to France, to Austria, to Australia [...] But foreigners are also beginning to live in Turkey [...] We have so many refugees coming to Turkey [...] In the Ottoman period we were a multicultural country, with people of different religion, ethnicity and culture [...] now again Turkey will be a place with this diversity. (İcduygu, 2014.)

Nonetheless, this welcoming portrayal is to some extent deceiving as it disguises its selectivity in terms of the laws and the policies that facilitate settlement for some groups rather than others.[5]

Migration flows transformed the domestic services sector which has a long history in the region. The Turkish domestic services sector has over the last decades developed into a multifarious system of live-in migrant workers and locals, paid on a daily basis (Toksoz, Erdogdu & Kaska, 2012). Many middle-class and upper-middle-class employers consider migrant domestic workers "European" and "civilised" as opposed to local women of rural origins who are thought of as uneducated (ibid.) and whose bodily labour marks them with "signs of peasantry" (Ozyegin, 2001, p. 125). In the case of nannies, the ethnic stratification of the labour market becomes even more pronounced. A remarkable study done by Danis (2007) portrays the complexity of and the hierarchies within the Turkish domestic labour industry. She suggests that English nannies, followed by Filipina nannies, take the place at the top of the ladder since they address Turkish upper-class aspirations for pre-school education. Turkish-speaking Bulgarians are ranked lower but still have the linguistic advantage. Finally, she states that women from Azerbaijan, Armenia and Georgia face significant obstacles in entering the Turkish domestic service market. Recently there has been a significant increase in work permits granted to Filipina women. The 36 permits granted to Filipina women in 2011 grew to 1,959 in 2017.[6] Moreover, unlike other migrant domestic workers, Filipina women are highly mediatised by employment agencies, employers themselves and television programmes, which presumably contribute to their perception, desirability and higher wages.

Female migration, transnational division of domestic labour and the Philippines

Women have been on the move for centuries. However, the early 1980s marked a difference in their mobility patterns, as women started to move on their own, rather than joining their husbands as family dependents. This shift attracted scholarly attention to female migration.

Upon arrival in a new country, job opportunities for these women remain highly limited, often boiling down to domestic work, care work and manufacturing jobs. The "care economy" (Zelizer, 2009) then becomes marked by the employment of a precarious workforce, which has gendered, raced and classed implications. These sectors are the largest venues for migrant women and they are asymmetrically filled by them. Presumably, it is the women from the Global South and East that move towards the Global North. The outcome of such movements is a transnational division of domestic labour, usually involving the delegation of non-biological reproductive work to "third world" women, while leaving intact gender ideologies regarding the family division of labour in sending and receiving countries. Parreñas (2000, p. 577) calls this unequal distribution the "international division of reproductive labour". She argues that the movement of women is embedded in "transnational capitalism" (ibid.), which is marked by structural inequalities regarding gender, race and class.

In the Philippines, overseas migration has become an institutionalised process in which the government plays a central role in facilitating overseas employment (Guevarra, 2014, p. 136). In the 1970s, the Philippine government started to export labour to oil-rich Gulf countries that needed workers (ibid, p. 135). In 1974, then president Ferdinand Marcos and his administration issued the Labour Code (Gonzales, 1996, p. 164), facilitating overseas contract employment to curb unemployment and payment deficits incurred as a result of IMF and the World Bank loans (ibid.; Guevarra, 2014, p. 135). The Labour Code promoted the establishment of institutions to implement the regulation of migration, such as the Philippine Overseas Employment Administration (POEA) and private employment agencies to expedite the recruitment process (Guevarra, 2014, p. 136). While initially men migrated to fulfil jobs such as those of mechanics, construction workers or engineers, the increasing need for care work led to the feminisation of the labour to be exported. The export of labour "has become one of the country's key programs of development" (ibid.).

Promotion of overseas employment that started with neoliberal policies still continues to this date. The economy of the country is contingent on the remittances sent by over 10 million Filipino migrant workers (Näre & Nordberg, 2016). In a 2003 statement, President Gloria Macapagal-Arroyo referred to herself not only as the head of state, but also as the CEO of a global company providing workforce recruits (2003, cited in Näre and Nordberg, 2016). This contributes to the image of the Philippines as exporter and Filipinas as exports. Moreover, state institutions and recruitment agencies are actively involved in "racial branding" to create a competitive advantage over other countries that export labour (Guevarra, 2014, p. 131). Through essentialising and racialising discourses, institutional actors brand Filipinas as "the Supermaid[s]" (Ibid, p. 140), thereby developing an "added export value" that positions Filipinas as better than the others in the foreign employer's eyes (Guevarra, 2010, p. 126). Guevarra (Ibid., p. 135) suggests that these discourses also contribute to the creation of "ideal labouring subjects" and this translates into "Filipina" becoming analogous to "maid" in Hong Kong (Constable 1997 in Barber 2000; Tyner 1994) and to "nanny" in certain urban settings in Canada (Barber, 2000).

Mediated representations in the receiving countries are crucial in understanding how these women are imagined and how imaginaries in turn create subjectivities; however, these representations have not been addressed extensively (see Gomes, 2011, and Piocos, 2018, for movies; Saroca 1997, 2006, 2007 for Filipina women's media portrayals in Australia; and Näre and Nordberg 2016 for media representations of Filipina nurses in Finland). There is a growing need to investigate the representations of migrants, and such investigation will help us to understand the dialectical relationship between imaginaries and representations which in turn contribute to the material dimensions of migration.

Methodology

In this chapter I analyse how Filipina nannies are depicted on 25 human resources agency websites in Turkey. The websites were chosen via an online search with the keyword "filipinli bakıcı" (Filipino caregiver). In other words, search engines for domestic workers and blogs with entries on domestic workers that my search yielded were excluded from the analysis. In addition, two newspaper interviews with the CEOs of a few bigger agencies were included among the data considered. All the websites were accessed during March 2018.

Following a constructionist approach to representation and taking a cue from Hall (1997, pp. 5–9), the chapter explores these representation practices to investigate how Filipina women are imagined. Drawing from Foucault's approach to discourse as producing social reality by "forming the objects of which [it] speaks" (Foucault, 1972, p. 49), the theoretical departure point of the study suggests that representations feed into imaginaries, produce social reality and subjectivities, and they in turn are fed by imaginaries. A study done by Angeles and Sunanta (2007) looks into the discursive representation of Thai and Filipina women on intermarriage websites to investigate how the intersections of gender, race and nation in these representations facilitate violence towards Third World women. The authors argue that these representations located in the nexus of consumerism, Orientalism and sexism shape how these women are treated and how they experience the world. In the same spirit, in this study I explore the constructions of Filipina women by employment agencies, to look into the ways social imaginaries of Filipina women are produced and result in preferential treatment on the labour market.

The Ideal Nanny

In representations on the selected agency websites, Filipina women were commonly depicted as highly desirable employees because of their presumed knowledge of English. They were portrayed as well-educated and their level of education was backed by statistics indicating that 80 per cent of Filipinas were college graduates and the remaining 20 per cent were high school graduates.[7] However, presumed personality traits seemed to be just as relevant. Filipina nannies were portrayed as disciplined, an alleged characteristic that was echoed across all websites. Yet, this discipline was carefully curated; it was the right amount of discipline implemented at the right times and in appropriate measure. Filipina nannies were said to be disciplined in their own work and when it came to children's education, sleeping and meal times, but they were equally cheerful during play time.[8] They would not implement hard and cold discipline on the children.[9] The common trope of nannies from the Philippines was one that highlights hard work, carefulness and meticulousness, as well as trustworthiness, and a task-oriented, energetic attitude.[10] Yet these more work-related traits were counterbalanced with another group of traits; they were "disciplined yet loving". Filipinas were portrayed as calm, easy-going, avoiding conflicts with their employers, tolerant, sweet-tempered and patient.[11] In contrast to the work-related traits, the second group related to docility and obedience. Nonetheless, this passivity was not an obstacle to dealing with a potential crisis like small accidents. They were seen as friendly, positive, sincere and clean.[12] They were loving, compassionate and merciful. One of the websites provides a comprehensive ten-item list to convey why Filipinas are the best choice on the market.[13]

> 10 reasons to prefer a Filipina child caregiver:
> 1) Language: English is the official language of Philippines
> 2) Discipline: hardworking, meticulous but not oppressive. Their discipline is limited to homework and sleep and meal times.
> 3) Kindness/grace: due to their culture, they are naturally graceful
> 4) Respectful/tolerant: a Filipina is respectful and does not get into conflict with you.
> 5) Exotic, Asian food: they are good cooks
> 6) Overnight stay
> 7) Service quality: the Philippines are known to provide a workforce for luxury cruises
> 8) Dynamism and energy: they have slender and agile physical traits, which enable them to do their jobs energetically and practically
> 9) Clean and well groomed: they have self-respect, they dress up in a clean and decent fashion all the time
> 10) Loving, compassionate and positive: they always smile and they are loving at all times.

On the websites it was stated that Filipina nannies fit perfectly in your family and will accompany you all the time: in vacations, in business trips and in special times. However, their presence would not be annoying because they were not chatterers and they were good at keeping secrets.[14] Moreover, the long journey from the Philippines and their visa, which is tied to their contract, elicit the promise of long-term commitment to an employer, which constitutes added value.

Overall, the combination of these traits made Filipinas successful at childcare and "better than other groups of nannies",[15] which turned them into the "Mercedes Benz" of nannies, as Guevarra (2014, p. 140) argued. Hence, these representations located Filipina women more highly in the hierarchy of the domestic labour market by constructing them as ontologically distinct. To keep the imagined ontological distinction intact, Filipina women's identities were depicted hiding the inconsistencies. The stereotypes were strategically used and maintained by the agencies because they marked the success of placement. They indicated agencies' "ability to render a perfect match between client and applicant in practice, their ability to stereotype in a way that is consistent with employers' expectations" (Bakan & Stasiulis, 1995, p. 317). The pride derived from a successful placement is clearly manifested in agencies' Instagram pages posting family photos of "perfect matches".

The knowledge of English, high levels of education and good work ethics and habits were wrapped up in the mantle of Asian female desirability, and personality traits were stressed rather than other characteristics like experience or age. Rollins (1985, p. 56) suggests that employers rank the "personality of the worker and the kinds of relationships employers were able to establish with them" "as more important considerations" than the job performance. By the same token, Akalin (2007) argues in her study on migrant and Turkish domestic workers that what was sought from the migrant domestics was "not their personalities as fixed entities, but the capacity to mould them". In this case, Filipina nannies' identities were imagined as fixed but at the same time mouldable, providing room for customisation if the employer needed it.

Filipina women are not perceived in the same fashion in different places. For instance, Humphrey (1990) found that in Jordan Filipinas were regarded as assertive. They were seen as optimistic and outgoing but "difficult to manage" in Taiwan (Lan, 2006, p. 77). Thus, the Philippines' neoliberal policies that led to the marketing of Filipina women as the "Mercedes Benz" of care work (Guevarra, 2014, p. 140) did not lead to homogenous imagination of Filipinas around the world. However, representations were consistent across all websites of agencies based in Turkey and constructed Filipina women as ideal nannies.

A Global Commodity

The representations of Filipina domestic workers as ideal nannies are part and parcel of the commodification of women's labour. As suggested by Tyner (1994, pp. 607–608), "when migrants are not viewed as individuals, but by the functions they perform, they become nonentities: products. Employers can select applicants through catalogues, order them through the mail (through the POEA), and have them delivered". The catalogues Tyner refers to in 1994 are now more commonly available in the form of video resumés or skype interviews, which have a more personal dimension. On the websites, statements such as "your selected nanny" prevail. Most agencies even promise a "replacement" if the client fails to get along with a nanny within the first six months.[16]

Moreover, when justifying the preference for Filipinas, the agencies advocate that families around the world look for Filipina nannies to employ.[17] They suggest that Filipinas receive training in childcare, cleaning, elderly care. They further argue that the Philippines has been a source of labour for more than 100 years and the country provides workforces especially in the services sector. This way, the export of nannies becomes normalised in global capitalism and hiring them comes to be framed as the right consumer choice.

In the process of Filipina women's construction as a universal commodity, racialisation or "racial branding" (Guevarra, 2014, p. 145) plays a central role. While in other countries in the region like Jordan (Liebelt, 2008), skin colour has been mentioned overtly, in Turkey racism and skin colour have a more complex relationship with each other. In the discursive construction, Filipina women's "culture" serves as a repository for a number of imagined qualities making them desirable labouring subjects. This is in line with the literature suggesting that culture has replaced race in the glorification of difference and declarations of superiority/inferiority (Todorov, 1993, pp. 156–157), and racism has been formulated through culture instead of "biological themes" (Balibar & Wallerstein, 1991, p. 26). As Blaut (1992, p. 280) maintains, "[t]oday's racism is cultural racism". Cultural racism exaggerates and radicalises differences and essentialises them by conceiving culture "along ethnically absolute lines, not as something intrinsically fluid, changing, unstable, and dynamic" (Gilroy, 1990 in Giroux 1993, p. 8). Attributing Filipina women's success in childcare to their culture justifies their place to serve and the "dominant group's place to be served" (Uchida, 1998, p. 14). While reproductive labour as a commodity has been purchased by women from privileged classes and links women to each other (Parreñas, 2000, p. 561), racialisation helps the division of labour in transnational capitalism to function. Through the "racial branding" engaged in by institutional actors in both the Philippines and the destination countries, Filipinas are imagined as global commodities with a superior export value and qualities. Thus, culture/race becomes the parameter by which the individual's potential for a job – her mobility across borders – is judged as desirable or undesirable.

A class-conscious item of consumption

Filipina nannies, in the Turkish context, were constructed not only as global commodities, but as valuable items of consumption linked to privilege. As in many countries, higher social standing can be claimed through consumption in Turkey (Ustuner & Holt, 2009, p. 52). This is reminiscent of Baudrillard's (2016) sense of consumption, by which individuals distinguish themselves from others and immerse in society. In the broader consumption field, domestic service is an essential commodity (Frantz, 2008, p. 614). Humphrey (1990, p. 13) argues that domestic servants in Jordan were "essentially an item of consumption with symbolic value", akin to "owning the right car" (Tyner, 1994, p. 605). Filipina nannies, branded as "supermaids" (Guevarra, 2014) or "supernannies" and as having "added export value" (Ibid.), appeal to higher classes and act as a status symbol. The agencies consistently mention that elite families' choices were Filipina nannies. In an interview, the CEO of the largest agency stated that she became an insider in high society; she knew which artists were pregnant and which were getting a divorce before everyone else (Hurriyet, 2016). This was a way of suggesting that, by employing Filipina nannies, one could be an insider to that high society as well. On the websites it is argued that children of the British monarchy have been and still are being raised by Filipina nannies.[18] Thus, through being able to afford the "Mercedes-Benz" of nannies, employers were constructed as members of the upper-middle classes who possessed the "best" out there, in relation to global standards.

The aspirational upper-middle-class status is further reified through photos shared on social media.[19] One of the agencies refers its users to its Instagram page[20]; on the Instagram page there are photo displays of families who are happy with their Filipina nannies. Posts include photos of families travelling to foreign countries, eating out or celebrating birthdays or New Year's Eve with their Filipina nannies. When at home, families are photographed in their decorated, spacious living rooms filled with pianos and staircases and their Filipina helpers. The communication of status via imagery is nothing new. John Berger (1972) in his influential series investigating the hidden ideologies behind visual imagery, argues that oil paintings were used as a means of depicting the wealth, status and possessions of the individuals who commissioned those works of art. Following his interpretation of European paintings, portrayals of families happily posing with their Filipina nannies circulating on social media, too, can be seen as akin to statements of possession. Furthermore, these representations were in line with "an essential aspect of what Bourdieu (1984) refers to as 'presentation', the ability of upwardly mobile classes to give the impression of living effortlessly and without apparent cost or sacrifice" (Humphrey, 1990, p. 10). Thus, within these respresentations Filipina women were constructed as status symbols that buttressed the performance of middle-class belonging by their employers.

Moreover, aspirations for an upper-middle-class life include desires for a cosmopolitan lifestyle. On one of the websites the agency argues that, growing up with a different culture, children will have a wider perspective.[21] This promise assumes a cosmopolitan mind-set as "having experience and engagement with the foreign or cultural other" (Glick Schiller & Salazar, 2013) without making any reference to different and less desirable "others". Less exoticised "others" such as Uzbeks or Tunisians are not imagined in the same way as offering children a cosmopolitan mind set. However, the employment of Filipina nannies was envisaged as a step into children's future of belonging to the transnational cosmopolitan class.

Class reproduction through the successful upbringing of the children is a crucial aspiration for the upper and upper-middle classes. Ustuner and Holt (2009, p. 50) argue that Bourdieu's cultural capital, which needed to be "sedimented" and reproduced quotidianly, can be imported into the Turkish context. They argue that "it is not the fruit of indigenous socialization as is the case in Bourdieu (1986)'s France" but it heavily depends on learning and internalising "deterritorialized cultural capital" (Ibid.) through such activities such as travel to the West. Thus, "perfect command of the English language" rather than knowledge of Turkish language, history and literature becomes a defining characteristic of elite education (p. 52). In this case, economic capital enables the privilege of having a Filipina nanny, which is convertible to the enriched and deterritorialised "cultural capital necessary for employability and social networking" (Skeggs, 2004, p. 75) in later life. Filipina nannies were imagined to put the children one step ahead in life.

In brief, Filipina nannies were constructed to reify one's claim to upper-middle-class status and equip children with the necessary skills to enable a successful adulthood in which structural problems such as insufficient language training at schools or widespread unemployment might be circumvented. On the other side of the coin, through contructing Filipina nannies as status symbols, these representations also constructed a transnational consumer middle-class in Turkey in pursuit of global, unique and pricier commodities. These imaginaries of Filipina women can influence how they are treated. The next section will explore how imaginaries may contribute to their material conditions.

Imaginaries and Mobility

Problematising sociology's approach to the "social", Latour (2005, p. 7) argues that the "social" is "not as a special domain, a specific realm or a particular sort of thing" but "a very peculiar movement of re-association and reassembling". He suggests that the "social" is visible only "when a new association is being produced between elements" (p. 8). Drawing from Castoriadis (1987) and Taylor (2002) primarily, these associations and connections that produce the "social" can be approached as social imaginaries (Valaskivi & Sumiala, 2014, p. 230). Social imaginaries are not the opposite of real, but they are "the condition of the perception and production of the real" (Kim, 2016, p. 62). Moreover, imaginaries generate and transform "realities". As Salazar (2010, p. 9) writes, "the imaginary can thus be conceived as a mental process, both individual and social, that produces the reality that simultaneously produces it". Griffiths and Maile (2014) provide an example of this co-productive relationship between reality and imaginaries. In relation to social imaginary of Berlin, they argue that the representation of the city is embroiled both in the "individuals' construction of place and in their embodied encounters with the city" (p. 142). Thus, they point out how imaginaries have the power to shape realities created personally or collectively.

As argued by a number of scholars (Castoriadis, 1987; Salazar, 2011; Camacho 2008), imaginaries have implications for mobilities. Imaginaries made and remade through the circulation of images, stories, representations, meanings and values make "certain types of mobile individuals become the subjects of praise or condemnation, desire, suppression or fear" (Glick Schiller & Salazar, 2013).

In the case of Filipina nannies in Turkey, the imaginaries may contribute to the material conditions of labour migration for these women. Benson (2012, pp. 1682–1683), looking at British migration to rural France, suggests that understanding of "how imagination is translated into action" requires a focus on "privileges and constraints". For Filipina nannies in Turkey, social imaginaries create various privileges. In an interview, the CEO of the biggest agency states that they are leading a legal action against a client who abused an employee (Hurriyet, 2016). Some of the agency websites clearly state that they protect the interests of both the families and the Filipina nannies.[22] Some agencies argue, moreover, that some families send these women to their countries by private jet and buy Filipina satellite channels for their entertainment.

Conclusion

This chapter looked into representations of Filipina nannies on human resource consultancy websites in Turkey. Investigation of websites suggests that Filipina women are constructed as ideal nannies. They were represented as ontologically different from and better than other groups of nannies due not to their job performance but to their imagination as the "other", constructed through the essentialisation of cultural practices, racialisation and gendering. Moreover, they were depicted as global commodities, ownership of which is presented as certifying one's belonging to transnational, cosmopolitan classes. Through these constructions, transnational consumer middle classes in Turkey were imaged as pursuing global, pricier commodities with particular symbolic significance. Market-based, racialised and gendered valuation of subjects consequently may harden or loosen the borders. These imaginaries of Filipina nannies in return seem to contribute to the material conditions for Filipina women in the form of mobility, preferential treatments, privileges and higher wages that are not granted to other nannies in the hierarchical domestic labour market. The market-oriented, racialised and gendered valuation of their subjectivities presumably leads to differential experiences in transgressing borders that are hardened or loosened through imaginaries of Otherness.

The maintenance of such positive imaginaries of Filipina nannies requires labour; studying the human resource agencies and interviewing their owners, Deniz (2018) finds that these agencies do not favour hiring Filipinas who have never left the Philippines. She suggests that they prefer women who have gone to Singapore or China through their personal means and who have worked in these places for a period of time and acquainted themselves with the use of electronic home appliances. The brokerage of nannies from the Philippines thus involves selection strategies that rely on previous cross-border labour mobility to maintain the image of the well-versed, ideal nanny. In the Turkish case, then, their mobility becomes contingent upon the imaginaries that are fed by previous mobilities. By looking into the representations of Filipina women in Turkey, I aimed to contribute to this dialogic relation between representation, mobility and imaginaries that create and perpetuate one another.

"Global capitalism, patriarchy, and racial inequalities are structural forces that jointly determine the subject-positions of migrant Filipina domestic workers in globalization", writes Parreñas (2015, p. 30). However, imaginaries of Filipina women should also be added to the equation as imaginaries work at the intersections of and through gender, class, race, contributing to the perpetuation of these structures of inequality. Thus, imaginaries complicate migration by adding layers to how migration is desired, perceived, realised, mediated, received and experienced, and looking at representations and imaginaries enhances and complicates our understanding of structural inequalities that are embedded in migratory projects for these women. The purpose of this chapter was to look at the intersection of discourses and imaginaries of Otherness and mobility. While this helps to unravel some complexities of mobilty in relation to neoliberal international divison of labour, I would like to note that as a form of political work we need more research that decentres dominant and privileged voices of academia and that opens up spaces that centre these women's epistemeologies and histories.

Notes

1 "Filipinli Yardımcı Ücretleri", [Filipino Helpers Fees], https://www.damladanismanlik.com/blog/filipinli-yardimci-ucretleri. (Accessed on 5 January 2019).

2 The employment agency websites use the terms nanny (*dadı*), child care giver (*bakıcı*) and domestic helper (*yardımcı)* interchangeably. One reason is that the Turkish equivalent of the term nanny is old-fashioned and replaced by caregiver and helper to refer to nannies as well. Despite having commonalities as well as differences, and despite the fact that boundaries between them rarely remain solid, I choose to use the word "nanny" as Filipina women are mostly employed to take care of children within a family setting.

3 On some of the webpages it is overtly stated that hiring Filipina nannies will require the payment of higher salaries.

4 I use the term in Hall's sense. Hall (2003, p.15) states that "[r]epresentation is an essential part of the process by which meaning is produced and exchanged between members of a culture. It does involve the use of language, of signs and images which stand for or represent things".

5 To illustrate: Armenians leaving Syria, which challenged the JDP's "Muslim brothers" rhetoric, were settled in Vakıflıköy, the only Armenian village in Turkey and were issued

with foreign-national certificates with which they could have access to healthcare services for births and operations, but only in hospitals within the region, unlike the nation-wide access given to Sunnite Syrians (Korkut, 2016). And as argued by Korkut (2016), "It may then be that Turkey's insistence on selective humanitarianism is forcing the Syrians to select more primordial associations rather than simply being Syrian".

6   These data were taken from the 2017 report of the Turkish Ministory of Family, Labour and Social Services on https://birim.ailevecalisma.gov.tr/media/11707/cal%C4%B1sma-hayati-istatistikleri-2017.pdf.

7   These numbers do not match the data on statistics tool offered by the Turkish Ministry of Family, Labour and Social Services on http://cibs.csgb.gov.tr/Istatistik/. According to the data published on this tool, only 20% of Filipinos who were granted work permits in 2017 and 2018 were college graduates.

8   "Filipinli Bakıcı", [Filipino Care Worker], https://yelkendanismanlik.com.tr/bakici -hizmetlerimiz/filipinli-bakici/ (accessed on 5 January 2019).

9   Filipinli Bakıcı", [Filipino Care Worker], https://www.evdekibakicim.com/filipinli-bakici (accessed on 24 January 2019).

10   "Filipinli Yardımcı Ücretleri", [Filipino Helpers Fees], https://www.damladanismanlik. com/blog/filipinli-yardimci-ucretleri (accessed on 5 January 2019).

11   "Filipinli Bakıcı Ariyorum", [I am looking for a Filipino Care Worker] http://www. filipinonanny.agency/tr/filipinli-bakici-ariyorum (accessed on 5 January 2019); "Filipinli Bakıcı", [Filipino Care Worker], https://yelkendanismanlik.com.tr/bakici-hizmetlerimiz/ filipinli-bakici/ (accessed on 5 January 2019).

12   "Filipinli Bakıcı", [Filipino Care Worker], https://www.evdekibakicim.com/filipinli -bakici (accessed on 24 January 2019).

13   "Filipinli Bakıcı", [Filipino Care Worker], http://www.damladanismanlik.com/ hizmetlerimiz/filipinli-bakici (accessed on 7 January 2019).

14   "Filipinli Bakıcı Arıyorum", [I am looking for a Filipino Care Worker], http://www. filipinonanny.agency/tr/filipinli-bakici-ariyorum.

15   "Filipinli Bakıcı", [Filipino Care Worker], http://www.filipinlibakicin.net/blog/detay/ filipinli-bakici-ankara/ (accessed on 19 January 2019).

16   "Fiyatlar ve Koşullar", [Fees and Terms], https://www.tontudanismanlik.com/blank.

17   "Filipinli Bakıcı Arıyorum", [I am looking for a Filipino Care Worker], http://www. filipinonanny.agency/tr/filipinli-bakici-ariyorum.

18   "Filipinler.. Uzakta bir ülke....", [The Philippines.... A far away land....], https://www. filipinlibakici.net/index.php/component/content/article?id=22.

19   While some agencies do have Instagram pages, they only post short videos of women introducing themselves. These introductions generally include names, ages, parental status

and work experience in terms of years and number of children taken care of. Some agencies on Instagram do not have any links to websites and operate only through these instagram pages. Nonetheless, this practice of posting photos of families is unique to this agency. Moreover, through this instagram account this agency organises Christmas parties for its employees.

20 https://www.filipinlibakici.net/ and https://www.instagram.com/filipinlibakici/.

21 "Filipinli Bakıcılar Dünyada 1 Numara" [Filipino Helpers are World Number 1] https://www.damladanismanlik.com/blog/filipinli-bakicilar-dunyada-1-numara.

22 "Filipinli Bakıcı", [Filipino Care Worker], https://www.evdekibakicim.com/filipinli-bakici (accessed on 24 January 2019).

References

Addati, L., U. Cattaneo, V. Esquivel & I. Valarino. (2018). *Care work and care jobs for the future of decent work*. Geneva: International Labour Organisation. Retrieved from https://www.ilo.org/global/publications/books/WCMS_633135/lang--en/index.htm.

Akalin, A. (2007). "Hired as a caregiver, demanded as a housewife: Becoming a migrant domestic worker in Turkey". *European Journal of Women's Studies*, 14:3, pp. 209–225.

Angeles, L., & S. Sunanta. (2007). "Websites, gendered representation, and the transnational migration of Filipino and Thai women". *Philippine Journal of Third World Studies*, 22:1, pp. 3–31.

Bakan, A. B., & D. K. Stasiulis. (1995). "Making the match: domestic placement agencies and the racialization of women's household work". *Signs: Journal of Women in Culture and Society*, 20:2, pp. 303–335.

Balibar, E., I. M. Wallerstein & S. R. I. Wallerstein. (1991). *Race, nation, class: Ambiguous identities*. London; New York: Verso.

Barber, P. G. (2000). "Agency in Philippine women's labour migration and provisional diaspora". *Women's Studies International Forum*, 23:4, pp. 399–411.

Baudrillard, J. (2016). *The consumer society: Myths and structures*. London: Sage.

Benson, M. (2012). "How culturally significant imaginings are translated into lifestyle migration". *Journal of Ethnic and Migration Studies*, 38:10, pp. 1681–1696.

Berger, J. (1972). *Ways of seeing*. Harmondsworth: BBC and Penguin Books.

Blaut, J.M. (1992). "The theory of cultural racism". *Antipode*, 24:4, pp. 289–299.

Bloch, A. (2011). "Intimate circuits: modernity, migration and marriage among post-Soviet women in Turkey". *Global Networks*, 11:4, pp. 502–521.

Bourdieu, P. (1984). *Distinction: A social critique of the judgement of taste*. Cambridge, MA: Harvard University Press.

Bourdieu, P. (1986). "*The Forms of Capital*". In J. G. Richardson (ed.), *Handbook of Theory and Research for the Sociology of Education* (pp. 241–258). New York: Greenwood Press.

Braun, V., & V. Clarke. (2006). "Using thematic analysis in psychology". *Qualitative Research in Psychology*, 3:2, pp. 77–101.

Camacho, A. S. (2008). *Migrant imaginaries: Latino cultural politics in the US-Mexico borderlands*. New York: NYU Press.

Castoriadis, C. (1987). *The Imaginary Institution of Society*. Translated by Kathleen Bliemen. Cambridge, MA: MIT University Press.

Chammartin, G. (2002). "The feminization of international migration" (pp. 37–40). International Migration Programme: International Labour Organisation.

Danis, D. (2007). "A faith that binds: Iraqi Christian women on the domestic service ladder of Istanbul". *Journal of Ethnic and Migration Studies*, 33:4, pp. 601–615.

Deniz, A. (2018). "Filipina Nanny Migration to Turkey: Understanding the Role of Intermediary Agencies". *Turkish Journal of Geographical Sciences, 16:2*, pp. 289–301.

Donato, K. M., & D. Gabaccia. (2016). "The global feminization of migration: Past, present, and future". Washington, DC: Migration Policy Institute.

Foucault, M. (1972). *The archaeology of knowledge*. Translated by A. M. Sheridan Smith. New York: Pantheon.

Frantz, E. (2008). "Of maids and madams: Sri Lankan domestic workers and their employers in Jordan". *Critical Asian Studies*, 40:4, pp. 609–638.

Gaonkar, D. P. (2002). "Toward new imaginaries: an introduction". *Public Culture*, 14:1, pp. 1–19.

Giroux, H. A. (1993). "Living dangerously: Identity politics and the new cultural racism: Towards a critical pedagogy of representation". *Cultural Studies*, 7:1, pp. 1–27.

Glick Schiller, N., & N. B. Salazar. (2013). "Regimes of mobility across the globe". *Journal of Ethnic and Migration Studies*, 39:2, pp. 183–200.

Gomes, C. (2011). "Maid-in-Singapore: Representing and consuming foreign domestic workers in Singapore cinema". *Asian Ethnicity*, 12:2, pp. 141–154.

Gonzalez, J. L. (1996). "Domestic and international policies affecting the protection of Philippine migrant labor: an overview and assessment". *Philippine Sociological Review*, 44:1/4, pp. 162–177.

Guevarra, A. R. (2010). *Marketing Dreams, Manufacturing Heroes: The Transnational Labour Brokering of Filipino Workers*. New Brunswick: Rutgers University Press.

Guevarra A. R. (2014). "Supermaids: the racial branding of global Filipino care labour". In B. Anderson and I. Shutes (eds.). *Migration and Care Labour. Migration, Diasporas and Citizenship Series*. London: Palgrave Macmillan.

Griffiths, D., & S. Maile. (2014). "Britons in Berlin: imagined cityscapes, affective encounters and the cultivation of the self". In M. Benson and N. Osbaldiston (eds.) *Understanding lifestyle migration* (pp. 139–159). London: Palgrave Macmillan.

Hall, S. (ed.). (1997). *Representation: Cultural representations and signifying practices* (Vol. 2). London; New York: Sage.

Humphrey, M. (1991) "Asian women workers in the Middle East: domestic servants in Jordan", *Asian Migrant*, 4(2): 53–60.

Hurriyet. (2016). "Filipinli dadılar anlatıyor: Jetiyle tatile gönderen de var kırılan bardağın hesabını soran da…". Retrieved from http://www.hurriyet.com.tr/kelebek/hayat/filipinli-dadilar-anlatiyor-jetiyle-tatile-gonderen-de-var-kirilan-bardagin-hesabini-soran-da-4024 2960.

İcduygu, A. (2014). "Turkey's migration transition and its implications for the Euro-Turkish transnational space". *Global Turkey in Europe II*, pp. 81–XXX.

IHA, (2018). "Türkiye'de çocuklar Filipinli bakıcılara emanet edildi". Retrieved from http://www.iha.com.tr/haber-turkiyede-cocuklar-filipinli-bakicilara-emanet-edildi-701509/.

Kaya, A. (2016). Syrian Refugees and Cultural Intimacy in Istanbul:'I Feel Safe Here!'. *Robert Schuman Centre for Advanced Studies Research Paper No. RSCAS, 59.*

Kim, S. S. (2016). "Imagining religion and modernity in post-colonial Korea: Neo-liberal brand culture and digital space". PhD thesis, Boulder, CO: University of Colorado at Boulder.

King, R., & Wood, N. (Eds.). (2013). Media and migration: Constructions of mobility and difference (Vol. 8). Routledge.

Lan, P. C. (2006). *Global Cinderellas: Migrant domestics and newly rich employers in Taiwan.* Durham, NC: Duke University Press.

Latour, B. (2005). *Reassembling the social: An introduction to actor-network-theory.* Oxford: Oxford University Press.

Liebelt, C. (2008). "On sentimental Orientalists, Christian Zionists, and working class cosmopolitans: Filipina domestic workers' journeys to Israel and beyond". *Critical Asian Studies*, 40:4, pp. 567–585.

Näre, L., & C. Nordberg. (2016). "Neoliberal postcolonialism in the media: constructing Filipino nurse subjects in Finland". *European Journal of Cultural Studies*, 19:1, pp. 16–32.

Ozyegin, G. (2010). *Untidy gender: Domestic service in Turkey.* Temple University Press.

Parreñas, R. S. (2000), "Migrant Filipina domestic workers and the international division of reproductive labor". *Gender & Society*, 14:4, pp. 560–580.

Parreñas, R. (2015). *Servants of globalization: Migration and domestic work* (2nd edition). Stanford, CA: Stanford University Press.

Piocos III, C. M. (2019). At home with strangers: social exclusion and intimate labor in Anthony Chen's Ilo Ilo (2013). *Feminist Media Studies*, 19(5), 717–731.Rollins, J. (1985). *Between women: Domestics and their employers*. Phildelphia, PA: Temple University Press.

Salazar, N.B., 2010. "Tanzanian Migration Imaginaries". *University of Oxford International Migration Institute Working Papers Series* (20), pp. 1–45.Salazar, N. B. (2011). "The power of imagination in transnational mobilities". *Identities*, 18:6, pp. 576–598.

Saroca, C. (2007). "Representing Rosalina and Annabel: Filipino women, violence, media representation, and contested realities". *Philippine Journal of Third World Studies*, 22:1, pp. 32–60.

Saroca, N. (1997). "Filipino women, sexual politics, and the gendered racist discourse of the mail order bride". *Journal of Interdisciplinary Gender Studies: JIGS*, 2:2, pp. 89–XXX.

Saroca, N. (2006). "Woman in danger or dangerous woman? Contesting images of Filipina victims of domestic homicide in Australia". *Asian Journal of Women's Studies*, 12:3, pp. 35–74.

Skeggs, B. (2004). "Exchange, value and affect: Bourdieu and 'the self'". *The Sociological Review*, 52:2 suppl., pp. 75–95.

Taylor, G. W., & J. M. Ussher. (2001). "Making sense of S&M: A discourse analytic account". *Sexualities*, 4:3, pp. 293–314.

Todorov, T. (1993). *On Human Diversity Nationalism, Racism, and Exoticism in French Thought*. Cambridge, MA: Harvard University Press.

Toksöz G., Erdoğdu S. & Kaşka S. (2012). *Irregular Labour Migration in Turkey and Situation of Migrant Workers in the Labour Market*. Ankara: International Organisation for Migration. http://www.turkey.iom.int/documents/IrregularMigration/IOM_Report_11022013.pdf. Tyner, J. A. (1994). "The social construction of gendered migration from the Philippines". *Asian and Pacific Migration Journal*, 3:4, pp. 589–618.

Uchida, A. (1998). "The orientalization of Asian women in America". *Women's Studies International Forum*, 21:2, pp. 161–174.

Ustuner, T., & D. B. Holt. (2009). "Toward a theory of status consumption in less industrialized countries". *Journal of Consumer Research*, 37:1, pp. 37–56.

Valaskivi, K., & Sumiala, J. (2014). Circulating social imaginaries: Theoretical and methodological reflections. European Journal of Cultural Studies, 17(3), 229–243.

Zelizer, V. A. (2009). *The Purchase of Intimacy*. Princeton, NJ: Princeton University Press.

Afterword: Changing Work, Changing Migrations

Russell King

Fiona-Katharina Seiger, Noel Salazar and Johan Wets opened this volume with a commentary on the current salience of international migration – always in the news, prominent in political debate and a major theme of academic research and scholarship. They also stated that there is no all-encompassing theory to explain international migration. I will try to answer this point by going back to one of the founder-figures of migration theory, E.G. Ravenstein (1885), who stated in one of his famous "laws": "the major causes of migration are economic". This statement, which I believe is as true today as it was in the late nineteenth century, helps us to unite the two keywords of this book: "migration" and "work". Seeking work through migration, or moving abroad to find a job which holds better income and career-development prospects than the one currently being done, remains a key driving force for international migration the world over; hence the economic motivation for migration is still paramount. Even when the main reason for migration is thought to be non-economic, as in lifestyle migration or international student mobility, economic factors are usually still operative, albeit in a hidden form. For instance, students move abroad to study in order to improve their career prospects by attending a prestigious university (Findlay et al., 2012) or as a step to switching from "student" to "immigrant" after graduation (Hazen & Alberts, 2006; Robertson, 2011). Lifestyle migrants, who are often international retirees, also do not overlook economic considerations: alongside their quest for a "better way of life" (Benson & Osbaldiston, 2014), they relocate to places with cheaper property prices and lower living costs in order to get better value for their incomes and pensions – a process of "geographic arbitrage" (Hayes, 2014).

The above introductory remarks are designed to reinforce my argument, *pace* Ravenstein, that the major driver of international migration is, indeed, economics. Most people move abroad to access work, higher incomes, improved career opportunities for themselves and their children and a better quality of life, the last of which is also reflected in a better material standard of living. Where migrations for family reunion take place, the reunifiers are usually joining family members who have already moved for economic reasons.

However, there is another dimension to the economics of migration: inequality. Economically motivated migration flows, built on aggregated micro-economic decisions about the costs and benefits of moving (cf. Sjaastad, 1962), are patterned across macro-economic structures of spatial inequality. At a variety of geographic scales, people move from economically deprived parts of the world, where incomes are low and unemployment is high, to economically advantaged areas where incomes and life-chances are significantly better. They move from the Global South to the Global North; within Europe they move from East to West, as well as from South to North; and within individual countries they migrate from rural peripheries to the major urban and industrial centres.

Within this landscape of economic inequality, which structurally underpins so much migration, both in the contemporary world and in the past, the role of work is fundamental: hence the well-known term "labour migration". However, the relationship between work and migration is undergoing change and it is this process of change, in what we might call the work-migration nexus, which is the focus of the rest of this concluding essay. My key argument is that, as the nature of work and the labour market has changed, so too has the type or regime of labour migration, which has responded in terms of changing skill level, temporality and rights. In sustaining this analysis, I touch base with many of the foregoing chapters as supporting evidence. Yet, at the end of the day – especially in Europe in recent years – we observe an unfortunate contradiction. On the one hand, labour migrants are needed, mainly as a resource to solve a problem – the shortage of certain types of worker in a diversified and segmented labour market. Yet on the other hand, in the eyes of the public, politicians and the media, immigrants are presented as a "problem" which has somehow to be "solved".

Historical perspectives on the economics of the work-migration nexus

Although labour migration is centuries old – including the brutal transatlantic slave migrations and the semi-forced migrations of indenture which succeeded them (Potts, 1990) – I start this historical account with the "boom" in labour migration in Europe during the early post-war period. For more than two decades, until the onset of the first oil crisis in late 1973, Western Europe witnessed the functioning of a classic regime of demand-driven labour migration. According to theories of dual labour markets (Kindleberger, 1967) and Marxist political economy (Castles & Kosack, 1973; Piore, 1979), these migrations sustained the growth of industrial capitalism by providing a "reserve army" of foreign, mainly rural-origin, workers drawn from the agricultural peripheries of Europe, especially to the south – Spain, Portugal, Italy, Greece, Yugoslavia, Turkey and the three Maghreb states of Morocco, Algeria and Tunisia. Other countries involved in this boom era in labour migration were Ireland (to Britain) and Finland (to Sweden), influenced by older relations of coloniality and proximity. Industrialising economies such as Britain, France and the Netherlands also drew labour supplies from their (ex-)colonies in the Caribbean, Africa, South Asia and elsewhere, completing the more global-scale spatial division of labour which sustained economic reconstruction and expansion in the "core" economies of North-West Europe (Massey, 1984).

Fielding (1993) called these mass migrations of the early post-war decades the migrations of Fordism in the sense that they supported the mass production of standardised goods for mass consumer markets. Whilst the colonial metropole countries mentioned earlier operated an open-door policy towards workers from their respective colonies (at least for a while), West Germany put in place a different recruitment model, that of *Gastarbeiter* ("guestworkers") who were regulated and rotated according to the needs of the economy for heavy-industry, manufacturing and construction workers. Starting around 1960, bilateral recruitment agreements with the Southern European and Maghreb countries fed supplies of manual labour to drive the German economy forward. Through the policy of *Konjunkturpuffer*, temporary migrant workers were used as a buffer to dampen the destabilising effects of economic cycles. They were imported on short-term work contracts when there was a boom period – as there was throughout the post-war years until 1973 – and sent home (by not renewing their contracts) during a slump. In this way, German workers could be protected from the worst effects of a recession. This mechanism of using migrants to cushion the impact of an economic downturn was seen in practice during the short-lived slump of 1966–1967 and in the longer recession which lasted for several years through the mid- and late 1970s and the early 1980s.

The ending of the model of organised recruitment of foreign labour by the industrialised countries in the early to mid-1970s was not a mere conjunctural phenomenon to be solved by the temporary repatriation of guestworkers. Rather, it reflected a longer-term and wider-scale restructuring of the system of (industrial) production and hence of the labour market (Castles & Miller, 1993, p. 77). In Fielding's analysis (1993, pp. 12–14), economic restructuring was the hallmark of the passage from Fordist mass production based on national sectoral specialisation and its corollary of mass migration, to a post-Fordist economic landscape of deindustrialisation, decentralisation, flexible production and a new "hierarchical" spatial division of labour which geographically separated different elements of the production process. In this new international division of labour (Fröbel et al., 1980), headquarter functions gravitated to major cities, research and development moved towards high-amenity regions and routine production was related to low-wage sites in European peripheral regions or the developing world. As, now, jobs were migrating to the workers rather than workers to the jobs, Fielding concluded (1993, p. 14, printed in bold in the original to emphasise the point) that the most important feature of mass migration under post-Fordist forms of production was its absence!

Soon, however, a new "age of migration" was portended by Castles and Miller (1993), shaped by the changing nature of the European and world economies and new trends in the supply and reproduction of labour. These authors (1993, p. 77) listed the following as relevant factors: the changing geography of global investment, including the transfer of low-skill production to low-wage regions; the mechanisation and computerisation of manufacturing processes, reducing labour needs; the decline of traditional manual skilled trades, such as carpentry (cf. Moderbacher, Chapter 7); the expansion of the service sector, with demands for both high-skilled and new types of low-skilled labour; the expansion of the informal sector in many countries, along with the casualisation and the precarisation of the workforce; and the increased segmentation of both labour supply and demand based on ethnic, citizenship, gender and age criteria. Accordingly, the geography and typologies of the new migration age exhibited different features from the mass migration flows of Fordism. Following again Castles and Miller (1993, p. 78), the main new trends included: a growth in family reunion and marriage migration; a surge in the movements of refugees and asylum-seekers; an increasing mobility of highly skilled and professional migrants, including students; an escalating migration to oil-rich countries, especially the Gulf States; continuing migration to the "settler" immigration countries (the USA, Canada, Australia); within Europe, the transition of southern EU countries from emigration to immigration; and, after 1990, the growth of East-West migration within Europe.

Finally, in this scoping of the new age of migration which spanned the period from the late 1980s into the new millennium, we can note how the technology of travel and communication changed, facilitating new regimes of mobility and staying in touch. This was closely linked to two new "turns" in migration research in these decades: the transnational paradigm, built on fundamental work by Nina Glick Schiller and her colleagues in the 1990s (see, for example, Glick Schiller et al., 1992; 1995), and the mobilities turn pioneered by John Urry in the 2000s (Urry, 2000; 2007). These changes in the way that migration was conceptualised and actualised were not unrelated to new interrelationships between migration and work. Faster, cheaper and more frequent travel enabled more flexible work-related regimes of circular and seasonal migration, transnational business development, "commuting" migrants and gender-specific forms of labour migration linked to burgeoning demands in the globalised market for care.

Migration, contemporary labour markets, gender and care

In the contemporary world of globalised, yet hierarchically ordered and segmented, labour markets, labour-related migrations and mobilities exist in many forms, as the foregoing chapters exemplify. The editors point out in their Introduction that mobility is a complex and contradictory form of freedom, closely related to national and international regimes of migration control and to the needs of global capital, especially the neoliberal demand for employment flexibility. The freedom to migrate is a right or privilege to be enjoyed or denied; conversely, poverty and unemployment may compel people to move, denying them the right to be immobile. Or immobility may be "forced" by visa regimes and other barriers to movement, as Carling (2002) has demonstrated for Cape Verde. The chapters in this book demonstrate the tensions between migrants' aspirations and imaginaries on the one hand and their migratory endeavours, achievements and disappointments on the other. Migrants' achievements may illustrate the synergy between spatial and socio-economic mobility but, often, this "success" comes at a price: family separation, cultural uprooting, linguistic challenges and deskilling.

One of the biggest challenges is how to combine migrant work with the responsibilities of transnational family care. The complex interrelationships between labour migration, paid care work and family duties of care emerge most clearly in the first two chapters. Lulle (Chapter 1) argues that labour migration regimes and theories need to be read through the lens of care, whereby employers' ideals of profit conflict with family ideals of togetherness and care. This conflict reaches a particularly poignant, even ironic, level when migrant women engage in paid care work for children and the elderly in a migration country but need simultaneously to manage the care and wellbeing of their own children and elderly parents in their home countries. Whilst, on the one hand, neoliberalised structures of flexible employment may blend well with mobile regimes of labour migration, on the other hand they do not always accommodate the flexibility needed to provide transnational care. Creative solutions based on collaboration and networking may emerge, such as in Marchetti's (2013) interesting study of job-sharing amongst Eastern European women who pair up with each other to be able to take alternate periods catering for their employers' needs in Italy and caring for family members at home.

The care lens continues in Chapter 2 by de Sousa Ribeiro, where the emphasis is on the "emancipation" of migrant health workers, both those immigrating to Portugal from Eastern Europe and Portuguese health professionals emigrating in the wake of the 2008 economic crisis. In focusing on the "infrastructures of emancipation" (recruitment fairs, regularisation schemes for residential status, recognition of qualifications, social-media networks, etc.) the author is able deftly to fill a conceptual gap between migration and national regimes of labour-market regulation.

Although de Sousa Ribeiro does not elaborate on this point, Portugal is a particularly interesting case in terms of its labour-market and migration dynamics in that it is simultaneously a labour-exporting and a labour-importing country, even in the same employment sector. How is it that Portugal can both export and import healthcare workers? We see the same phenomenon in the construction sector: Portuguese construction workers have a tradition of migrating to other European countries, notably France, Germany and Switzerland; meanwhile, vacant jobs in the building industry in Portugal are filled by migrants from the Portuguese ex-colonies – such as Cape Verde – and from Eastern Europe, notably

Ukraine. The answer lies in hierarchical, spatial divisions of labour (Massey, 1984) and different wage levels for the same kind of work in different assemblages of countries (North-West Europe, Southern Europe, Eastern Europe and Portugal's African ex-colonies). Portugal has a dual position within the global economy and migration system: it is peripheral to the "core" economies of North-West Europe – which offer higher wages and better job prospects – and is the centre of a former colonial empire and thus a traditional destination for labour migration flows from its ex-colonial periphery (King, 2019).

The focus on gender, migration and access to work is continued in the remaining two chapters of Part 1. In Chapter 3, Ncube and Mkwanazi pose a dual question. Does migration empower women economically by enabling them to access employment, increase their independence and break the glass ceiling of the country of origin? Or does migration act to reinforce traditional gender roles and inequalities and expose women to new vulnerabilities in an unfamiliar environment, including their precarious position in an exploitative labour market? Further questions ensue. How valid is the "triple jeopardy" hypothesis that migrant women suffer three exclusions because of their migrant status, their gender and their ethnicity/colour? Or is migration an escape route from multiple exclusions and abuse in their home countries? The authors sensibly reject extremes of answers to these questions and take a more nuanced view, based on their "capabilities approach" to research on Zimbabwean and other black African migrant women in South Africa. Reflecting neoliberal labour values, the authors found that resilience, networking, adaptability and entrepreneurial skills were instrumental in migrants accessing work in South Africa and in creating jobs for themselves which enabled them to both sustain their lives in the host country and support family members in their home countries through remittances.

Chapter 4 (Wajsberg) switches the focus to six West African men and the way in which their experiences of intra-EU mobility are interwoven with different residence statuses, increasingly restrictive national and EU migration policies, access to different kinds of work, and decisions to onward-migrate. The six men exemplify "moving stories" of "status mobility" ("legal" worker, undocumented worker, asylum-seeker, refugee, student, tourist) in which successive moves from one country to another were a logical response to constantly changing circumstances. This chapter, albeit based on only a few case studies, demonstrates the fluidity of the interaction between mobility and work, as it evolves across an increasingly hostile terrain of EU and national regulations for third-country nationals from poor countries. Repeat onward mobility is seen as a navigational tactic in which both the actors (migrants) and their environment are moving. Yet episodes of involuntary immobility – "waithood" – often punctuate their lives, when they get stuck, wasting time and not advancing their livelihoods and careers in any way.

Imaginaries of work, place and migrants

The nexus between work and migration is mediated by a variety of intervening elements: aspirations, perceptions and mediating actors – above all, employers. Place also plays a fundamental role, since work is spatially specific, even if the work itself is mobile. Migrants have idealised images of "other" places where, metaphorically, the streets are paved with gold and riches are easily acquired. These images, provided through films, television and the global media, may be further distorted by previous waves of migrants who exaggerate the success of their migration project. For their part, employers also have idealised imaginaries of "desirable"' migrant workers – generally young, healthy and reliable but also docile. These images are gendered, racialised and ethnicised and are dependent on the type of work to be performed in the current segmented labour market, where different "niches" require different skills and attitudes.

The second part of the book focuses on the imaginaries mediating the two-way relationship between migrants and the labour market: on the one hand, migrants' imaginaries of different types of work and of the places where that work takes place; on the other hand, employers' imaginaries of different types of migrant, based on gender, age, skills endowment, nationality/ethnicity and so on.

Underpinning these imaginaries, once again, are basic economic principles and perceptions – above all regarding wage levels. The prospective incomes that migrants (think they) can earn must be sufficient to incentivise them to migrate, discounting the financial and psychological costs of the move. There may be trade-offs to be calculated between short-term and longer-range prospects. Target-earners, who aspire to earn as much as possible in a limited time, will go for higher-paying jobs, including the possibility of overtime, in order to accumulate the sum needed for a particular purpose – to build a house in their home country, to finance children's education, to set up a business or to pay off a loan. Other migrants may sacrifice short-term gain if there are good chances of career development through training, language learning, on-the-job experience, etc. This is part of the notion of "migratory careers" (Martiniello & Rea, 2014) used by Di Martino, Maiztegui and Aristegui (Chapter 5) in their analysis of European and Latin American women's working lives in the Basque Country.

Di Martino et al. open up an important discussion on the definition and measurement of "skill" in migrants who transfer from one national labour market to another. The dichotomisation between "skilled" and "unskilled" (or "higher-skilled" versus "lower-skilled") migrants is hugely problematic. This is so even in a non-migratory context. The conventional criterion for highly skilled (possession of a tertiary-level educational qualification, typically a bachelor's degree) is controversial since it makes a double assumption – that a graduate is automatically "skilled" and that an experienced professional such as a business manager is not highly skilled if they finished their education at secondary level. In reality, many people possess what could be regarded as "medium" skills, which are accumulated over a period of training and experience (such as carpentry – see Chapter 7 by Moderbacher) but which do not require higher education.

The issue of skill becomes more complicated with migration, leading to the common syndrome of "deskilling": migrants are classified as highly skilled in their home countries but are able to perform only unskilled or lower-skilled jobs abroad. The wide gap in wage levels between rich and poor countries is the economic justification for deskilling. In my own research on Albanian migration to different West European countries, I came across multiple examples of this – teachers working as child-minders or cleaners, academics working as chauffeurs and graduate agronomists working as casual gardeners. Barriers of language, the non-recognition of qualifications, and social and employer prejudice prevent migrants from transferring their human capital and diplomas to an equivalent job abroad (King & Mai, 2008).

Returning to the interesting results of Chapter 5, Di Martino et al. find that highly skilled women from Europe and Latin America face challenges in "job-matching" when they move to Spain, partly due to their gender and ethnicity and partly reflecting their wish to create a satisfactory work-life-family balance. Three arrival pathways are noted, which surely hold resonance for other studies of migratory women. These are: (i) women who moved to Spain for sentimental reasons – by definition, with or to join a romantic partner; (ii) those who moved for professional reasons, often on their own; and (iii) those who fled situations of oppression and violence in their home countries. The first and third categories, especially, end up doing jobs for which they are over-qualified. Whilst, for those seeking to escape an abusive situation, the improvement in their life is tangible, for others, frustration and disappointment are the dominant reactions.

The interplay between structural opportunities and obstacles on the one hand, and personal lives and coping strategies on the other, produces a diversity of "migratory careers" which are rarely linear and progressive but subject to frequent changes and "bifurcations" – significant choices and dilemmas over which path to take. An initial period of deskilling may be followed by recouping trajectories of "upskilling" (regaining or recognition of the skills lost and advancing them further) or "reskilling" (switching to a new skillset related to existing employment opportunities). However, reskilling may not always be successful, as Moderbacher's poignant portrait of Guinean migrant Cisé (Chapter 7) demonstrates. Retraining as a carpenter was seen as a waste of time for this long-stay immigrant, with the result that his protracted life in limbo in Belgium turned into a "waiting room" for something to happen, which it never did.

The notion of a migratory career is also implicit in Chapter 6 (Dimitriadis), which looks at the imaginaries of Albanian construction workers in Italy and Greece regarding their onward migration to somewhere "better". Taking Salazar's (2011) definition of imaginaries as "socially shared and transmitted representational assemblages that interact with people's personal imaginings", Dimitriadis interrogates the narratives of Albanian building workers against the background of economic recession in the host countries. Actual or potential unemployment, reduced hours, falling incomes and worsening labour conditions are the recession's main impacts on workers in a vulnerable economic sector like the building industry. In contrast to other studies of onward migration, which survey respondents who have actually moved on to a new destination (e.g. Della Puppa & King, 2019; Ramos, 2018), Dimitriadis interviews only those who have not (yet) moved. Whilst this might be thought a limitation, it enables the author, through the words of his interlocutors, to draw a nuanced picture of the positive and negative imaginaries of moving on to the likes of Germany, Sweden or the UK. Economic advantages (higher wages, more secure contracts, better working conditions) are balanced – and often outweighed – by the costs and upset of moving, the perceived more "boring" lifestyle, the colder weather and the feeling that social life and the lives of their children are better in southern Europe, closer to Albania.

Important research still needs to be done on the imaginaries of different categories of migrant worker held by employers, recruiting agents and host societies at large. Whilst large-scale comparative research across many countries and migrant ethnicities would generate some useful broad parameters, Chapter 8 (Ayaydin) is an intriguing case study of how one migrant nationality and one gender (Filipina women) achieve the coveted status of "desirable migrant" for the job of domestic helper and childcare-giver in Turkey. This example fits the framework suggested by Findlay et al. (2013) for the social and cultural construction of the "good migrant" as the "ideal worker". Findlay et al. pose two questions. First, how is the "goodness" of the migrant worker represented in bodily form and psychological make-up on the part of significant actors and agencies within the migration system? Second, how is "goodness" enacted, performed and produced in the recruitment process?

For the case of the Filipina "nannies" employed by upper- and middle-class families in Turkey, recruitment agencies create an image of Filipinas as "supermaids" and therefore able to earn higher wages than other nationalities, including Turkish rural-origin women, who are regarded as "rough" and "uncivilised". Amongst the specific embodied features of the Filipinas, as portrayed on employment agency websites, are their generally high levels of education, knowledge of English (hence "free" English lessons for the children of the family) and behavioural and attitudinal characteristics: calm yet hard-working, trustworthy, clean, meticulous, patient and sweet-tempered. In short, in the globalised commodification of women's labour, which siphons millions of women from the Global South to "serve" in the Global North (including Turkey and Middle Eastern countries with substantial wealthy classes), Filipinas are seen as *the* ideal nannies, not just as workers but also as valuable items of consumption linked to the demonstration of status and upward mobility.

Conclusion

This Afterword has attempted to draw together some of the key threads woven through the chapters of this book and to present them in a broader frame of history and economics. The evolution of regimes of labour mobility is seen to be closely linked to a sequence of macro-structural economic trends, notably those relating to systems of production and the changing character of national, European and global labour markets. Fordism, post-Fordism, economic restructuring, globalisation and neoliberalism are the key stages in the development of the work-migration nexus over the past 70 or so years. In this brief overview, I have touched on colonial-era migrations, continued in the post-colonial era; "guestworker" migrations, many of which matured into migrations of permanent settlement as family reunion replaced temporary labour migration;

and the much more diverse regimes of mobility co-involved with the "new age of migration", linked to the globalisation of production, consumer demand and labour markets, new regimes of migration control, the rise of the service sector and its demands for post-industrial workers, and the neoliberal turn which requires flexible labour regimes and arguably looser systems of control.

Encased within these longer-term developments in global political economy are more discrete events which also provoke episodes of migration and mobility – and their perceived need for control. From a European perspective, some obvious examples are the EU enlargements of 2004 and 2007, which revolutionised intra-European migration flows, opening up new reservoirs of reserve-army labour in ten countries in Central and Eastern Europe; the 2008 economic crisis and its aftermath of austerity policies which likewise had a profound impact on migration trends, especially in those countries hardest hit by the crisis, such as Greece, Spain and Portugal; the so-called "refugee crisis" of 2015–2016 which saw Europe struggle to cope with the sudden influx of more than one million refugees from Syria, Iraq and Afghanistan; and, most recently, the decision of the UK to leave the European Union.

In all these stages and events, if migration is "the story", it is for good reason. That reason is economics. The exception might be refugee flight, but even refugees are concerned in most cases to seek asylum in countries which offer them the best economic opportunities. When speaking about economics, I do not follow any one single orthodoxy. As far as migration is concerned, equally relevant are the neoclassical perspective of push and pull factors, supply and demand, costs and benefits; and the neo-Marxist school which stresses the dominance of global capital, class relations and the high levels of socio-economic and spatial inequality which both shape migration flows and are reinforced by them. As Shamir (2005, p. 199) states, mobility regimes are "constructed to maintain high levels of inequality in a normatively homogenized world".

It is also the case that, as far as migration is concerned, imaginaries dominate realities. I illustrate this final point with reference to the vexing issue of Brexit, uppermost in my mind as I am writing these words in the days immediately following the official exit date of 31 January 2020. Immigration played a leading role in the Brexit debate in the months leading up to the referendum of 23 June 2016 and has re-emerged as a live issue now that the departure has formally taken place.

The referendum itself was called by the then-Prime Minister David Cameron, who had been spooked by the electoral success (at local and European elections) of the UK Independence Party (UKIP) and its outspoken leader, Nigel Farage, alongside the increasingly vocal Eurosceptic wing of the Conservative Party. The idea was to neutralise this threat by winning the referendum with a "Remain" majority. Farage and the far-right "Tories" succeeded in creating a "moral panic" over immigration, supported by a trio of high-circulation tabloid newspapers (the *Daily Mail*, the *Daily Express* and the *Sun*) which manipulated the populist vote to "Leave". The image was relentlessly created of a Britain overrun by EU migrants from the "East", putting British workers out of jobs, creating pressure on housing and health services and changing the character of British towns and cities. As soon as the referendum was announced, in February 2016, a feeding frenzy over immigration developed, with the "Leave" campaign and its tabloid mouthpieces deploying all the standard negative tropes about migration – exaggeration of numbers, military metaphors of "armies" and "invasion", frequent reference to "uncontrollable floods" and links to criminality (drug-smuggling, sex-trafficking, abuses of the benefits system etc.). The reality was that EU migrants, the vast majority of whom came to the UK to work and to study, made a significant net contribution to the economy, especially in sectors such as agricultural labour, the food processing industry, hotels and catering, construction and allied trades, the health and care services, finance and business, and academia and research.

Fast-forward four years to February 2020 and we witness the UK Home Office's first attempts to formulate a post-Brexit immigration policy which respects the referendum pledge to "take back control" of the UK border against "free-movement" migration from the EU. Home Secretary Priti Patel aims drastically to reduce low-skill immigration – and overall net immigration – by setting a minimum income cap of £25,600 per year and selectively favouring higher-skill migration. Under the proposed new points system (at least 70 points are required) three criteria are mandatory: a job offer from an approved sponsor (20 points), a job at an appropriate skill level (20) and the ability to speak English (10). Other points, needed to get to the threshold of 70, can come from the level of salary of the job (over £25,600, 20 points), a job offer in a "shortage occupation" (20) and a PhD (10 points – 20 if it is in science, technology, engineering or maths). Effectively, this set of criteria means that the UK will be closed to unskilled and low-skilled workers.

Quite apart from whether the Home Office has the administrative capacity to handle the change to such a radically new and complex immigration filtering system, a bigger question arises as to how the labour market will cope with the dramatic fall in labour supply. In response, Patel argues that large numbers of the

8.5 million "economically inactive" people aged 16–64 in Britain will take up these erstwhile "immigrant" jobs in agriculture, the care sector, hospitality and construction. Two objections can be raised against this supposition. First, the vast majority of the 8.5 million are students, full-time homemakers/carers, retired or sick. Second, as past experience has shown, British-born workers tend not to offer themselves up for these tough, low-paid jobs which are generally under-valued by society. In other words, the UK government has not understood the relationship between migration and the labour market, the subject of this book.

References

Benson, M., & N. Osbaldiston (eds.). (2014). *Understanding Lifestyle Migration: Theoretical Approaches to Migration and the Quest for a Better Way of Life*. Basingstoke: Palgrave Macmillan.

Carling, J. (2002). "Migration in the age of involutary immobility: theoretical reflections and Cape Verdean experiences". *Journal of Ethnic and Migration Studies*. 28:1, pp. 5–42.

Castles, S., & G. Kosack. (1973). *Immigrant Workers and Class Structure in Western Europe*. London: Oxford University Press.

Castles, S., & M. J. Miller. (1993). *The Age of Migration: International Population Movements in the Modern World*. Basingstoke: Macmillan.

Della Puppa, F., & R. King. (2019). "The new 'twice migrants': motivations, experiences and disillusionments of Italian-Bangladeshis relocating to London". *Journal of Ethnic and Migration Studies*, 45:11, pp. 1936–1952.

Fielding, A. (1993). "Mass migration and economic restructuring". In R. King (ed.), *Mass Migration: The Legacy and the Future* (pp. 7–18). London: Belhaven.

Findlay, A.M., R. King, F.M. Smith, A. Geddes & R. Skeldon. (2012). "World class? An investigation of globalisation, difference and international student mobility". *Transactions of the Institute of British Geographers*, 37:1, pp. 118–131.

Findlay, A., D. McCollum, S. Shubin, E. Apsite & Z. Krisjane. (2013). "The role of recruitment agencies in imagining and producing the 'good' migrant". *Social and Cultural Geography*, 14:2, pp. 145–167.

Fröbel, F., J. Heinrichs & O. Kreye. (1980). *The New International Division of Labour*. Cambridge: Cambridge University Press.

Glick Schiller, N., L. Basch & C. Blanc-Szanton. (1992). "Transnationalism: a new analytic framework for understanding migration". *Annals of the New York Academy of Sciences, 645*, pp. 1–24.

Glick Schiller, N., L. Basch & C. Szanton Blanc. (1995). "From immigrant to transmigrant: theorizing transnational migration". *Anthropological Quarterly*, 68:1: pp. 48–63.

Hayes, M. (2014). "'We gained a lot over what we would have had': the geographic arbitrage of North America's lifestyle migrants in Cuenca, Ecuador". *Journal of Ethnic and Migration Studies,* 40:12, pp. 1953–1971.

Hazen, H. D., & H. C. Alberts. (2006). "Visitors or immigrants? International students in the United States". *Population, Space and Place*, 12:3, pp. 201–216.

Kindleberger, C. P. (1967). *Europe's Postwar Growth – The Role of Labor Supply*. Cambridge, MA: Harvard University Press.

King, R. (2019). "New migration dynamics on the south-western periphery of Europe: theoretical reflections on the Portuguese case". In J. Azevedo and C. Pereira (eds.). *New and Old Routes of Portuguese Migration: Uncertain Futures at the Periphery of Europe* (pp. 267–281). Cham: Springer.

King, R., & N. Mai. (2008). *Out of Albania: From Crisis Migration to Social Inclusion in Italy*. New York: Berghahn.

Marchetti, S. (2013). "Dreaming circularity? Eastern European women and job sharing in paid home care". *Journal of Immigrant and Refugee Studies*, 11:4, pp. 347–363.

Martiniello, M., & A. Rea. (2014). "The concept of migratory careers: elements for a new theoretical perspective on contemporary human mobility". *Current Sociology*, 62:7, pp. 1079–1096.

Massey, D. (1984). *Spatial Divisions of Labour*. London: Macmillan.

Piore, M. J. (1979). *Birds of Passage: Migrant Labor and Industrial Societies*. New York: Cambridge University Press.

Potts, L. (1990). *The World Labour Market: A History of Migration*. London: Zed Books.

Ramos, C. (2018). "Onward migration from Spain to London in times of crisis: the importance of life-course junctures in secondary migrations". *Journal of Ethnic and Migration Studies*, 44:11, pp. 1841–1857.

Ravenstein, E. G. (1885). "The laws of migration – 1". *Journal of the Statistical Society*, 48:2, pp. 167–227.

Robertson, S. (2011). "Student switchers and the regulation of residency: the interface of the individual and Australia's immigration regime". *Population, Space and Place*, 17:1, pp. 103–115.

Salazar, N. B. (2011). "The power of imagination in transnational mobility". *Identities*, 18:6, pp. 576–598.

Shamir, D. (2005). "Without borders? Notes on globalization as a mobility regime". *Sociological Theory*, 23:2, pp. 197–217.

Sjaastad, L. A. (1962). "The costs and returns of human migration". *Journal of Political Economy*, 70:5, suppl., pp. 80–93.

Urry, J. (2000). *Sociology Beyond Societies: Mobilities for the 21ˢᵗ Century*. London: Routledge.

Urry, J. (2007). *Mobilities*. Cambridge: Polity.

About the Authors

Iratxe Aristegui is Associate Professor of Social Work and Sociology at the University of Deusto. She holds a PhD in Political Science and Sociology. She is part of the "Deusto Social Barometer" work team and conducts research as part of the "Deusto Social Values" team that works on the European Values Survey. Iratxe Aristegui has written several articles on employment, leisure, the elderly, human capital and social vulnerability.

Deniz Berfin Ayaydin is a sociology PhD student at Boston College. She received her MSc degree in Media and Communication Studies at the London School of Economics and Political Science in 2013 and her BA degree in Management Science from Bogazici University in 2011. Her research interests include global capitalism, feminist praxis and counter-hegemonic struggles.

Maria Luisa Di Martino received her PhD in Human Rights from the University of Deusto. She held an MA in Development Studies from the University of the Basque Country. Her research interests are focused on the socio-cultural transformations in the migration trajectories of migrant women and their agency; on the relationships between power and oppression in the construction of women's migratory career from a feminist perspective.

Iraklis Dimitriadis is a Research Fellow at the Department of Social and Political Sciences of the University of Milan. He obtained his PhD in Sociology and Methodology of Social Research from the Universities of Milan and Turin with the distinction of Doctor Europaeus. His current research focuses on migration governance and asylum crisis within the Horizon 2020 "MAGYC" project, while in recent years he has developed research on labour migration, informal employment, citizenship, and religion and immigration.

Russell King is Professor of Geography at the University of Sussex and Visiting Professor in Migration Studies at Malmö University. He has long-standing research interests in many forms of migration, including labour migration, and has carried out research projects in a variety of countries, mostly in Europe. From 2000 to 2013 he was the editor of the *Journal of Ethnic and Migration Studies*.

Aija Lulle is a lecturer in Human Geography. Her area of expertise is family and youth migration and psycho-social wellbeing of migrants. She acts as an advisor on migration and diaspora policies, and as an EU- and national-level expert. Lulle has extensive research experience on migration from children's, youth and ageing perspectives.

Concepción Maiztegui-Oñate is currently tenured lecturer at the Department of Social Pedagogy and Diversity in the Faculty of Psychology and Education (University of Deusto, Bilbao). As a senior researcher, she is part of the "Intervention: Quality of Life and Social Inclusion" research team. Her research areas are mainly focused on social participation and citizenship, especially from the perspective of interculturality. Her other axis of interest is related to participatory methodologies.

Faith Mkwananzi is a Postdoctoral Research Fellow with the Higher Education and Human Development Research Group at the University of the Free State, South Africa. Her research is on higher education and development with particular facets of poverty, migration and creative research methods. In addition to this, she is interested in education policy and philanthropy in higher education.

Christine Moderbacher is an anthropologist and documentary filmmaker. Having completed her PhD at the University of Aberdeen in 2019, she is currently part of the Max Planck Research Group entitled "Alpine Histories of Global Change: Time, Self, and the Other in the German-Speaking Alpine Region" in Halle, Germany. Her documentary films, *A Letter to Mohamed* (2013) and *Red Earth White Snow* (2018), were shown in international film festivals and received a number of prizes.

Alice Ncube is a senior lecturer at the Disaster Management Education and Center for Africa (DiMTEC) at the University of the Free State, South Africa. She has over ten years of experience in disaster (risk) management teaching, training, and researching on gendered migration, social vulnerability, and resilience. Her research interests are in social vulnerability, resilience and international migration, with particular emphasis on gendered migration in the face of climate change.

Noel B. Salazar is Research Professor in Anthropology at KU Leuven, Belgium. He is editor of the Worlds in Motion (Berghahn) book series and author of *Momentous Mobilities* (2018), *Envisioning Eden* (2010) and numerous peer-reviewed articles and book chapters on human mobility. Salazar is founder of the EASA Anthropology and Mobility Network (AnthroMob). In 2013, he was elected a member of the Young Academy of Belgium.

Fiona-Katharina Seiger is a sociologist by training who has worked with women, children and youth in Japan and the Philippines. She holds a PhD from the National University of Singapore. Her intellectual project centres on the politics of belonging in a world in flux, to which she now adds a burgeoning interest in urban spaces and in qualitative research involving "the digital". Her education and research career took Fiona to Vienna, Paris, Kyoto, Tokyo, Manila, Singapore and Antwerp, before she joined Erasmus University Rotterdam.

Joana de Sousa Ribeiro is a researcher at the Centre for Social Studies (NHUMEP Research Group – Humanities, Migration and Peace Studies Research) and a PhD student at the School of Economics, University of Coimbra. In her PhD thesis she looks at the de-skilling and re-skilling process of migrants in the healthcare sector. Her main research interests include the socio-professional mobility of migrants and refugees, longitudinal studies, intercultural studies and citizenship.

Mirjam Wajsberg is a PhD candidate at the Department of Geography, Planning and Environment at Radboud University. Her research focuses on themes of (im)mobility, migration, border struggles and solidarity movements in Europe.

Johan Wets has a PhD in Social Sciences and is migration research manager at the Research Institute for Work and Society (HIVA), an interdisciplinary research institute of the University of Leuven, Belgium (KU Leuven). He has a record of academic and policy-oriented research on international migration and integration. His main research topics concern migration and the labour market, family migration, irregular migration, integration, migration policy, migration and development (including brain drain and migrant remittances), the attitude towards (new) migrants, etc. He teaches Political Sociology at the Université Saint Louis Bruxelles.